Critical Comparison of Low-Carbon Technologies

A practical guide to prioritizing energy technologies for climate change mitigation

Tushar Choudhary, Ph.D.

Copyright ©2020 Tushar Choudhary

All Rights Reserved. This book is for personal use only. The distribution of this book by any means without the permission of the author is illegal and punishable by law. Your support for the author's rights is appreciated.

Cover Design Credit: R. Choudhary
Cover Images Credit: NASA, Z. Cebeci, S. Burchell, and A. Rietveld

Dedication

I would like to dedicate this book to my amazing Mom (Asha Choudhary) and Dad (Vasant Choudhary) who have always been there for me.

Dear Mom/Dad, words cannot express how grateful I am for your unconditional love and support through the years. Your sacrifices for me have not gone unnoticed. You are the biggest reason for everything I am today, and I could not have hoped for more perfect parents.

Acknowledgements

I would like to take the opportunity to thank the people who have made many valuable contributions to this book.

I would like to start with thanking my awesome wife. She has contributed to the book cover design, enhancing the appearance of Figure and Tables, formatting and provided suggestions for improving readability. This book would not have been possible without her contributions and support. Thank you Rajeshree!

Providing robust technical feedback on a book like this requires a significant time commitment. I am thankful to Dr. V.R. Choudhary, and several other technical experts who took the time to review the technical content of the book and provide valuable suggestions.

Last but not the least, I would like to thank my dear sister, Rashmi, for copy editing the book.

Table of Contents

PREFACE   **9**

CHAPTER 1: INTRODUCTION   **11**

1.1 Background   **11**

1.2 Key elements of the book   **15**

CHAPTER 2: ISSUES & CHALLENGES FOR CO_2 REDUCTION AND RELATED IMPLICATIONS   **17**

2.1 Major issues related to CO_2 reduction   **17**
     2.1.1 Stringent time-line requirements   17
     2.1.2 Extraordinary size of the problem   17
     2.1.3 Global nature of the problem   19
     2.1.4 Competition from other extremely important global problems   20
     2.1.5 Severity of CO_2 impact remained misunderstood for several decades 21

2.2 Critical challenges related to CO_2 reduction   **24**
     2.2.1 Need for urgency and substantial impact   24
     2.2.2 Cost control: Low cost requirement   25
     2.2.3 Potential for severe (yet unknown or misunderstood) environmental impact from CO_2 reduction solutions at the required scale   27

2.3 Implications: Framework for comparing CO_2 reduction solutions   **35**

CHAPTER 3: KEY CHARACTERISTICS OF THE TECHNOLOGY SOLUTIONS   **38**

    3.1 Key characteristics of the CO_2 reduction solutions for electricity generation   **41**
     3.1.1 Natural gas fueled plants   44
     3.1.2 Solar-Utility Plants   47
     3.1.3 Solar-Distributed   53
     3.1.4 Solar with energy storage   54
     3.1.5 Wind technology-onshore   57
     3.1.6 Wind technology: offshore   60

3.1.7 Wind technology with energy storage   62
3.1.8 Biomass   62
3.1.9 Nuclear Energy   65
3.1.10 Hydropower   67
3.1.11 Power plants with CO_2 Capture and Storage   71

3.2 Key characteristics of the CO_2 reduction solutions for the transportation sector   73
3.2.1 Hybrid Electric Vehicles   74
3.2.2 Battery Electric Vehicles   78
3.2.3 Biofuels   84
3.2.4 Shared Transportation   87

3.3 Brief discussion on key characteristics for direct CO_2 capture from air   90

CHAPTER 4: COMPARISON OF TECHNOLOGY SOLUTIONS   93

4.1 Comparison of solutions within the electricity generation sector (EGS)   93
4.1.1 Comparison of EGS solutions: Cost   93
4.1.2 Comparison of EGS solutions: Magnitude of impact   95
4.1.3 Comparison of EGS solutions: Potential for severe environmental impact at the required scale   97
4.1.4 Comparison of EGS solutions: Dependence on another new technology   98
4.1.5 Comparison of EGS solutions: Speed of impact   98

4.2 Comparison of solutions within the transportation sector (TS)   99
4.2.1 Comparison of TS solutions: Cost   99
4.2.2 Comparison of TS solutions: Magnitude of impact   101
4.2.3 Comparison of TS solutions: Potential for severe environmental impact at scale   102
4.2.4 Comparison of TS solutions: Dependence on another new technology   102
4.2.5 Comparison of TS solutions: Speed of impact   103

4.3 CO_2 Reduction Cost   103
4.3.1 Comparison of EGS solutions: CO_2 reduction costs   105
4.3.2 Comparison of TS solutions: CO_2 reduction costs   107

CHAPTER 5: PRIORITIZATION OF TECHNOLOGIES FOR EFFICIENT CO_2 REDUCTION   110

5.1 Prioritization discussion for the United States   112

5.1.1 Prioritization of EGS solutions for the United States	112
5.1.2 Prioritization of TS solutions for the United States	116
5.1.3 Prioritization across the EGS & TS sectors for the United States	119

5.2 Global Prioritization Discussion — 122
5.2.1 Global prioritization of EGS solutions — 123
5.2.2 Global prioritization of TS solutions — 126
5.2.3 Summary discussion on global implementation of technology solutions — 128
5.2.4 General comments on robustness of the prioritization methodology — 131

CHAPTER 6: EXECUTIVE SUMMARY PLUS — 134

6.1 Challenges Associated with CO_2 Reduction — 134

6.2 Prioritization of CO_2 Reduction Technologies — 137
6.2.1 Prioritization of technology solutions within the electricity generation sector — 137
6.2.2 Prioritization of technology solutions within the light duty vehicle transportation sector — 139
6.2.3 General comments about prioritization of technology solutions within the next decade — 140

6.3 Other critical aspects — 142
6.3.1 Implications of the global nature of the problem — 142
6.3.2 Strategic importance of climate change adaptation — 146

GLOSSARY & UNITS — 147

APPENDIX — 149

ABOUT THE AUTHOR — 157

REFERENCES AND NOTES — 158

Preface

About twenty years ago, I had a remarkable conversation with my mentor, Dr. Marvin M. Johnson, who was the recipient of the first U.S. Medal of Technology & Innovation[1]. During that conversation, he asked me about my thoughts on widescale technology commercialization in a promising new area. I responded by enthusiastically outlining my thoughts for two whole hours. What came next would have a *lifelong impact on me*!

He congratulated me on my in-depth technical knowledge on the topic, following which he identified a practical aspect that I had not fully factored into my analysis. This led to significant reassessment of my thoughts on the subject. I realized that I had missed out on one practical aspect that turned out to be a critical element in determining the problem solution. The two main reasons were a) I was distracted by the numerous scientifically interesting *aspects* of the complex problem which in retrospect were less important, and b) I was biased due to emotional attachment to certain aspects.

It became apparent to me that, in addition to innovative science/engineering, efficient solutions to complex problems required a robust practical understanding of all critical aspects and subsequent dispassionate addressing of all critical challenges. Since that day, I made it a mission to improve my ability to look at problems in a *holistic manner* by first identifying all critical aspects and then focusing on them in an unbiased manner.

CO_2 reduction via technology-based solutions is a topic that has been close to my heart for the past several years. This book is my attempt to share the critical aspects related to this topic in a concise manner. I have strived to be concise (which ironically was very time consuming) to ensure that the critically needed information is available to the readers without burden from irrelevant data.

Public opinion on anthropogenic CO_2 emissions and climate change varies over a wide spectrum- Some want to take immediate action to drastically reduce emissions, some are in favor of a cautious approach, some others are either disinterested and/or disengaged from the issue, while some are dismissive of the relationship between anthropogenic CO_2 emissions and climate change. I am hopeful that everyone, irrespective of their thoughts on climate change, will gain some *fresh insights* from the comparative analysis of technologies used for CO_2 reduction. I have ensured that the analysis provided in this book is based on data compiled from the most credible sources available.

Tushar V. Choudhary
Houston, Texas

Chapter 1: Introduction

Headlines from some articles that were issued a few weeks before work on this book began.

> "Offshore wind could power the world". CNN Business
>
> "Offshore wind production forecasts are inflated, world's largest developer warns". S&P Global Market Intelligence
>
> "Offshore windfarms can provide more electricity than the world needs". The Guardian
>
> "Developers Struggle to Get Wind Projects Going in India". Bloomberg news

There are a large number of articles released every year about different CO_2 reduction technology solutions. These articles are typically narrow in scope, and therefore provide only a certain limited viewpoint. Unfortunately, this does not allow the needed *big picture* understanding about the technologies. In fact, it can create confusion and misunderstandings. The primary goal of this book is to provide a holistic understanding about the popular low-carbon technologies and their widescale implementation.

1.1 Background

Fossil fuels, which have been a low cost and abundant resource for energy and materials, have played an important role in the phenomenal progress that mankind has achieved over the last century in wide-ranging fields from *agriculture to medical to telecommunications to space programs*. On the flip side, energy production from fossil fuels, and other human activities have led to release of extremely large amounts of CO_2 (Figure 1)[2,3]. This has resulted in an increase in CO_2 concentration in the earth's atmosphere. The atmospheric CO_2 content has increased by ~30% from its 1960 level to above 400 ppm currently[4].

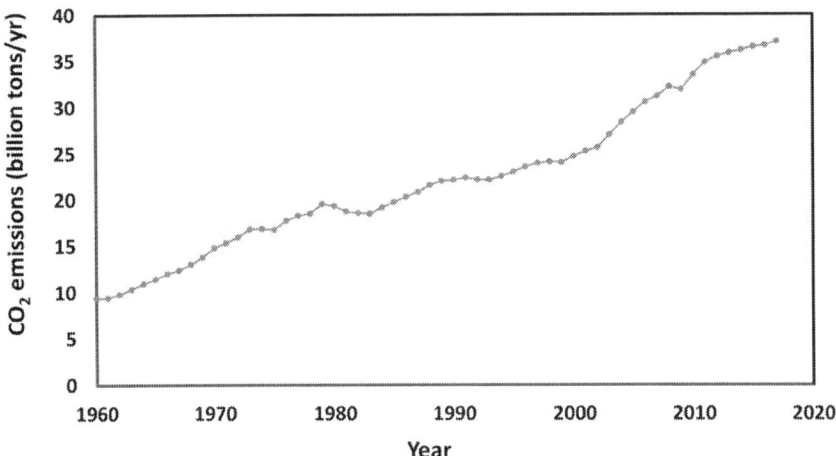

Figure 1. Global CO_2 emissions per year from fossil fuel use (power plants, industry, transportation, etc.) and cement production. Data sources: World Bank & Netherlands Environmental Assessment Agency.

Studies related to ancient air bubbles trapped in ice have shown that the current atmospheric CO_2 content is *higher* than any time in the *past several hundred thousand years*[5]. Atmospheric content of CO_2 is important because it belongs to an important group of compounds known as greenhouse gases, which trap some of the heat radiated by the Earth's surface[6]. This blanketing effect from greenhouse gases present in the atmosphere is essential for maintaining comfortable temperatures on Earth. However, excess of the greenhouse gases can increase the Earth's temperature beyond optimum. Some of the compounds in this group such as CO_2, methane, nitrous oxides, and certain fluoro/chloro compounds are long-lived in the atmosphere and do not respond to temperature changes. These compounds can "force" climate change (e.g. can cause global warming due to their excess production from human activity)[7]. Amongst the targeted greenhouse gases, CO_2 has been identified as the major contributor to climate change forcing (Figure 2)[8].

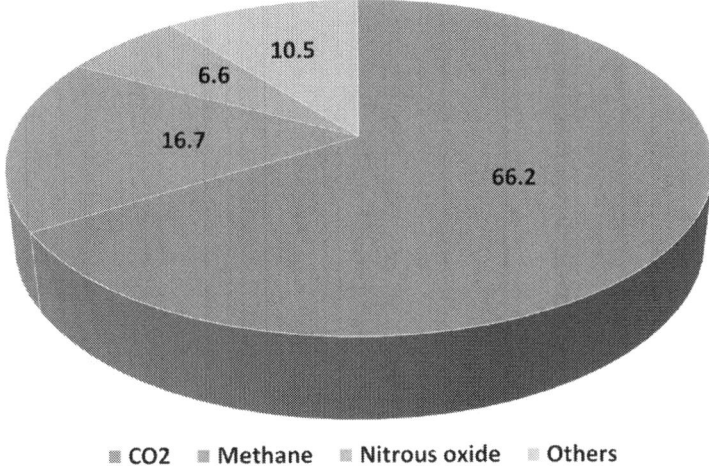

■ CO2   ■ Methane   ■ Nitrous oxide   ■ Others

Figure 2. Contribution from the targeted greenhouse gases to the overall climate forcing in 2017. The category *Others* include the following compounds: HFCs, PFCs, SF$_6$, CFCs, HCFCs and CH$_3$CCl$_3$. Data source: European Environment Energy.

The Intergovernmental Panel on Climate Change (IPCC) was specifically set up in 1988 as the Intergovernmental body responsible for assessing the science of climate change[9]. The recent, Fifth Assessment Report of IPCC, based on a collaboration of a large number of scientists and a wide representation of countries, reported the following key findings related to the *observed changes*, *causes of climate change* and *future climate change risks and impacts*[10]:

- "Human influence on the climate system is clear, and recent anthropogenic emissions of green-house gases are the highest in history. Recent climate changes have had widespread impacts on human and natural systems".
- "Continued emission of greenhouse gases will cause further warming and long-lasting changes in all components of the climate system, increasing the likelihood of severe, pervasive and irreversible impacts for people and ecosystems. Limiting climate change would require substantial and sustained reductions in greenhouse gas emissions which, together with adaptation, can limit climate change risks".

Several Intergovernmental initiatives have been undertaken to address climate change in recent years. Amongst these, the *Paris*

Climate Agreement has been the most important initiative considering that it has been ratified by Governments of 189 countries[11]. The key objectives of the Paris Agreement are listed below[12]:

- "Holding the increase in the global average temperature to well below 2°C above pre-industrial levels and pursuing efforts to limit the temperature increase to 1.5°C above pre-industrial levels, recognizing that this would significantly reduce the risks and impacts of climate change".
- "Increasing the ability to adapt to the adverse impacts of climate change and foster climate resilience and low greenhouse gas emissions development, in a manner that does not threaten food production".
- "Making finance flows consistent with a pathway towards low greenhouse gas emissions and climate-resilient development".

The countries that have ratified the Paris Agreement have quantified their nationally determined contribution targets towards decreasing greenhouse gas emissions[13]. Public support is one of the key requirements for meeting the proposed targets. Some public opinion data is available from a related large study covering 40 countries conducted in 2015 by the non-partisan fact tank Pew Research Center[14]. A majority from all the countries polled agreed that climate change was *at-least a some-what serious problem*, with a global median of 54% considering it a very serious problem. More importantly, a median of 78% supported their country signing the Paris Agreement, and thereby the goal of limiting greenhouse gas emissions. Recent polling across different countries also showed a significant concern about climate change; moreover, a general global trend of *increasing concern about climate change* has been observed with passing years[15].

The *vast majority of the relevant global scientific organizations* have come forward in support of the findings related to climate change[16,17,18,19,20,21,22,23,24], with several requesting increased action from people and the governing bodies. In response, governments (local and national) around the world are considering the increased implementation of low-carbon technologies.

1.2 Key elements of the book

There are several low-carbon technologies such as solar, wind, batteries, biofuels, electric cars etc., which are being aggressively considered as the solutions for CO_2 reduction[25,26]. It is therefore important to develop a **practical understanding** of how these proposed technology solutions compare with each other taking into consideration all the critical challenges related to CO_2 reduction. A large number of books have been written to discuss the different low-carbon technologies. However, these books do not provide the much-needed practical comparison between the different proposed technology solutions.

An effective solution to CO_2 reduction is going to require the global population to develop a practical understanding of all critical aspects of the problem; which is essential for driving holistic discussions, and thereby enabling robust policy making across the globe. This book is specifically written to address the gap discussed above, i.e. discuss the *critical challenges* associated with reducing CO_2, provide *key characteristics* of the proposed technology solutions, *compare* the key characteristics of the technology solutions in relation to these challenges and *prioritize* the technologies based on the comparison.

The information provided in this book is broadly applicable, as opposed to the abundant localized data available in different forms of media, which can be either overly optimistic or overly pessimistic. Most importantly, the data used for the analysis in this book has been compiled from the **most credible sources available** (e.g. World Bank, United Nations, European Environment Agency, United States, Energy Information Administration, etc.).

Low-carbon technology solutions are already being implemented globally to some extent or another, and this implementation is expected to increase significantly in the coming years. The information provided in this book should be relevant to everybody irrespective of their beliefs about climate change as it is focused on ensuring the **most efficient use of our limited resources**.

Some salient points to note:
- The collective information about the technology solutions presented in this book will enable the readers to undertake their own analysis. Overall, the discussion in the book has been developed such that it will provide the readers with a holistic understanding of the technology solutions that could be

considered in the short-to-midterm (10 to 15 years) to efficiently address the CO_2 reduction problem. The book also provides an *evergreen technology prioritization framework* for climate change mitigation.
- Examples/discussions provided in the book are simplified so that the messaging is concise and easy to understand.
- Links to useful references are provided so that the reader can obtain further details as needed. If the provided links do not work (due to change in the location of the information from the website owners), the descriptive titles of the references should hopefully lead the reader to the updated website location.

...§§§-§-§§§...

Chapter 2: Issues & Challenges for CO_2 Reduction and Related Implications

In order to compare the different low-carbon technologies, first and foremost, it is necessary to understand the issues and challenges associated with reducing CO_2. This chapter will discuss the *major issues* associated with CO_2 reduction, the *critical challenges* that arise from these issues, and *corresponding implications* for the technology solutions.

2.1 Major issues related to CO_2 reduction

For the purpose of this book, major issues are defined as those which absolutely must be considered to develop a practical understanding of the CO_2 reduction (a major component of *climate change mitigation*) problem.

2.1.1 Stringent time-line requirements

As discussed earlier, one of the key goals from the Paris Agreement is to limit the increase in global average temperature to well below 2° C above preindustrial levels[27]. According to a recent IPCC report (2018), human activities have already resulted in ~ 1° C temperature increase above preindustrial levels and the current rate of increase is ~ 0.2° C per decade[28]. This means that the efforts related to CO_2 reduction will need to meet stringent time-line requirements to limit the risk and impact from climate change.

2.1.2 Extraordinary size of the problem

The size of the problem can be defined by the total amount of CO_2 emitted globally. In 2017, the total amount of CO_2 emitted globally was 37 billion tons[29]. To put this in perspective, the weight of the global human population was 0.4 billion tons in 2017[30]; i.e. the amount of CO_2 emitted globally in *just four days* in 2017 exceeded the *weight of the entire human population on the planet*. Energy production is responsible for the majority of the global CO_2 emissions. This is because fossil fuels (natural gas, coal and liquid hydrocarbons) are by far the most dominant source of energy (Figure 3)[31], with about 80% contribution. The enormous size of CO_2 emissions may be attributed to the immense need for energy in homes, industries, transportation, etc. Due to the strong relationship between energy and CO_2 emissions, *the amount of energy consumed globally can also be considered as a measure of the size of the CO_2 reduction problem.*

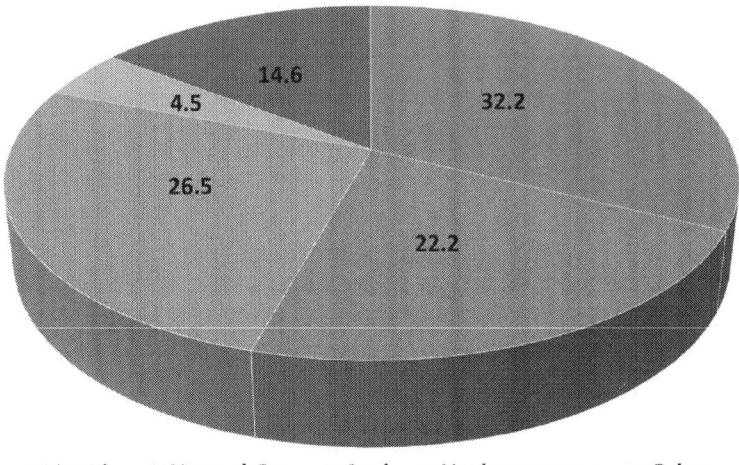

Figure 3. Global energy consumption by fuel type (2017 data). "Liquids" category includes >95% petroleum liquids; "Other" category includes hydroelectric plus other renewables. Data source: United States, Energy Information Administration (U.S. EIA)

Population and gross domestic product (economic activity) have historically been excellent indicators of energy requirements. The world population has more than doubled, from 3.7 billion in 1970 to 7.6 billion in 2018[32]. The world gross domestic product has increased from 19 trillion dollars to 83 trillion dollars from 1970 to 2018[33]. Correspondingly, the global demand for energy has almost tripled over the past few decades (Figure 4)[34].

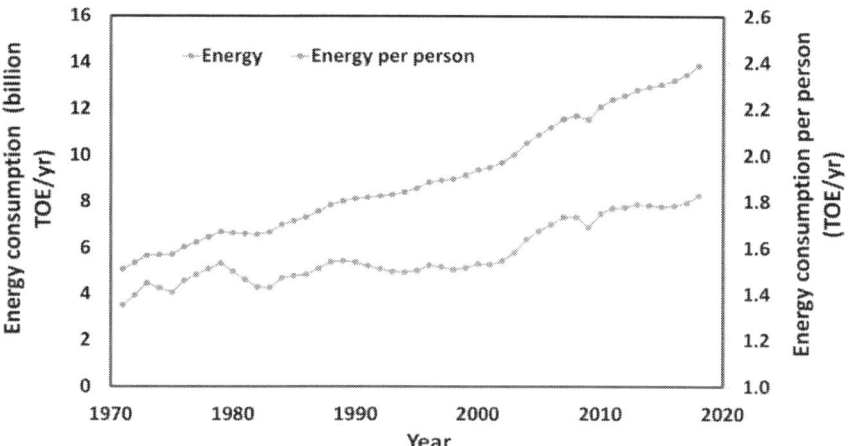

Figure 4. Trend in primary global energy consumption (total) and energy consumption per person. TOE/yr = Tons of Oil Equivalent per year. Data source: Energy data: BP statistical review of world energy 2019; Population data: World Bank

The Figure shows an increase in both the total energy consumption as well as the average energy consumed per person per year. In 2018, the total energy consumed by the global population was an enormous 13.9 billion tons of oil equivalent. Furthermore, the global energy demand is expected to further increase by 50% from 2018 to 2050[35], corresponding to the expected increase in world population and gross domestic product. Thus, it is clear that the CO_2 problem is extraordinarily large and expected to get even larger.

2.1.3 Global nature of the problem

Since CO_2 is a long-lived gas (up to two hundred years)[36], it stays for sufficient time in the atmosphere to get well mixed; i.e. it spreads more or less evenly around the earth, independent of the source. As a result, the amount that is measured in the atmosphere is roughly the same anywhere in the world[37]. Over the years, the different countries in the world have emitted CO_2 at different rates depending on their population, economic state, available resources, etc. For reference, the yearly CO_2 emissions from representative countries are shown in Figure 5[38].

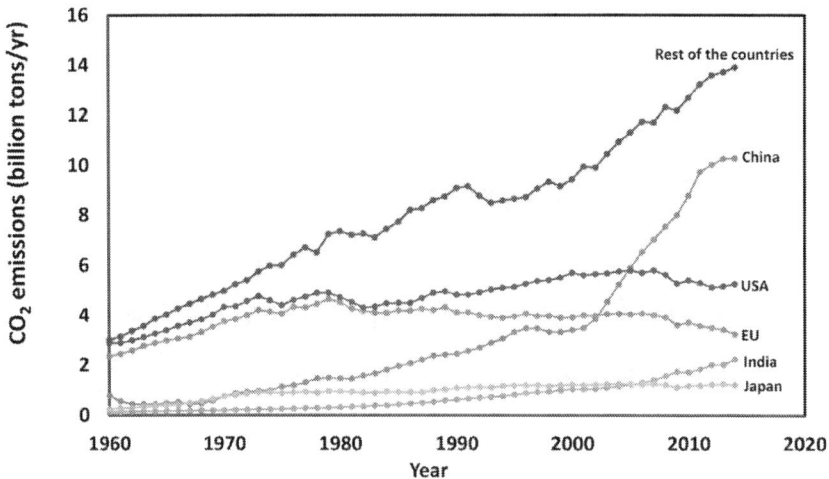

Figure 5. Yearly CO_2 emissions trend from representative countries and rest of the world. Data source: World Bank.

Since the year 2000, the annual CO_2 emissions have decreased for developed economies such as United States, European Union and Japan. On the other hand, the emissions have increased considerably for China and India. In particular, there has been an exponential increase in China's emissions since 2000. As a result, China is currently the greatest CO_2 emitter in the world in terms of total emissions. The sum of contributions from the United States and European Union to the global CO_2 emissions on a percentage basis has decreased from 56% to 24% from 1960 to 2014 and is expected to further decrease with time. Essentially, Figure 5 indicates that the CO_2 emissions are becoming larger and relatively more evenly distributed across the different parts of the world with time; i.e. the CO_2 reduction is a global problem.

2.1.4 Competition from other extremely important global problems

There are several urgent problems that the world has yet to overcome. These include problems such as child deaths, malnutrition, lack of access to clean drinking water, electricity, and medical facilities. These problems are due to a significant fraction of the global population living under extremely poor economic conditions. Related highlights of data from the United Nations are provided below[39,40]:

- Over **500 million** people are living under **1.9 $/day**, which is considered by the World Bank as the level defining extreme poverty. Correspondingly, several hundred million people remain undernourished, are without basic drinking water and have no access to electricity. For example, it was estimated that more than **800 million** people were undernourished in 2018[41].
- About **5 million children** die before their fifth birthday each year[42].
- **Half** of global population lacks access to essential health services[43].
- Advanced economies such as the U.S. also have several million people living under poverty[44]. Clearly, several other urgent problems are competing for the *limited available resources*.

2.1.5 Severity of CO₂ impact remained misunderstood for several decades

Figure 6 provides a historical timeline related to achieving scientific consensus about the detrimental impact of CO_2 emissions on the climate[45]. The figure and the corresponding text clearly show that that the severity of CO_2 impact remained misunderstood for an extraordinarily large period of time.

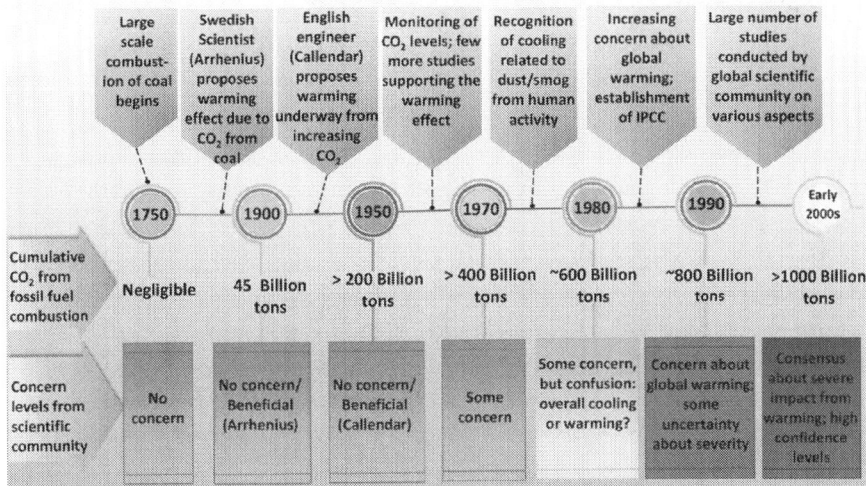

Figure 6. Timeline related to understanding the severity of impact from CO_2.

Large-scale combustion of fossil fuel (coal) roughly started along with the industrial revolution in the middle of the eighteenth century. Towards the end of the nineteenth century, a well-known Swedish Scientist (Svante Arrhenius) proposed that CO_2 released from burning coal would increase the Earth's temperature[46]. However, his proposal did not receive any significant attention from the scientific community. It is noteworthy that the cumulative global amount of CO_2 released from fossil fuel combustion had already reached a substantially large value of **45 billion tons** at the end of the nineteenth century[47]. To put this value in perspective, the cumulative amount of plastics (one of the most widely used materials) produced globally since its invention has been **less than 10 billion tons**[48]. In the 1930s an English engineer (Guy Callendar) speculated that warming of earth was already underway due to emission of CO_2 from fossil fuel combustion. Like the Swedish scientist, the English engineer was interested in this phenomenon primarily to better understand the ice-age. Interestingly, he believed that this effect would be beneficial in the long term[49]. By 1935, the cumulative global amount of CO_2 released from fossil fuel combustion had crossed an imposing 150 billion tons.

Callendar's work eventually prompted more studies in the 1950s and 1960s. These studies generally agreed with the main thesis that warming was occurring due to CO_2 emissions from human activity. In spite of recognizing the warming effect caused by increased CO_2 emissions, the scientific community made no significant recommendations besides increased monitoring. In 1965, a comprehensive report was published by the *United States President's Science Advisory Committee* titled "Restoring the quality of our environment", wherein several important recommendations were made to ensure the future sustainability of the environment[50]. The final recommendations in this important report help us understand the *then existing* level of concern of the scientific community towards the different environmental issues. There were several concrete recommended actions related to air, water pollutants, etc., in this report. *However, the only recommendation by the esteemed panel of scientists related to the CO_2 impact topic was to continue the precise measurements of CO_2 and temperature at different heights in the stratosphere.* This cogently demonstrates the inadequate understanding of the severity of the effect from CO_2 emissions back then. By the year 1970, the cumulative global amount of CO_2 released from fossil fuel combustion had exceeded **400 billion tons**[51].

In the 1970s, several studies supported the long-term impact of warming from greenhouse gases. However, there were also few studies that raised an alarm about potential global cooling due to blocking of sunlight from the dust and smog produced from human activities. Reports from premier scientific organizations clearly reveal that the scientific community lacked adequate understanding of the climate change problem at that time[52,53]. By the end of 1980, the cumulative global amount of CO_2 released from human activity had exceeded 600 billion tons[54].

The studies related to the warming from greenhouse gases started getting increased attention in the 1980s. With more and more climate experts agreeing that human activity was systematically causing significant warming, the Intergovernmental Panel on Climate Change (IPCC) was established in 1988 to guide global Governments on this issue[55]. The first IPCC report for policymakers was issued in 1990 followed by a supplement in 1992[56]. The report concluded the following: a) there was increased warming of the Earth's surface due to emissions from greenhouse gases, b) some greenhouse gases were more potent than the others and that CO_2 was the major contributor to the warming, and c) scenario studies showed that the Earth's mean temperature and sea levels would increase significantly by the year 2100, and d) there were uncertainties in the predictions in terms of timing, magnitude and regional patterns due to incomplete understanding of certain aspects, which could be mitigated via further research.

Around this timeframe, there was a transition from the topic being investigated by a relatively small number of scientists to becoming an extremely large field of study. Large amount of experimental and computational work was undertaken to develop robust understanding of the many issues related to the complex problem. The subsequent IPCC reports[57] took this additional work into consideration, which included contribution from thousands of scientific experts across the globe. By the early part of the twenty first century, there was a strong agreement within the vast majority of the climate experts in the scientific community about the impact of greenhouse gas emissions from human emissions and related aspects[58]. The cumulative global amount of CO_2 released from human activity had exceeded 1000 billion tons by year end 2000, and more than two centuries had passed since the first large-scale combustion of fossil fuels.

The above discussion clearly shows that the severity of impact from the CO_2 emissions **remained misunderstood until an extraordinary amount of CO_2 had been released into the atmosphere**. Perhaps the strongest evidence for this is that it took until 1988 (more than 700 billion tons of cumulatively emitted CO_2) to form an intergovernmental organization (IPCC) to advise global governments on the matter. Clearly, if the severity of the CO_2 impact had been adequately understood earlier, *the needed efforts to address the problem would have also been taken several decades earlier* (for example when CO_2 emissions were still below 100 billion tons).

2.2 Critical challenges related to CO_2 reduction

The major issues associated with CO_2 reduction, discussed in the previous section, serve as indicators for the critical challenges related to resolving the problem (Figure 7). These critical challenges, which can be broadly classified into three categories, are discussed in this section.

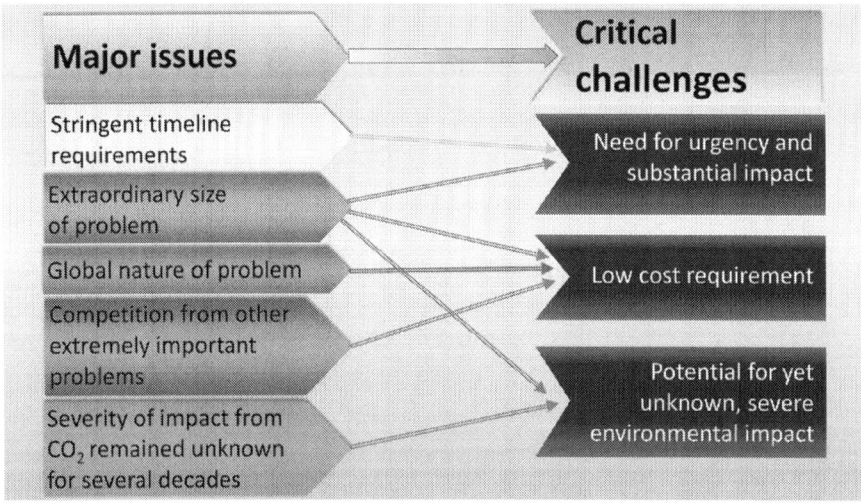

Figure 7. CO_2 reduction: Issues and corresponding challenges

2.2.1 Need for urgency and substantial impact

Need for urgency and substantial impact is directly related to the major issues of stringent timeline requirements and extraordinary size of the CO_2 reduction problem. Earth has already warmed by ~ 1° C above pre-industrial levels due to human activity and is expected to increase a further ~ 0.2° C per decade[59]. More the delay in taking substantial action towards CO_2 reduction, the more difficult it is going to be to avoid major detrimental impact in the future years. Hence, it is important that substantial CO_2 reduction efforts are taken urgently. The data discussed in a previous section related to the extraordinary size of the problem is useful for defining what substantial means in this context. Considering that >35 billion tons of CO_2 is being emitted globally every year and this number is increasing due to increasing demand for energy, there is an urgent need to reduce global CO_2 emissions by *several billion tons per year* within the next few years (as a starting point).

2.2.2 Cost control: Low cost requirement

The *cost control* challenge arises from three major issues associated with CO_2 reduction: extraordinary size of the problem, competition from other extremely important problems and the global nature of the problem. Over the past several years, the CO_2 emissions from fossil fuel combustion for energy related applications have consistently *exceeded 30 billion tons per year*. Because of the extraordinary amount of the energy used, the total global cost of the current fossil-fuel based infrastructure, which includes the electricity, transportation, industry, and miscellaneous sectors, can be roughly estimated to be *several tens of trillions of dollars*. Several of the technology solutions proposed for CO_2 reduction involve the replacement of the current fossil fuel-based energy infrastructure. Considering that the absolute costs are extremely large, any incremental cost for the fossil fuel replacement technologies (CO_2 reduction solutions) can be expected to result in a *tremendously large price tag to the society*. For illustrative purposes, let us consider the example of passenger cars. The number of conventional cars on the roads globally are estimated to be about 1 billion[60,61]. A simplified scenario is provided to give the reader a feel for the CO_2 reduction cost associated with the replacement of 1 billion conventional cars with electric cars. The retail price for an average electric car is currently about 60% higher than an average conventional fossil fuel-based car[62]. If the 1 billion existing passenger cars are replaced with new electric cars as opposed to new conventional cars, the additional cost to the society will be **10+**

trillion dollars[63]. Three important data points are provided to develop an appropriate perspective about the *magnitude of these costs to the society*: a) Passenger cars contribute to ~10% of the global CO_2 emissions[64], b) the annual total gross domestic product (monetary value of all goods and services) of India, which has a population of over 1 billion, is currently ~3 trillion dollars[65], and c) total *global cost for eliminating extreme poverty* is estimated to be ~*3.5 trillion dollars* (175 billion dollars per year for 20 years)[66]. From the above discussion, it is clear that the extraordinary size of the CO_2 produced globally can result in extraordinary costs to the global society.

The importance of cost control for the CO_2 reduction solutions is evident from the fact it faces competition from other extremely serious problems that need to be resolved very urgently. Over 0.5 billion people live in extreme poverty[67]; with millions of child deaths each year, wide-spread malnutrition, and lack of access to electricity, basic drinking water and medical facilities. An additional ~2.5 billion people are struggling to meet their basic needs (are living on less than $5.5/day)[68]. In other words, **about 40%** of the people in the world are currently living in such poor economic conditions that just meeting **basic daily necessities** is their most important problem[69,70]. It is well-established that availability of low-cost energy is essential for robust progress of the economically affected population[71], and consequently it is critical that the CO_2 reduction solutions do not have a significant impact on the cost of energy. The importance of keeping the energy cost low can also be seen from the strong correlation between human development index and energy consumption per capita for developing countries[72,73].

Although majority of the economically affected population is living in less developed economies, poverty is still a significant problem in advanced economies. For example, a sizeable number of people in the United States are living under very poor economic conditions. Based on the data from the U.S. Census Bureau, the number of people living in poverty in 2018 in the United States was **38 million**[74]. Also, it is well documented that even countries with advanced economies have budget restrictions[75]; i.e. there is far more *expenditure* compared to the available budget, which is resulting in a **massive budget deficit**[76]. The expenditure/projects include financial assistance and opportunities for the economically affected, affordable medical care, maintaining/improving infrastructure, national defense, etc. The budget situation is even more challenging for less developed economies. It is critical that cost from the CO_2 reduction solutions are kept as low as possible in view of all the other projects that are also extremely important and urgent.

As discussed in the previous section, large CO_2 emissions are not restricted to the advanced economies such as the United States and the European Union alone. In fact, the total CO_2 emissions are currently the highest in China. Furthermore, they are increasing rapidly in India and are expected to start increasing rapidly in the world's poorest nations in the coming decades. It is apparent that achieving the targeted CO_2 reduction is going to require reduction of CO_2 levels from countries all over the globe in the decades to come. Correspondingly, given that there are *several hundred million people* currently living under very poor economic conditions in countries where CO_2 emissions are expected to increase substantially in the coming years,[77] the CO_2 reduction cost needs to be kept as low as possible.

2.2.3 Potential for severe (yet unknown or misunderstood) environmental impact from CO_2 reduction solutions at the required scale

In a previous section, the historical timeline of understanding the severity of detrimental impact from CO_2 emissions was discussed. The severity of impact from CO_2 emissions resulting from fossil fuel combustion remained misunderstood for an extraordinarily long time despite the enormous CO_2 emissions. This issue is an indicator of the potential for severe environmental impact from *any proposed CO_2 reduction technology* that will be applied at a *wide scale* for energy production in the future. In this book, **"wide scale"** refers to the level of implementation **comparable to the implementation scale of fossil fuel-based technologies**.

Some points from the previous section will be repeated here to drive home the significance of perhaps the most important and **yet ignored** challenge related to reducing CO_2. Combustion of fossil fuels began around the mid eighteenth century, which started the relentless upward march of CO_2 emissions. Our inability to understand the severity of the detrimental impact from human actions is clearly seen from the fact that even after 200 years (from 1750 to 1970) and cumulative release of over 400 billion tons of CO_2

from fossil fuel combustion[78], there was still no substantial alarm raised by the global scientific community. Along with the extraordinary achievement of the first human landing on the moon in 1969[79], humans had also made significant advances in science and technology in several fields by 1970. In other words, the overall state of science and technology was sufficiently advanced back then. The severity of the impact from CO_2 was missed because a) climate/environmental issues are enormously complex with a large number of unknowns, b) the number of researchers working on the specific problem was small compared to the difficulty of the problem, and *most importantly* c) the CO_2 levels, although over 400 billion tons, were still too low (**below threshold level**) to provide a warming effect that could be modeled with high confidence. It took focused efforts from the global scientific community for more than a decade after IPCC was set up in 1988, to achieve the needed high confidence about the impact severity from CO_2 emissions[80]. This high confidence was ironically helped by the fact that the amount of CO_2 emitted via human activity had **exceeded 1000 billion tons** by the end of the year 2000[81]; the corresponding larger impact *provided the needed confidence* in the efforts related to modeling/understanding of the increase in the global mean surface temperature.

The cumulative implementation of the popular low-carbon technologies is currently on an extremely tiny scale compared to the cumulative implementation of fossil fuels. As a result, the global scientific community is in a *similar situation currently with respect to these technologies* compared to what it was with fossil fuel-based technologies several decades ago. The tiny scale of current implementation levels of the popular technology solutions can be clearly seen from the following primary energy consumption data[82]: a) in the year 2019 *alone* the energy consumption from fossil fuels was about **14 billion** tons of oil equivalent, b) *cumulative* solar energy consumption (*from 1965 to 2019*) has been only **0.7 billion** tons of oil equivalent, c) *cumulative* wind energy consumption (*from 1965 to 2019*) has been only **2.2 billion** tons of oil equivalent, and d) the scale of energy storage from batteries is even smaller.

Even **back in the year 1900**, the cumulative primary energy consumption from fossil fuels was *two+ times higher* than the *cumulative to-date consumption of solar and wind energy combined*[83]. From the above discussion it is evident that several CO_2

reduction solutions are currently implemented at a scale that is **trivial** compared to the scale at which the severe impact of CO_2 was appropriately understood by the global scientific community. The importance of scale is further highlighted in the following discussion. By 1950, the global cumulative CO_2 emissions from fossil fuel combustion had exceeded 200 billion tons. Remarkably, these extremely large levels were so low from a *threshold* perspective, that even after the speculation that CO_2 could cause warming, the related impact was grossly misunderstood until 1950. This is evident from the fact that the two key researchers, Arrhenius in ~1900 and Callendar in 1930s/1940s, who had speculated that CO_2 release from human activity would cause warming, believed that this effect could actually be **beneficial for mankind**[84,85].

The critical importance of the threshold scale is further illustrated in the next example. By 1989, the global cumulative CO_2 emissions had exceeded 750 billion tons. However, the **minimum threshold CO_2 levels,** at which the impact could be indisputably attributed to human-driven fossil fuel combustion, had not yet been reached. This is clear based on the following judgement points made in the first IPCC assessment[86]:

- "Global mean surface air temperature has increased by 0.3°C to 0.6°C over the last 100 years, with the five global average warmest years being in the 1980s."
- *"The size of the warming is broadly consistent with predictions of climate models, but it is also of the same magnitude as natural climate variability."*
- *"The unequivocal detection of the enhanced greenhouse effect from observations is not likely for a decade or more."*

Considering that the CO_2 reduction technology solutions are currently implemented at an extremely tiny scale, it is likely that there is potential for severe environmental impact from any proposed CO_2 reduction technology solution when implemented at the required scale. Three other examples are discussed next to provide evidence about prior serious misunderstandings about environmental impacts of technologies, until the implementation scale reached a certain threshold.

Example 1: The timeline related to the unfolding of the first example is shown in Figure 8.

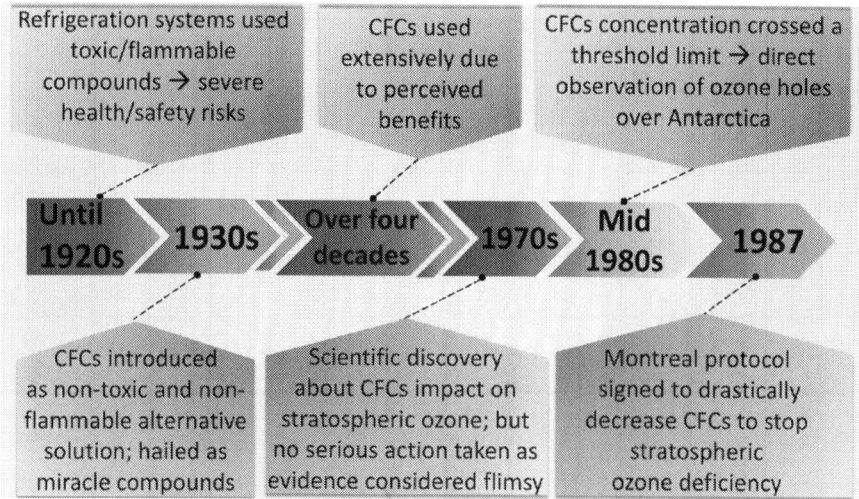

Figure 8. Timeline related to impact from Chlorofluorocarbon (CFCs)

Chlorofluorocarbon compounds (CFCs) were developed in the 1920s and 1930s as a replacement solution to the toxic compounds such as ammonia and sulfur dioxide[87] that were used in refrigerants before then. Exposure to these previously used compounds was a serious concern from a health and safety perspective because of their toxicity and inflammable nature. The replacement chlorofluorocarbon compounds, which were supposedly safe, non-flammable, and non-corrosive, were hailed as a **miracle compounds** at that time because these compounds were considered as an exceptionally robust solution to the prior refrigerant problems[88]. These "miracle" compounds were used extensively across the globe for several decades[89], during which the severity of impact from these compounds remained misunderstood.

It was only in the 1970s that the scientific community started recognizing the potential severity of the impact from these compounds[90]. It was realized that these compounds could potentially decrease the concentration of ozone in the stratosphere. In the 1980s, the concentration of the compounds in the stratosphere finally reached the **minimum threshold** value *needed for direct detection*; i.e. these compounds decreased the ozone levels to the extent that scientists were able to observe (find direct proof) ozone holes over Antarctica in the mid-1980s. It was also established that even a relatively small decrease in stratospheric ozone concentration could result in an increased risk for skin cancer and eye damage in humans, reduced agricultural productivity, and disruption of marine ecosystems[91].

Finally, about five decades after the introduction of these (previously considered as miracle) compounds, a global agreement (Montreal Protocol) was finalized in 1987 with the goal of **phasing out** production and consumption of CFCs[92]. As a result of the Montreal protocol, several compounds were introduced in the early 1990s to replace CFCs. Unfortunately, some of these replacement compounds, known as hydrofluorocarbons, also are powerful greenhouse gases[93]. In fact, some hydrofluorocarbons are more than a thousand times more potent (impact on warming on a per unit basis) than carbon dioxide in contributing to climate change. The seriousness of the impact from greenhouse gases was misunderstood when the original Montreal Protocol was developed. To address this issue, the Protocol was amended in 2016 to include control measures to reduce the warming impact from hydrofluorocarbons (the Kigali Amendment)[94].

In other words, there was a major environmental problem (ozone depletion) caused by the first *technology replacement* solution (CFCs) and then there was another major environmental concern (very high warming potential) with the subsequent *technology replacement* solution (hydrofluorocarbons).

Example 2: Due to desirable characteristics such as low cost and versatility, plastics find applications in packaging, building construction, textiles, consumer products, transportation, electronics, and industrial machinery[95]. Their superior properties make them the perfect solution for most material-related problems. Examples of some commonly used plastics are polypropylene and polyethylene. Due to the benefits offered by the plastics to the society, the demand for plastics has increased rapidly from about 2 million tons per year in the middle of the twentieth century to over 350 million tons per year currently[96]. About 80% of the cumulatively produced plastics (over 5 billion tons) have either ended up in landfills, dumps or in the environment[97]. As the scale of plastics production has increased, previously misunderstood impacts from plastics on the environment have been increasingly recognized.

Severe environmental impacts from plastics which are now well understood include[98]: a) blockage of waterways and worsening of natural disasters, b) increased transmission of diseases such as malaria due to clogging of sewers, which can serve as a breeding ground for mosquitoes and other pests, c) blocking of airways and stomachs of hundreds of species, d) transfer of toxic/carcinogenic materials present in the plastics to humans via the food chain, and e) release of harmful gases such as furan and dioxin during disposal of plastic waste by burning in open air pits. Furthermore, most plastics do not degrade but instead break down into smaller particles known as microplastics. These microplastics are even more difficult to remove from the ocean and because of their extremely long lives (thousands of years) can contaminate both soil and water. When consumed by fish, these microplastics become a part of our food-chain. These microplastics have been found in table salt, bottled water and tap water. Considering that this is a relatively recent phenomenon, the health effects of these microplastics on humans are yet unknown, which is significantly worrisome.

As a result of increased recognition of the severity of the detrimental impact from plastics[99], more than **sixty countries** have taken steps to address plastics pollution in recent years[100]; for example, certain countries and states/cities have banned use of disposable plastic bags.

Example 3: Due to the increased focus on greenhouse gas emissions in early 2000s, several initiatives were implemented to address the issue. One example of the initiatives promoted around that timeframe was to decrease greenhouse gas emissions from fossil fuels by using vegetable oils such as palm oil, rapeseed oil, soy oil etc., to produce biodiesel for transportation[101]. In this example, palm oil which has one of the highest yields per unit area of land, will be discussed.

Due to the favorable climate conditions, certain countries such as Indonesia are large producers of palm oil. The production of palm oil has increased significantly over the last two decades for food and industrial use (which includes biodiesel)[102]. The corresponding *large increase in palm oil production* has allowed for the quantitatively understanding the environmental impact from palm crops. Studies undertaken over the past few years have shown that the increased palm crop production has led to significant *deforestation*. For example, it was found that the proportion of deforestation caused by expansion of palm oil production in Indonesia was about 11% from 2000 to 2010[103]. The above deforestation estimate includes direct land impact (where forest area is replaced by palm crop) and indirect land impact (where palm crop replaces another crop, which relocates to a forest area). Deforestation has a strong detrimental impact on atmospheric CO_2 content. A series of studies for the European commission have indicated that use of palm oil for transportation as replacement of fossil fuels could result in increase in net greenhouse gas emissions instead of reductions[104]. Based on the revelation of this previously misunderstood impact of the palm oil-to-biodiesel solution[105], the European Union has recently taken **corrective actions** to address the issue[106,107].

The above examples illustrate the *potential for severe environmental impact* from any technology solution when the implementation scale is significantly increased. Further light can be shed on this aspect by considering some basic concepts. The current state of the planet's environment compared to the past state (i.e. before the industrial revolution) is unambiguous proof that widescale human driven activity has and will continue to impact the environment. Well established examples of our impact on the environment include significantly *increased air and water pollution, decrease in number/extinction of certain species, and accumulation of enormous amounts of waste*[108,109,110]. This is not surprising considering our increasing population, resourcefulness to get what we need, and limitless needs. The increasing needs of the increasing human population requires activity (i.e. human driven actions) to address those needs. Unfortunately, any activity conducted on a wide scale is expected to have a significant impact on the environment. For example, activity done for supplying food for our growing population involves clearing of land, production of fertilizers, production of pesticides, packaging, transportation of the food and so on. Each of these steps involves use of energy, materials, generation of waste and correspondingly results in certain amount of pollution and thereby an impact on the environment.

Everything else being the same, the magnitude of impact on the environment will depend on the efficiency of the activity; *more activity needed for the same problem equals more impact on the environment*. However, even for an efficiently undertaken activity, the environmental impact is expected to be significant at a widescale undertaking of the activity.

The above discussion does not suggest that humans need to stop progress, however, it does indicate that we need to be aware of these issues and **be realistic when we consider alternative solutions** to our current problems. It would be unfortunate if we ignore key lessons from the past, and unrealistically hope that that the alternative solutions will not have any severe environmental impact at the scale at which these will need to be deployed in the future.

When we consider any alternative CO_2 reduction technology solution, it is well understood that any of the solutions when deployed at the *extraordinary scale necessary to address the global energy needs*, will require **extraordinarily large amounts of resources** such as land, minerals, materials, water, etc., and correspondingly an extraordinarily large amount of activity. Based on fundamental logic and the large amount of historical data, it is very likely that there will be severe environmental impacts due to alternative technology solutions for CO_2 reduction, when implemented on a wide scale. **The severe impact from any proposed technology solution at scale could a) be local or global, b) impact health and/or safety and/or environment, and c) impact air and/or water and/or land.** Any of these impacts, depending on the severity, could essentially disallow or limit the further use of the technology solution. Each technology solution is expected to have its own threshold level of implementation at which these effects become severe enough to limit further implementation. Currently, it is not known *how severe* the specific impacts will be, nor is it known at *what threshold scale* they will be detectable, for a proposed technology solution. The above is apparent from the fact that we misunderstood the environmental impact from fossil fuel combustion for several decades and until several hundred billion tons of CO_2 had been released, and also from the three other examples discussed previously. On the bright side, if we acknowledge this important challenge associated with CO_2 reduction solutions, through a systematic approach, we should be able to identify and deploy solutions in a manner that will have the least relative impact on the environment.

2.3 Implications: Framework for comparing CO_2 reduction solutions

The most discussed challenge associated with CO_2 reduction has been the need for urgency and substantial impact. Based on recent reports from climate experts this is indeed an extremely important challenge. If this was the only important challenge associated with CO_2 reduction, the path forward would be quite straight forward; i.e. it would simply entail the implementation of the CO_2 reduction technology solutions that would provide the quickest relief from the CO_2 problem. However, there are other critical challenges associated with reducing CO_2. Correspondingly, the prioritization of solutions is far from straightforward. The requirement that the reduction solutions be as low cost as possible is critical because even a modest cost increase would make the budgeting impractical considering the a) extraordinary size of the problem, b) other extremely important problems faced by the society and c) global nature of the problem. Unlike the fortunate few who have the luxury to worry about the issues that will be an extremely serious problem in the *next few years/decades*, about 40% of the global population is currently far more concerned about *just meeting their basic needs* such as food, clean water, basic medical, etc., on a day-to-day basis. A significant poverty problem also exists in advanced economies such as the United States as discussed previously[111]. Considering that the poverty problem is currently far from being solved and budgeting is quite tight even in countries with advanced economies, it is apparent that the global society does not have unlimited funds. Therefore cost/impact-based prioritization between the different reduction solutions is essential.

Perhaps the most important challenge is the *inevitability* that each of the technology solutions is expected to have some form of severe environmental impact when implemented on a wide scale. The high-quality historical data and fundamental logic discussed in the previous section, clearly shows the importance of this challenge. Unfortunately, this challenge is currently not on the radar because of the inadequacy of the current understanding of the long-term impact from the proposed technology solutions (when implemented on a wide scale). Efforts until this point have been unable to recognize this challenge due to the **unavailability of relevant data** and **unrealistic optimism driven by emotions**. Unfortunately, not considering this challenge appropriately could result in a massive setback to the global society, recovery from which would be extremely difficult. For example, it could potentially result in other serious environmental problem(s) being generated due to an injudicious *widescale implementation* of one or more CO_2 reduction technology solutions. Considering the associated enormous cost, this will also be a massive setback to the credibility of global environmental efforts.

There is another critical challenge, which was purposely not discussed previously because it is not directly related to the major issues associated with CO_2 reduction; however, it is very important for comparing technologies from a practical viewpoint. This challenge is related to the *forced interdependency* between certain technology solutions. If successful widescale implementation of one CO_2 reduction technology requires the successful widescale implementation of another *relatively* new technology, this significantly increases the difficulty of implementation. For example, there is increased project risk, increased uncertainty in defining and meeting timelines, and increased potential for severe environmental impact from two less established technologies. In other words, a technology solution that is dependent on another less established technology will be significantly disadvantaged.

The discussion in this section can be directly used to develop a framework of characteristics for comparing the different CO_2 reduction technology solutions. The key comparison characteristics included in the framework are provided below:
- Ability to make a quick and substantial impact
- Cost
- Potential for severe environmental impact at a scale comparable to the historical use of fossil fuels. Note, severe environmental impact as used in this book refers to a level of detrimental impact to the environment, health or safety, that will limit or disallow the use of the technology solution.
- Dependence on another new technology

Thus, based on the above comparison framework, an ideal CO_2 reduction solution would be the one that has a) an ability to make a quick and substantial impact, b) a low relative cost, c) a low potential for unknown severe environmental impact at scale, and d) no dependence on another new technology.

...§§§-§-§§§...

Chapter 3: Key Characteristics of the Technology Solutions

This chapter will focus on the framework of key characteristics identified for comparing the different CO_2 reduction technology solutions. Based on this framework, the characteristics that need to be considered for comparing the different solutions are a) cost, b) CO_2 reduction impact in terms of magnitude, c) CO_2 reduction impact in terms of speed, d) potential for, yet unknown, severe environmental impact at widescale implementation and e) dependence on another new technology.

The general approach undertaken to discuss the key characteristics of the technology solutions is provided below:
- The *cost characteristic* is an indicator of the budget requirements. Since, technology cost is influenced by multiple factors, there are several challenging aspects related to comparison of the cost characteristic. For example, it is important to consider the effect of *location* and *time* on the costs appropriately. Also, considering that there are several inaccurate costs available in open literature for the different technologies, it is essential to use cost data from **credible sources**. Finally, it is important to avoid the inclusion of subsidies and costs from localized cases (i.e. based on few specific projects). Costs which do not satisfy the above criterion, are not representative and, therefore, are inappropriate for comparison between technologies. To enable robust relative cost comparisons between different technologies, it is crucial to a) standardize for location, time, and other factors, b) exclude subsidies and c) only consider data from credible sources. These conditions are satisfied herein by using the recent, unsubsidized, average cost data for the United States, which is publicly available from credible sources such as the U.S. Department of Energy[112]. While the cost discussion is *initially focused* on the United States, the discussion is later expanded to include the other regions of the world. Unless mentioned otherwise, all the cost data presented herein is in 2019 dollars[113].

- *The magnitude of impact* characteristic relates to the magnitude of CO_2 reduction by the proposed solution *relative to the reference technology* for the given sector. Herein, the magnitude of impact will be discussed in terms of the amount of life cycle CO_2 emissions avoided relative to the reference technology. Reference technology is defined as the conventional technology that currently produces the majority of the CO_2 emissions for a given sector. The entire life cycle must be considered for a realistic comparison of magnitude of impact on CO_2 reduction from different technology solutions[114]. Correspondingly, the CO_2 emissions reported herein are based on the complete life cycle. For example, electric vehicles have zero tail-pipe emissions; however, a life cycle analysis includes CO_2 emissions from the production of the electricity and the manufacturing of the electric vehicle. The CO_2 emissions data is provided in *terms of CO_2 equivalent* so that the impact from other greenhouse gas emissions from that technology can also be included. Another example, the methane emissions are also included in the life cycle analysis of natural gas fueled power plants[115].
- *The potential for severe environmental impact at scale* characteristic relates to the possibility of a, yet unknown, severe environmental impact from a *widescale implementation* of the proposed technology solution. *Widescale implementation,* for the purpose of this book*,* refers to an implementation scale comparable to the **implementation scale of conventional fossil fuel-based technologies**. *Severe environmental impact* as defined in this book is an impact level that will **limit or disallow** the further use of the technology solution. The impact could be local or global and is all inclusive- it includes air pollution, water pollution, water scarcity, land erosion, land contamination, health, safety and so on. Herein, the potential for such severe impact from a CO_2 reduction technology solution will be evaluated in terms of data on its *current scale of implementation* and *required human activity on a life cycle basis*. Essentially, if the CO_2 reduction technology solution has *already* been implemented widescale (i.e. it already represents a substantial fraction of total energy production), the environmental impact of the technology *should be well understood* and correspondingly should have a lower potential for unknown severe environmental impact. However, if the proposed solution has not yet been

extensively implemented, then based on previously discussed examples, a significant potential for severe environmental impact from the technology may be expected for a wide scale of implementation. The relative potential for severe environmental impact will depend on the extent of current implementation; i.e. lower the current scale of implementation, higher will be the statistical probability for severe unknown environmental impact. The relative amount of required *human activity* is the other important indicator for the potential existence of a severe impact from a technology solution. The required amount of human activity for the proposed technology solution depends on the *efficiency of the assistance provided by nature* for the technology solution on a *life cycle basis*. Efficient assistance from nature would result in a lower requirement of human activity[116] and correspondingly a lower potential for severe environmental impact on a relative basis. The efficiency of assistance by nature may be evaluated in terms of the *accessibility of the energy source* (e.g. sunlight, wind, crude oil, natural gas, biomass etc.) and the *process efficiency for extracting useable energy from the energy source*. Significant human activity is required to access the energy source for fossil fuels-based technology solutions (e.g. extraction of crude oil); however, minimal human activity is required for accessing sunlight which is the energy source for solar photovoltaics technology solution. As for process efficiency, the amount of human activity depends on the difficulty in extracting the energy from the energy source. One way to evaluate this energy extraction difficulty is in terms of the energy density of the energy source. Energy density is essentially the amount of energy available per relevant unit (e.g. mass, volume, etc.) from the energy source. Therefore, for a technology solution which uses an energy source with low energy density (i.e. dilute energy source), a much higher level of human activity will be required due to the **inherent inefficiency** of such a process. Higher requirement of human activity typically involves *larger requirement of land*, and/or *water*, and/or *materials production*, and/or *component fabrication* and/or need for *mining of difficult-to-access metals*. It is important to keep in mind that the severe impact on the environment will be **directly observable** only after a certain

threshold level of implementation of the technology is reached (similar to the examples discussed previously).
- *The dependence on another new technology* characteristic relates to the additional need for widescale successful implementation of another less established technology. Herein, this characteristic will be discussed in terms of the level of co-dependence between the two technologies and corresponding issues that could arise as a result of the co-dependence.
- *The speed of impact* characteristic relates to the speed of implementation of the CO_2 reduction solutions based on technical and practical issues. Herein, the speed of impact will be discussed primarily in terms of the technology maturity levels, compatibility with existing infrastructure and other related practical issues. For example, more the amount of *change* required for the proposed solution relative to existing infrastructure, greater would be the challenge for a high-speed implementation. This is related to the extraordinary size and complexity of the problem, which involves massive resource requirements, complicated logistics, etc.
- To enable practical cost comparisons, the discussion will focus on the current state-of-the-art technology solutions; i.e. currently preferred technology solutions based on commercial applications. This is related to the fact that the average time for a new technology in the energy field (e.g. new materials that replace existing materials in solar technology)[117] to advance from a promising R&D phase to reasonably high levels of implementation is more than 10 years.

For facilitating the discussion of the above characteristics, the different technology solutions have been categorized in the following groups: electricity generation, transportation, and direct CO_2 capture from air.

3.1 Key characteristics of the CO_2 reduction solutions for electricity generation

Fossil fuel-based technologies, such as coal and natural gas, are often lumped together in comparison discussions with different CO_2 reduction technology solutions such as wind, solar etc.[118]. However, this approach suffers from practical concerns, considering that there is an enormous difference between the characteristics of coal fueled power plants and natural gas fueled plants. The natural-gas fueled technology is substantially superior to the coal-fueled technology from a capital cost and CO_2 emissions perspective[119,120] (further details in section 3.1.1). *Lumping of these technologies is not very practical* when the objective is to reduce CO_2. Replacement of coal-fueled plants with natural gas-fueled plants should also be considered as one of the CO_2 reduction solutions[121], which is not possible if the two technologies are lumped together. This is especially important considering that nearly 40% of the global electricity production is currently based on coal, and that the global CO_2 produced from coal fueled power plants alone is *~10 billion tons per year*[122]. Therefore, for future discussions in this book, the existing coal plants are considered as the primary reference case for replacement by the CO_2 reduction technologies in the electricity generation sector.

As discussed previously, it is important to have credible and representative cost data. The representative cost data for the current state-of-the-art electricity generation technologies has been primarily sourced from the United States Energy Information Administration (U.S. EIA)[123]. The cost data (presented in 2019 $) includes the capital cost, fixed *operating and maintenance* (O&M) cost, variable O&M cost and the levelized cost of electricity for typical electricity generation units in the United States[124,125]. Further details about the capital cost estimations, if needed, are available from the U.S. EIA[126]. The capital cost values for the electricity generation units are provided in terms of a per unit *capacity output* ($/kW) basis. Capacity output refers to the maximum electricity output of the plant. In reality, the actual output is lower than the capacity output because of issues such as availability of energy sources (e.g. sunlight and wind), downtime due to regular maintenance schedule, electricity supply/demand, etc. Therefore, a capacity factor term is required for each technology, which is a ratio of the actual output over a period of time to the capacity output. Since the capacity factors can be significantly different for different technologies, a robust comparison of investment for the electricity generation projects needs both, the capital cost in terms of per unit capacity and the capacity factor for each technology. The fixed and variable O&M costs provide a comparison of on-going operations and maintenance costs.

Levelized cost of electricity is one of the commonly used metrics for comparing the competitiveness of the different technologies. The levelized cost of electricity provides a comparison of the technologies in terms of the *total* electricity production cost for constructing and operating a generating plant over *an assumed financial life and duty cycle*. The levelized cost of electricity data has been reported from the recent related report published by the U.S. EIA[127]; detailed information/assumptions related to their estimations can be obtained directly from that report.

The data for CO_2 emissions from the power plants, which has been used herein for comparing the magnitude of impact on CO_2 reduction, includes the entire life cycle and is expressed in terms of *CO_2 equivalent* (CO_2e)[128,129]. The life cycle data consists of direct emissions, infrastructure and supply chain emissions, and so on. For example, the life cycle emissions from coal and natural gas fueled plants include all greenhouse gas emissions (CO_2e) from fuel extraction, fuel processing, fuel transportation, power plant emissions, and transmission/distribution systems.

The discussion related to the potential for severe environmental impact at scale is based on the overall scale of implementation and required human activity based on the *efficiency of assistance from nature* for a given technology solution. The efficiency of nature has been considered in terms of accessibility of the energy source (i.e. activity required to access the energy source) and the process efficiency to extract energy from the energy source (i.e. activity required to extract useable energy from the energy source).

Certain technologies such as natural gas fueled, coal fueled, nuclear, biomass, etc., are considered to be *dispatchable* since electricity generation from these can be scheduled on demand[130] However, technologies such as solar energy and wind energy are considered to be *non-dispatchable*, as these produce electricity *intermittently* and therefore cannot produce electricity on demand. Considering that electricity demand can depend on the time of the day, season and/or location, the dispatchable technologies have a *substantial advantage* over the non-dispatchable technologies[131]. Therefore, the characteristics such as costs, magnitude of impact etc., **cannot be considered in an isolated manner** to make overall efficiency decisions between dispatchable and non-dispatchable technologies. To address this problem, the overall efficiencies of the CO_2 reduction technology solutions are compared in this book *by* *simultaneously considering all the critical aspects* (overall comparison discussion is provided in a later chapter).

3.1.1 Natural gas fueled plants

In case of coal and natural gas power plants, burning of the fuel (coal or natural gas) produces heat energy, and a turbine-generator combination is used to convert the heat energy to electrical energy[132]. In practice, the conversion of energy from the fuels to electrical energy can be achieved via various plant configurations. Over the past decades, the most efficient configurations have been identified and these are considered as the state-of-the-art technologies. Herein, the cost characteristics of the state-of-the-art *natural gas* fueled technology (combined cycle) is compared with the state-of-the-art *coal* fueled technology (ultra-supercritical), when discussing new plants.

Cost: The capital cost per unit capacity for the natural gas fueled technology is substantially lower than the coal fueled technology (Table 1)[133], which can be attributed to the relatively greater technical challenges associated with conversion of coal to electricity. Also, the on-going operating and maintenance costs are also significantly lower for the natural gas fueled technology.

	Capital Cost (\$/kW)	**Variable O&M** (\$/MWh)	**Fixed O&M** (\$/kW-yr)
Coal	3661	4.5	40.4
Natural gas	1079	2.5	14.0

Table 1. Capital Cost, operating and maintenance cost (O&M) comparison: natural gas and coal plants. Data source: U.S. EIA[134]

As seen from Figure 9, the levelized cost of electricity is substantially lower for a new natural gas fueled plant compared to a new coal fueled plant in the United States[135,136].

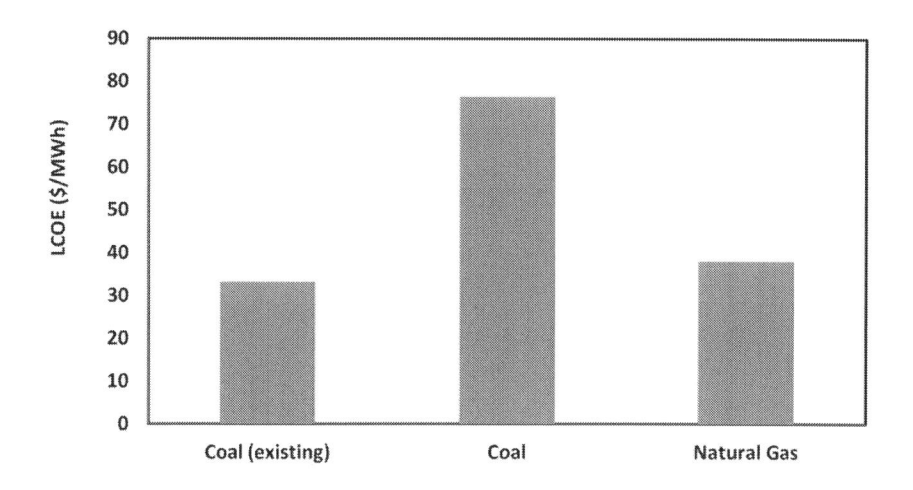

Figure 9. Levelized cost of electricity (LCOE) comparison: new natural gas plant and coal (existing and new) plants. Data source: U.S. EIA[137]

From this data it is evident that there is a considerable cost advantage for a new natural gas fueled plant compared to a new coal fueled power plant in the United States. However, the levelized cost of electricity for *existing coal plants* is more important for comparison purposes, considering that the existing coal plants are the *reference case* for replacement by the different CO_2 reduction technologies. The levelized cost of electricity for existing coal plants obviously does not involve any capital cost, as these are currently operational plants. Therefore, the levelized cost of electricity for existing coal plants is based only on the operating and maintenance costs and is expectedly low. Interestingly, the levelized cost of electricity from a new natural gas fueled plant is only modestly higher than the levelized cost of electricity from an existing coal plant (Figure 9). This shows that the replacement of an existing coal plant with a natural gas fueled plant is a relatively low-cost option in the United States. The overall electricity production economics is very sensitive to the specific country as it also depends on the feedstock cost differential between coal and natural gas, which is country dependent. For example, the United States historically has much cheaper natural gas prices compared to countries such as Japan[138]. Therefore, unlike in the United States, where natural gas fueled plant is a low-cost option, it is expected to be a higher cost option in countries wherein natural gas prices are considerably higher relative to coal[139].

Magnitude of impact: On a life cycle basis, natural gas fueled technology (~500 gCO$_2$e/kWh) produces about half the CO$_2$ emissions per unit of electricity produced compared to coal fueled (~1000 gCO$_2$e/kWh) technology[140,141]. The replacement of an existing coal plant with a natural gas plant, thus, reduces the CO$_2$ emissions by ~500 gCO$_2$e/kWh. The magnitude of impact of CO$_2$ reduction resulting from replacement of existing coal plants with natural gas plants can be considered as medium when compared to reductions from other technology solutions. Considering that there are currently a very large number of existing coal plants (total CO$_2$ emissions from coal plants ~ 10 billion tons per year)[142], the overall impact is expected to be substantial from replacing existing coal plants with natural gas plants. For example, if 60% of the global coal-fired power plants were replaced by natural gas power plants, that by itself would reduce the CO$_2$ emissions by around *3 billion tons per year*.

Potential for severe environmental impact at scale: Natural gas plants and the associated infrastructure (from fuel extraction to electricity transmission) has been extensively implemented across the globe in the last few decades[143,144]. It is well established that natural gas technology produces *significantly fewer pollutants* than coal-based technology. Considering that natural gas fueled power plants have been one of the major producers of electricity for several decades, the life cycle environmental impacts (pollutants, land impact, etc.) from natural gas technology are now well understood[145]. Consequently, when applied for CO$_2$ reduction by replacing the reference technology (i.e. existing coal plants), there is a relatively low potential for any hitherto unknown severe environmental impact from conventional natural gas technology. In recent decades there has been a change from conventional production of natural gas to unconventional production (i.e. hydraulic fracturing/fracking). Anytime there is a change in any part of the lifecycle, the potential for severe environmental impact needs to be re-evaluated in terms of the scale of deployment of the change. The scale of implementation of natural gas production from fracking has increased rapidly over the past two decades. The percent of natural gas produced by fracking in the United States increased from less than 7% of the total output in 2000 (3.6 billion cubic feet per day) to 67% in 2015 (53 billion cubic feet per day)[146]. The environmental impact from fracking has been reasonably well identified in the United States[147]. However, compared to conventional production, the fracking-based production is still relatively small on a global cumulative basis. Based on the above discussion, there is medium potential for yet unknown severe impact from natural gas fueled technology.

Dependence on another new technology: The upstream (natural gas production, distribution) and downstream (electricity transmission and distribution) network required for natural gas fueled power plants is well established considering the massive implementation[148]; consequently, there is no dependence on any other new technology.

Speed of impact: The speed for replacing coal fueled power plants with natural gas fueled power plants is expected to be high considering the high maturity of the technology and excellent compatibility with the existing energy infrastructure.

3.1.2 Solar-Utility Plants

Solar photovoltaic technology converts sunlight directly into electricity[149]. This technology can be used for large-scale[150] applications such as utility power plants as well as smaller scale applications such as residential/commercial. There are several different types of solar photovoltaic technologies such as silicon (monocrystalline, poly-crystalline, amorphous), cadmium telluride thin film, copper indium gallium selenide thin film, organic polymer, quantum dot, and hybrid organic-inorganic[151]. These different solar photovoltaic technologies can primarily be differentiated based on the materials used in each technology for the conversion of sunlight. The choice of the materials leads to different cost and performance characteristics. The silicon-based photovoltaic technology has consistently been the most widely used technology globally[152] based on its overall advantage over other solar photovoltaic technologies in terms of cost, conversion efficiencies, and long-term robustness.

Since, sunlight is not available for certain time-periods (night-time, cloud cover, etc.), solar energy can only provide electricity in an intermittent manner and is therefore categorized as non-dispatchable[153]. As discussed earlier, there is a significant advantage for dispatchable technologies compared to non-dispatchable technologies due to electricity supply/demand issues. Therefore, the characteristics such as cost, and magnitude of impact cannot be used for evaluating the overall efficiency of technologies in a *standalone fashion* between dispatchable and non-dispatchable technologies. However, these characteristics when considered together with other key characteristics can provide the necessary information for an overall comparison between the different technology solutions.

Cost: As seen from Table 2, the capital cost per unit capacity of solar photovoltaic technology for utility plant applications is comparable to natural gas fueled plants, but substantially lower than coal fueled plants [154].

	Capital Cost ($/kW)	Variable O&M ($/MWh)	Fixed O&M ($/kW-yr)
Coal	3661	4.5	40.4
Natural gas	1079	2.5	14.0
Solar-Utility	1331	0.0	15.2

Table 2. Capital Cost, operating and maintenance cost (O&M) comparison: solar utility and fossil-fueled plants. Data source: U.S. EIA[155]

Since solar photovoltaic technology has a much lower capacity factor than the fossil fueled plants, there is a corresponding detrimental impact on the total initial investment cost. However, the on-going operating and maintenance costs, which includes the feedstock costs, are very low for the solar photovoltaic technology, thus lowering the levelized cost of electricity (Figure 10)[156].

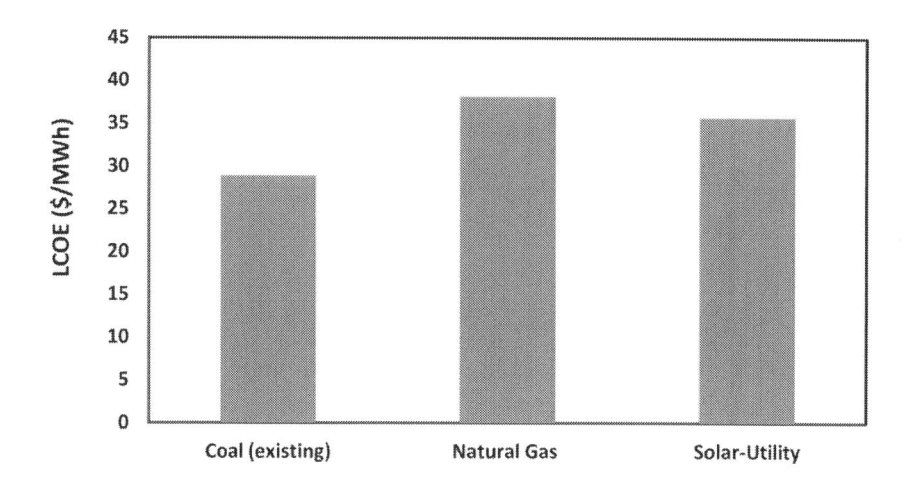

Figure 10. Levelized cost of electricity (LCOE) comparison: solar-utility, coal (existing) and natural gas plants. Data source: U.S. EIA[157]

Magnitude of impact: On a life cycle basis, solar photovoltaics technology produces very little CO_2 (~ 50 gCO_2e/kWh) emissions per unit of electricity produced, compared to coal fueled (~1000 gCO_2e/kWh) technology[158,159]. The extremely low emissions from solar technology makes it an attractive solution for CO_2 reduction. The magnitude of impact for CO_2 reduction via solar technology, therefore, is high (~ 950 gCO_2e/kWh) for replacement of existing coal fueled plants. However, it is important to note that direct replacement of dispatchable technologies with non-dispatchable technologies is **only possible on a limited scale**[160]. To illustrate this point, consider a small town, which is currently being powered by a combination of coal and natural gas plants. If 100% production of electricity is replaced by solar technology, the town will not receive adequate electricity for a significant fraction of a 24-hour time period (e.g. evening through dawn, or when there is a cloud cover). A more practical solution would be the elimination of the coal fueled plant and using an appropriate combination of solar energy, wind energy and natural gas fueled plants. Another alternative that would allow a much wider application of solar technology involves the inclusion of energy storage options. However, there are several new challenges to this approach, which are discussed in a subsequent section.

Potential for severe environmental impact at scale: As discussed previously, the potential for severe environmental impact at scale of any technology can be evaluated by considering its *current scale of implementation* and *efficiency of assistance provided by nature.* In case of solar technology, mass production first started in 1963[161]. However, the cumulative amount of energy consumed from solar technology since then has only been around ~0.7 billion tons of oil equivalent. The cumulative amount of solar energy consumed (i.e. when including all years) is **about 15 times lower** than the energy consumed from *fossil fuels in a single year*[162]. This data suggests that implementation is still far below the threshold scale at which any *potentially severe environmental impact* will be appropriately understood. Environmental impact studies for any technology solution are based on the information related to the scale of implementation at that point in time. Since solar energy is currently at an extremely small scale of implementation, researchers currently do not have the appropriate information for understanding potential environmental impacts at the required wide scale of implementation. Therefore, the information from the current studies *could be misleadingly optimistic*. This is similar to scientists not raising any substantial concern about fossil fuels, plastics, and chlorofluorohydrocarbons when they were still implemented on a small scale. Consider the fact until 1950, the leading scientists who proposed the potential of earth warming from CO_2 emissions believed that this effect could be *beneficial* in the long term[163]. It is important to note that by 1950 (i.e. from 1750 to 1950), more energy had been consumed from fossil fuels than the cumulative energy (i.e. *total from all years until 2019*) consumed **from all non-fossil fuel technologies combined**[164,165]. On account of current extremely low levels of implementation of solar photovoltaics technology, it is not possible to say with any certainty that there would be no severe impact at widescale implementation. In fact, based on historical data discussed earlier, it is probable that there will be some type of severe environmental impact from the technology solution when implemented at the required enormous scale.

One approach to estimating the probable environmental impact of the technology solution at scale is by considering the fundamentals of the technology, i.e. by considering the efficiency of assistance provided by nature for the technology. In case of solar photovoltaics, there is no need for human activity for accessing the energy source. Also, there are no direct environmental pollutants related to the energy source. However, sunlight is a very dilute source of energy with several orders of magnitude lower energy density compared to fossil fuels. Since sunlight is a very dilute source of energy[166], the overall electricity production process is relatively inefficient, and a large amount of material and land is required to produce electricity and therefore there is significant need for human driven activity. The human activity involves preparation of land, extraction/production of the material(s) required for the many different components, fabrication of the components, disposal/recycling of components, etc.[167] Therefore, at a scale that is *several orders of magnitude higher* compared to the current implementation scale of the solar technology (i.e. widescale- comparable to fossil fuel scale), there is medium-to-high potential for one or more factors related to solar-utility such as the material extraction/use, production of various components, disposal/recycling, land impact, plant operations, etc., to result in some type of severe environmental impact.

Dependence on another new technology: Due to intermittent production of electricity from solar photovoltaics, the solar photovoltaic technology cannot be exclusively used as a standalone solution. The current implementation of this technology has only been possible because it represents a relatively small fraction of the overall electricity production. Consider a region, where electricity is provided by natural gas fueled plants, coal fueled plants, and nuclear plants. Due to the dispatchable nature (ability to match demand with electricity production) of the power plants and the significant flexible features of natural gas power plants, the region can be reliably powered with electricity 24 hours a day and 7 days a week (24X7) for the entire year with the above discussed combination of power plants. Now, let us consider the case where significant amount of solar power is added to replace some of the older coal plants. Solar technology will provide electricity only in the hours when there is sunlight. The other power plants will have to be ramped up or down depending on the electricity demand to address the problems attributed to the non-dispatchable solar plants. Unfortunately, there are technical and economical limitations to the extent to which the other plants can be ramped up and down, which will result in sub-optimization (i.e. inferior performance) of the overall electricity production[168]. Thus, more the solar power penetration (as a percentage of the total electricity produced), more sub-optimization would typically be expected, thus increasing the challenge for meeting the 24X7 electricity demand reliably for the entire year.

In an actual electricity grid, there are several different types of plants such as hydroelectric, wind, biomass, etc., and correspondingly there is more complexity. The increased addition of renewables such as solar power in recent years in the state of California has clearly shown the sub-optimization associated with integration of large amounts of solar technology in the electricity grid. This sub-optimization problem has been described as a "duck curve", so named because of the shape of the electric load met by conventional plants when increasing levels of solar capacity is added to the system[169]. As a result, solar power has had to be turned off (i.e. electricity generation *curtailed*) during certain time-periods since the past few years[170]. This sub-optimization has an *adverse impact* on the economics and environmental benefit. The problem has increased with increasing penetration of solar power in California.

As a result of the sub-optimization caused by solar power integration into the grid, only a limited implementation of solar technology is practical in any existing mix of conventional power plants without energy storage technology. A widescale implementation of solar utility plants is possible if there is also a widescale implementation of *energy storage technology* (discussed in the subsequent section), which will allow the storage of the electricity for later use when sunlight is not available. Thus, the widescale implementation of solar photovoltaic technology is strongly dependent on energy storage technology. Currently the implementation of energy storage technology is extremely small; related issues will be discussed in a subsequent section.

Speed of impact: Solar photovoltaic utility plants are based on a mature and robust technology, which is favorable from the viewpoint of speed of implementation. On the flip side, solar technology has poor compatibility with the conventional electricity grid, especially at high penetration levels. When coupled with energy storage systems, the challenge related to compatibility with the electricity grid can be eliminated, however there are several new challenges. Challenges for speed of impact when considering energy storage systems are discussed in a subsequent section. Another potential challenge for quickly implementing utility-scale solar photovoltaic technology in regions where suitable land is scarce, is the large land requirement. Solar utility plants require over 100 times more land compared to natural gas fueled power plants per unit electricity produced[171,172]. Based on the above discussion, the speed of impact from solar photovoltaics technology is expected to be medium-to-high until a certain threshold level of implementation (i.e. favorable speed of impact *only* until there is reasonable compatibility with the grid).

3.1.3 Solar-Distributed

Solar-distributed includes applications such as residential and small scale non-residential. Since there are several similarities between solar-utility and solar-distributed, only the key differences will be discussed herein. The capital cost per unit capacity is about 2 times higher for solar-distributed compared to solar-utility[173]. The levelized cost of electricity is also considerably higher for solar-distributed. The cost advantage for solar-utility is related to economy of scale advantage (due to superior hardware, labor, etc. efficiencies at the much higher scale) and potentially higher capacity factors due to greater opportunities for optimization. Apart from a cost disadvantage, solar-distributed also has some practical disadvantages related to operation and maintenance, considering that it involves multiple very small, widely spread locations, as opposed to a large single point source for solar-utility.

However, solar-distributed does have certain important advantages. For implementations such as roof top installations, additional land is not required. Transmission losses are also lower since solar-distributed is located at the site where electricity is consumed[174]. Thus, solar energy-distributed has a higher cost, lower potential for severe environmental impact, but similar magnitude of impact, speed of impact and dependence, when compared to solar-utility.

3.1.4 Solar with energy storage

Due to the intermittent nature of sunlight, a widescale implementation of solar technology will also require a widescale implementation of an energy storage technology. Correspondingly, several combinations of solar technology and energy storage technologies are being considered[175]. Herein, two of the more popular choices, concentrated solar with thermal storage system[176] and solar photovoltaic with Li ion battery system[177], will be considered as representative technologies to understand the key characteristics related to widescale implementation of solar with energy storage.

Concentrated solar technology collects and concentrates sunlight to produce heat energy, which is subsequently converted to electricity[178]. The inclusion of a thermal energy storage system allows the storage of heat to produce electricity when sunlight is not available.

In case of solar photovoltaic with Li ion battery energy storage, the electricity produced by solar photovoltaic technology is stored using Li ion battery technology for later use.

Cost: The levelized cost of electricity production for concentrated solar thermal power with energy storage (CSP) is more than two times that for solar photovoltaic technology[179,180]. This is due to very high capital cost per unit capacity for concentrated solar thermal power with storage (Table 3)[181].

	Capital Cost ($/kW)	Variable O&M ($/MWh)	Fixed O&M ($/kW-yr)
Coal	3661	4.5	40.4
Natural gas	1079	2.5	14.0
Solar Thermal/Storage	7191	0.0	85.0

Table 3. Capital Cost, operating and maintenance cost (O&M) comparison: concentrated solar thermal power with storage and fossil-fueled plants. Data source: U.S. EIA[182]

The capital cost presented in Table 3 for concentrated solar thermal with storage is only for eight hours of energy storage[183,184];

therefore, from a standalone operational perspective, longer duration storage hours will be required[185], and correspondingly higher cost will be incurred[186]. As discussed earlier, the capital cost for natural gas fueled plants and utility-scale solar photovoltaic plants is comparable. However, when energy storage is included with solar, the natural gas fueled technology has *a very large capital cost advantage*. To illustrate this, a natural gas fueled plant is compared with a solar-utility photovoltaic plant with a Li ion battery energy storage system. Data for the natural gas fueled and solar-utility plants is directly obtained from the U.S. Energy Information Administration[187]. For this illustrative comparison, it is assumed that either a natural gas fueled plant in a standalone mode or a solar with battery storage system in a standalone mode will be used to power a small town. For the Li ion battery energy storage system, the capital cost ranges from 380 to 469 $/kWh based on recent studies by leading US. National Laboratories[188,189]. To provide a more optimistic estimate for solar with battery energy storage, the lower end value of 380 $/kWh is used herein. Using this data, the capital investment required for the solar-utility plant with the battery energy storage system is about *seven times higher* than that of the natural gas fueled system to power the small town, on a standalone basis. Please see Appendix for more information about the estimations.

Reductions in the capital cost of energy storage systems is expected to help in the future years. The impact of such future potential cost reductions is discussed next. A collaborative study by various U.S. National Laboratories indicated a 23% cost reduction from 2018 to 2025 for the Li ion battery energy storage system[190]. To develop a *very optimistic* case, a 50% capital cost reduction for energy storage system, a 20% capital cost reduction for solar photovoltaic, and no cost reduction for natural gas fueled plant, is assumed by the year 2025. Even with these *very optimistic assumptions* in favor of solar photovoltaic with battery storage, the capital investment requirement for the combined solar and energy storage system is still found to be about *five times higher* than a natural gas fueled plant to provide electricity for the town in the year 2025.

Magnitude of impact: The CO_2 released per unit of electricity produced by solar with energy storage, irrespective of the type of solar/storage combination used, is expected to be very low (< 100 gCO$_2$e/kWh) compared to coal plants, especially when a significant fraction of the energy used for manufacturing the energy storage systems is from renewable sources[191,192]. Thus, the CO$_2$ reduction magnitude of impact for replacing existing coal plants by solar with energy storage technology is high.

Potential for severe environmental impact at scale: An effective indicator for the potential for severe environmental impact at scale for a given technology, is the current level of implementation of that technology. As discussed previously, the amount of implementation for solar has been extremely small compared to energy produced fossil fuels. Furthermore, the implementation of energy storage (such as thermal energy storage and batteries) has been even smaller[193]. Therefore, in case of solar with energy storage there is a significant possibility for severe environmental impact(s) at scale.

Due to the dilute nature of sunlight, a substantial amount of human activity is required in terms of material, land requirement, etc., for extracting electricity from sunlight. When considering both solar and energy storage, human activity is further required for the energy storage component. The energy storage component requires substantial human activity (e.g., metals/materials, production of different components, recycling/disposal, etc.)[194] due to the very low energy densities of current energy storage systems[195]. Considering the very low scale of implementation and substantial human activity required for the solar and the energy storage component, there is a high potential for (yet unknown) severe environmental impact at scale for the solar with energy storage technology solutions.

Dependence on another new technology: As long as solar is coupled with adequate energy storage to meet the electricity demand 24X7, there should be no dependence on any other new technology for the solar with energy storage technology solution.

Speed of impact: There should be good compatibility with the existing infrastructure as long as solar is coupled with adequate energy storage to meet the electricity demand (24X7). However, the technology is *much less mature* and there are considerable practical challenges related to implementation of this fairly complex combination of functionalities (electricity production and energy storage). Based on the discussion above, the speed of impact for the solar with energy storage solution is expected to be low-to-medium.

3.1.5 Wind technology-onshore

Wind is a result of a combination of uneven atmospheric temperatures, irregularities of the earth's surface and earth's rotation[196]. In case of the wind technology, wind turbines convert the energy in the wind into electricity. Modern wind turbines fall into two basic groups: horizontal axis turbines and vertical axis turbines. The wind technology market is currently dominated by the horizontal axis turbines[197]. Wind-driven utility scale plants, which consist of a group of large turbines, are often described as wind farms. Electricity produced by wind technology is only intermittently available depending on when the wind is blowing, which varies by the day and season. Similar to solar technology, the wind technology is also categorized as *non-dispatchable*. Wind-onshore technology will be discussed in this section, while the salient features of the offshore wind technology will be discussed in the next section.

Cost: As shown in Table 4, the capital cost per unit capacity of wind-onshore technology is comparable to natural gas fueled plants, but substantially lower than coal fueled plants[198].

	Capital Cost ($/kW)	**Variable O&M** ($/MWh)	**Fixed O&M** ($/kW-yr)
Coal	3661	4.5	40.4
Natural gas	1079	2.5	14.0
Wind-Onshore	1319	0.0	26.2

Table 4. Capital Cost, operating and maintenance cost (O&M) comparison: wind-onshore and fossil-fueled plants. Data source: U.S. EIA[199]

The ongoing operating and maintenance costs are low for wind technology. Since there are no feedstock costs for the wind technology, as seen from Figure 11, it has an attractive levelized cost of electricity[200]. As discussed earlier, there is a substantial disadvantage for non-dispatchable technologies due to electricity supply/demand issues. Therefore, the characteristics such as costs and magnitude of CO_2 reduction impact cannot be considered in a standalone fashion for deciding between non-dispatchable technologies and dispatchable technologies. However, the key characteristics when considered together can provide the necessary information for an overall efficiency discussion between the different technology solutions (an overall efficiency discussion for the technologies is provided in a later chapter).

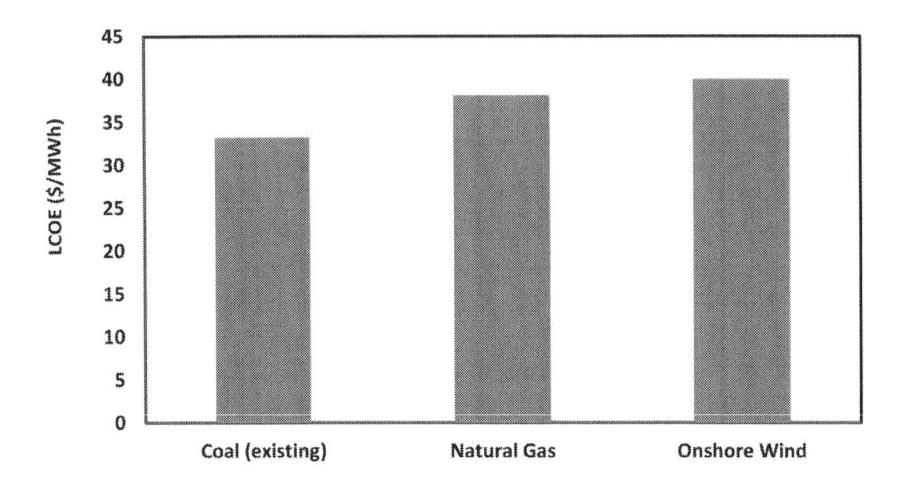

Figure 11. Levelized cost of electricity production (LCOE) comparison: wind-onshore, coal (existing) and natural gas plants. Data source: U.S. EIA[201]

Magnitude of Potential impact: Wind technology produces very little CO_2 (~ 25 gCO_2e/kWh) emissions per unit of electricity produced compared to coal fueled (~1000 gCO_2e/kWh) technology[202,203]. The extremely low emissions from wind technology makes it a very attractive solution from a CO_2 reduction perspective. The magnitude of impact for CO_2 reduction via wind technology, therefore, is high (~ 975 gCO_2e/kWh) for replacement of existing coal fueled plants. However, it is important to reiterate that direct replacement of dispatchable technologies with non-dispatchable technologies is only possible on a *limited scale* due to practical constraints arising from a supply/demand mismatch (i.e. it involves similar issues to those discussed earlier with regards to solar technology).

Potential for severe environmental impact at scale: For facilitating this discussion, the current scale of wind technology implementation is considered first. The cumulative amount of energy produced from wind technology since its commercialization has been around 2.2 billion tons of oil equivalent[204]. Although the implementation scale for wind technology has been larger than solar technology, it is still extremely small compared to fossil fuels. The cumulative implementation for wind technology considering *all the years* so far is about *5 times lower* than the energy produced from fossil fuels in a *single year*[205]. Correspondingly, based on practical constraints of the available data (just as in the case of the examples discussed earlier), environmental studies undertaken to-date are not expected to anticipate potential severe environmental impact for wind technology that could arise when implemented at a scale. Based on historical data on the other systems, it is probable that there will be some type of severe environmental impact from widescale implementation.

The environmental impact of wind technology at scale can be further discussed by considering the efficiency of assistance from nature for the technology and the related human activity requirements. No human activity is required to access the energy source and also, there are no environmental pollutants that are directly related to the energy source. However, wind is a very dilute source of energy with several orders of lower energy density compared to fossil fuels[206,207,208]. Correspondingly, the overall electricity production process is relatively inefficient, and large amount of material and land is required to extract energy from wind to produce electricity and therefore requires significant human activity. Therefore, at a scale which is more than an order of magnitude larger compared to the current implementation scale (i.e. at a scale comparable to fossil fuel scale), there is medium-to-high potential for one or more factors related to wind technology such as the extraction of metals, fabrication of components, disposal/recycling, turbine operation, land requirements, etc., to result in some type of severe environmental impact.

Dependence on another new technology: Wind technology can be implemented only on a limited scale because there will be a need for curtailment if the scale of implementation increases beyond a certain threshold[209,210]. Similar to solar technology, curtailment of electricity production from wind also results from grid and generator constraints and transmission inadequacy. For example, over-generation of electricity can occur when wind-based generation is high, and dispatchable generators cannot feasibly ramp down any further or quickly enough or transmission capacity is insufficient to transfer the excess generation to other locations. Since curtailment is detrimental from an economic (causes sub-optimization of the grid) and environmental viewpoint, standalone implementation of wind technology is not practical beyond a certain level. A widescale implementation of wind technology will only be possible if there is also a widescale implementation of energy storage technology, which will allow the storage of the electricity for later use as required. Thus, widescale implementation of wind technology is strongly dependent on energy storage implementation.

Speed of impact: From a speed of implementation perspective, wind technology has one favorable technical factor in that it is a mature/robust technology. However, as discussed earlier, wind technology has poor compatibility with the conventional electricity grid at high penetration levels. When coupled with adequate energy storage, the challenge related to compatibility can be eliminated but there will be several new challenges. Challenges for speed of impact when considering energy storage systems are discussed in a later section. Also, wind farms require more than 100 times land compared to natural gas fueled plants per unit electricity produced[211]. Therefore, another issue that could be a challenge for quickly implementing wind technology in regions where suitable land is relatively scarce is the large land requirement[212]. Based on the above discussion, the speed of impact from wind technology is expected to be medium-to-high until a certain threshold level of implementation (i.e., favorable speed of impact *only* until there is reasonable compatibility with the grid).

3.1.6 Wind technology: offshore

Since there are several similarities between offshore and onshore wind technologies, only the key differences will be discussed herein. Wind-offshore technology can benefit from the fact that the wind resource is more abundant and consistent in case of offshore locations[213]. Also, being located close to major coastal load centers, wind-offshore technology involves shorter transmission distances and does not require valuable land resources. However, the capital cost per unit capacity is about 3 times higher for wind-offshore technology compared to natural gas and wind-onshore technology[214] (Table 5).

	Capital Cost ($/kW)	Variable O&M ($/MWh)	Fixed O&M ($/kW-yr)
Coal	3661	4.5	40.4
Natural gas	1079	2.5	14.0
Wind-Offshore	5446	0.0	109.5

Table 5. Capital Cost, operating and maintenance cost (O&M) comparison: wind-offshore and fossil-fueled plants. Data source: U.S. EIA[215]

The levelized cost of electricity is also much higher for wind-offshore (Figure 12)[216]. Higher costs are expected considering the obvious advantages that land-based projects have in terms of installation and robustness issues compared to offshore based projects[217].

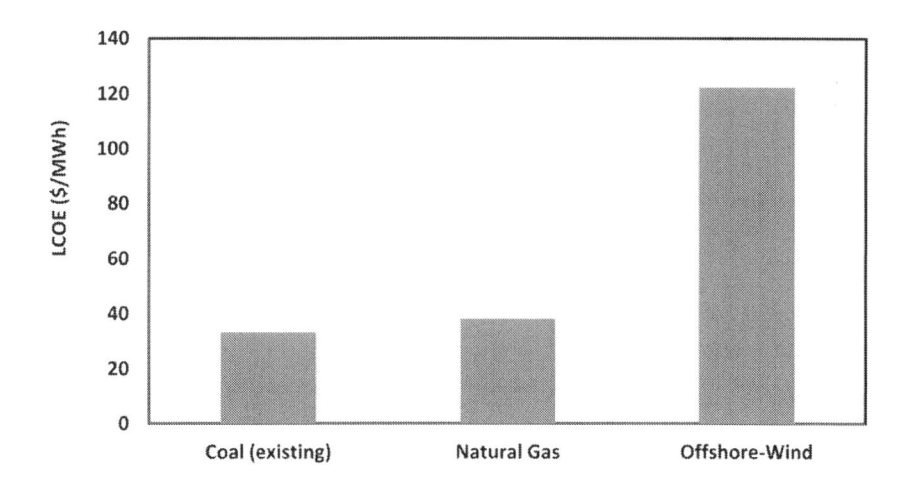

Figure 12. Levelized cost of electricity (LCOE) comparison: wind-offshore, coal (existing) and natural gas plants. Data source: U.S. EIA[218]

Correspondingly, more human activity is required for wind-offshore projects compared to onshore projects. This in turn indicates a higher potential for severe environmental impact when applied at a much higher scale. Due to the much higher costs and project complexity, the speed of potential impact is also expected to be slower for wind-offshore technology compared to wind-onshore technology.

3.1.7 Wind technology with energy storage

Considering that the solar (section 3.1.2) and wind (section 3.1.5) technology solutions are fairly comparable in all key characteristics, it follows that wind with energy storage applications should also have similar key characteristics as solar with energy storage (section 3.1.4). In other words, wind with adequate energy storage has a high cost, large magnitude of impact on CO_2 reductions, high potential for yet unknown severe impact on environment, no dependency on other solutions and low-to-medium speed of implementation for potential CO_2 reductions.

3.1.8 Biomass

Biomass, which is basically organic material from plants, contains stored energy from the sun[219]. Major applications of biomass include heating, transportation and electricity generation[220]. Since wood is a commonly used feedstock for biomass power plants[221], this section will use wood as a representative example for biomass. Similar to fossil fueled power plants, the heat energy produced from the burning of biomass is converted into electricity in biomass power plants.

Cost: As seen from Table 6, biomass power plants have significantly higher capital cost per unit capacity compared to natural gas fueled power plants[222].

	Capital Cost ($/kW)	Variable O&M ($/MWh)	Fixed O&M ($/kW-yr)
Coal	3661	4.5	40.4
Natural gas	1079	2.5	14.0
Biomass	4104	4.8	125.2

Table 6. Capital Cost, operating and maintenance cost (O&M) comparison: biomass and fossil-fueled plants. Data source: U.S. EIA[223]

Considering that the operating and maintenance costs, are also significantly higher than natural gas fueled plants, the levelized cost of electricity for biomass plants is also substantially higher than natural gas fueled plants[224] (Figure 13) in the United States. For countries where labor is cheap and cost of fossil fuel feedstocks is much higher (e.g., India), the cost of electricity production from biomass power plants is expected to be significantly more competitive than it is in the United States.

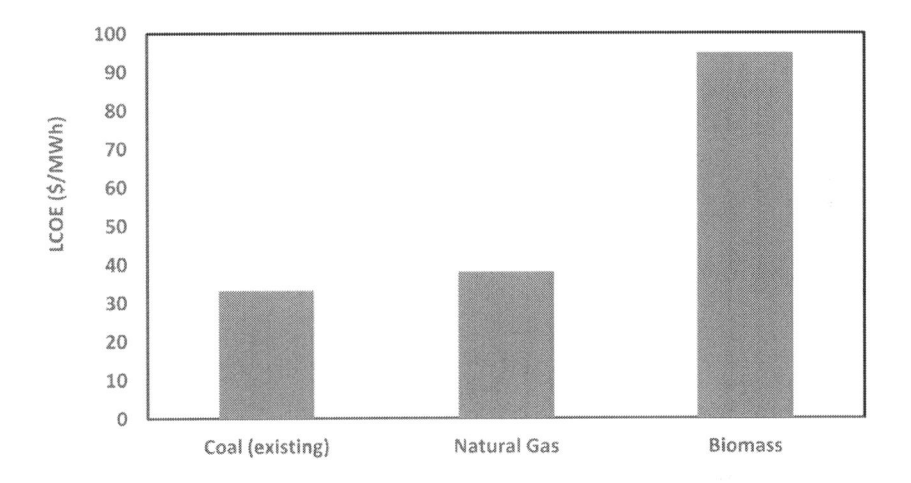

Figure 13. Levelized cost of electricity (LCOE) comparison: biomass, coal (existing) and natural gas plants. Data source: U.S. EIA[225]

Magnitude of impact: Although the burning of biomass releases comparable amount of CO_2 to fossil fuels, the CO_2 released from biomass burning is balanced by the CO_2 captured during its own growth[226]. Thus, burning of biomass is expected to produce much lower net CO_2 compared to burning of fossil fuels[227]. The CO_2 emissions produced per unit electricity from biomass (wood fueled) powerplants are estimated to be about 150 gCO_2e/kWh[228]. For the use of dedicated energy crops, and crop residues as feedstocks, the CO_2 emissions are expected to be higher (about 250 gCO_2e/kWh) for the biomass-to-electricity process due to higher infrastructure and supply chain emissions[229]. Therefore, the magnitude of impact for CO_2 reduction using biomass power plants for electricity production is medium-to-high when replacing existing coal plants. However, it is important to note that the life cycle greenhouse gas emissions related to biomass feedstocks are not adequately understood due to the complexity arising from issues such as *land use and change* impact[230]. Thus, the magnitude of impact for CO_2 reduction will need to be revisited as the understanding of life cycle greenhouse gas emissions from biomass-to-energy continues to evolve.

Potential for severe environmental impact at scale: Use of biomass for modern applications such as electricity and transportation has been on an extremely small scale compared to fossil fuels[231]. But even when considering the heating application of traditional biomass, the scale of the application has been an order of magnitude smaller compared to fossil fuels[232]. The small scale of biomass application up to this point indicates the possibility for severe environmental impact when applied at a scale that is representative of fossil fuel use. Due to the low energy density of biomass (related to its very high moisture/oxygen content)[233], significant human activity is required to grow, transport and covert biomass on a per unit of electricity produced basis. As a comparison, the human activity required to use the highly energy dense fossil fuels for producing electricity, which have been formed by millions of years of nature's action of pressure and heat on past remains of organisms, is considerably smaller. Based on the very large requirements of water and land for growing biomass and related issues[234,235,236], a high potential for severe environmental impact can be expected from biomass *at a wide scale*.

Dependence on another new technology: Similar to fossil fueled plants, biomass powered plants are also not dependent on any other new technology.

Speed of impact: The biomass to electricity technology can be considered to be a fairly mature technology. However, the speed of implementation of biomass power plants is still expected to be slow-to-medium because of practical issues such as logistics related to transportation/storage of the low-density biomass feedstock and requirements of large amounts of water and land.

3.1.9 Nuclear Energy

Nuclear power plants leverage nuclear fission reactions, wherein splitting of atoms produces heat energy[237]. The heat energy is used to produce steam that drives large turbines to produce electricity by using generators[238]. Nuclear power plants employ nuclear reactors, which are designed to contain nuclear chain reactions and release heat at a controlled rate. These nuclear reactors use a certain type of Uranium, U-235, because it's atoms can be easily split apart. The state-of-the-art advanced nuclear power plants are considered herein for discussing the cost characteristics[239].

Cost: As seen from Table 7, the capital cost per unit capacity for advanced nuclear power plants is substantially higher than even coal fueled power plants[240]. However, due to a high capacity factor and relatively low variable operating and maintenance costs, the levelized cost of electricity (Figure 14)[241] for nuclear plants is not as high as the capital cost would suggest.

	Capital Cost ($/kW)	Variable O&M ($/MWh)	Fixed O&M ($/kW-yr)
Coal	3661	4.5	40.4
Natural gas	1079	2.5	14.0
Nuclear	6317	2.4	121.1

Table 7. Capital Cost, operating and maintenance cost (O&M) comparison: advanced nuclear and fossil-fueled plants. Data Source: U.S. EIA[242]

The capital cost for advanced nuclear plants is much higher than coal and natural gas plants on a *global basis*. However, the relative cost comparison of levelized cost of electricity for each country will depend on the natural gas and coal feedstock price for that country. For example, due to the very low natural gas price in the United States, the levelized cost of electricity for nuclear plants is higher compared to natural gas fuel plants, however this could be reverse in countries where natural gas price is much higher.

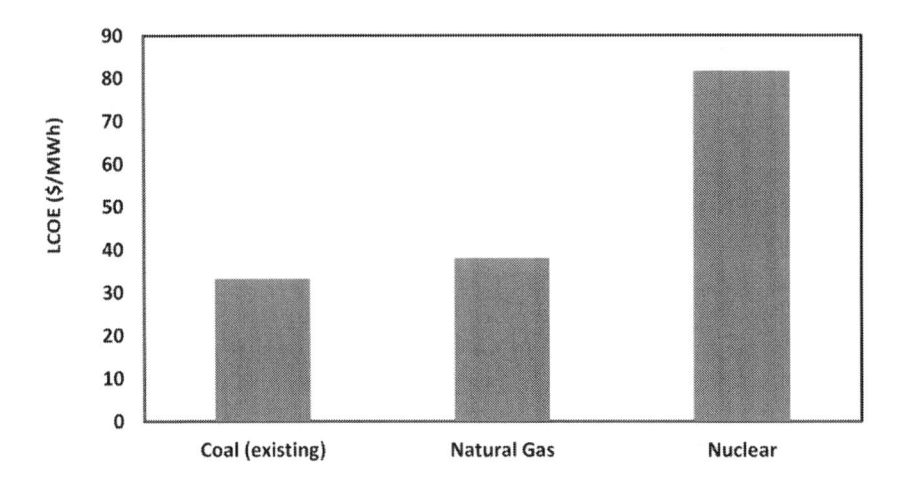

Figure 14. Levelized cost of electricity (LCOE) comparison: advanced nuclear, coal (existing) and natural gas plants. Data source: U.S. EIA[243]

Magnitude of impact: The CO_2 emissions from advanced nuclear power plants are extremely low (< 20 gCO_2e/kWh) on a per unit of electricity produced basis compared to coal (about 1000 gCO_2/kWh)[244,245]. Consequently, the magnitude of impact for CO_2 reduction from nuclear technology is large for replacing coal power plants.

Potential for severe environmental impact at scale: Nuclear energy along with hydropower, has been the dominant source of low carbon electricity for the past several decades[246]. The cumulative amount of energy produced by nuclear energy power plants from 1965 to 2018 has been more than *seven times* the cumulative energy produced from solar and wind together during that timeframe[247]. However, the cumulative amount of energy produced from nuclear energy has been *lower by more than order of magnitude* compared to fossil fuels [248].

Over the last few decades, several environmental concerns have been recognized related to nuclear technology. Environmental concerns include potential of contamination of water and air (due to natural disasters such as earthquakes, human actions, etc.), and dealing with radioactive waste and associated equipment[249]. Significant efforts have been directed towards developing strategies to decrease the environmental concern from the nuclear energy projects. As discussed earlier, although the implementation of nuclear technology has been substantial, there has not yet been enough implementation to ensure an excellent understanding of issues related to environmental impacts at a wide scale. As a result, there is still some potential for a severe impact at a much larger scale of implementation of nuclear technology.

The energy density of nuclear fuel is orders of magnitude higher than fossil fuels[250]. This is excellent from the viewpoint that only a very small quantity of fuel is required per unit of electricity produced; however, it results in a new challenge. This extraordinarily high energy density and radioactive nature of the fuel introduces formidable challenges related to controlling the energy release/handling, which requires significant human activity in terms of materials and processes to ensure reliable/safe operations[251]. Based on the overall discussion above, there is a medium potential for severe environmental impact from nuclear energy at a wide scale due to potential issues from nuclear fuel production, logistics, operations and recycling/storage at that scale.

Dependence on another new technology: Similar to fossil fueled plants, nuclear power plants are also not dependent on any other new technology.

Speed of impact: Nuclear technology is quite mature and has no significant compatibility issues with the existing energy infrastructure. On the flip side, a nuclear plant project requires much longer lead times. From a practical perspective, the rapid implementation of this technology is expected to face significant obstacles. This is related to the substantial negative perception that has developed towards this technology over the decades due to some widely publicized incidents[252]. Therefore, the speed of implementation of a nuclear technology is expected to be medium.

3.1.10 Hydropower

The energy in flowing water is converted into electricity in case of hydropower. The most common type of hydropower plant consists of a dam to store water in a reservoir. When the water from the reservoir is released, it drives a turbine, which in turn activates a generator to produce electricity[253]. Hydropower is considered as a renewable source as it leverages the global water cycle which consists of evaporation driven by heat from the sun, cloud formation, precipitation, and collection of the precipitated water in different water bodies[254]. Hydropower is currently the most dominant source of renewable electricity[255].

Cost: The capital cost of hydropower plants varies significantly depending on the suitability of location/geological conditions[256]. As seen from Table 8, the capital cost per unit capacity for hydropower plants is substantially higher than natural gas fueled plants[257]. The levelized cost of electricity on the other hand is relatively competitive (Figure 15) with fossil fueled plants due to low variable operating and maintainence costs[258]. A significant number of hydropower projects have been completed around the globe in the past few decades. Considering that an appropriate location is very important for hydropower plants and that several suitable locations have already been utilized, fewer locations will be available in the future. As a result, it is possible that higher capital costs will be expected for future hydropower projects.

	Capital Cost ($/kW)	Variable O&M ($/MWh)	Fixed O&M ($/kW-yr)
Coal	3661	4.5	40.4
Natural gas	1079	2.5	14.0
Hydropower	2752	1.4	41.6

Table 8. Capital Cost, operating and maintainence cost (O&M) comparison: hydropower and fossil-fueled plants. Data source: U.S. EIA[259].

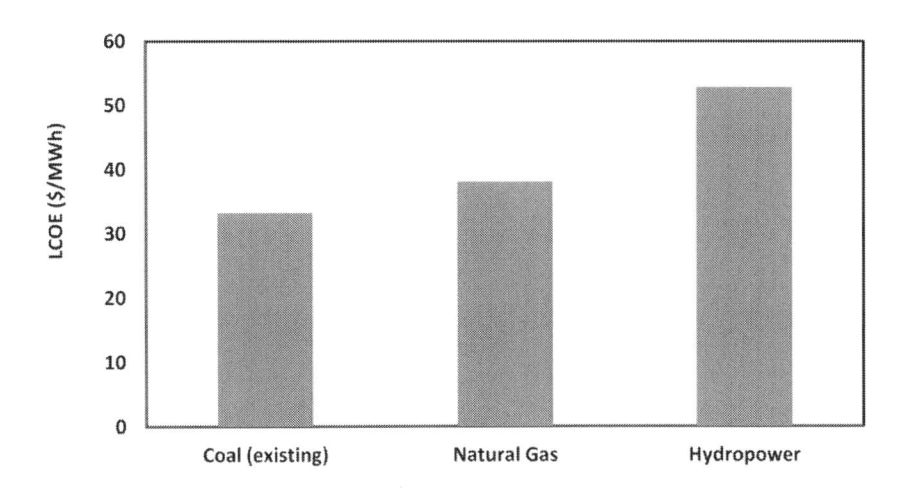

Figure 15. Levelized cost of electricity (LCOE) comparison: hydropower, coal (existing) and natural gas plants. Data source: U.S. EIA[260]

Magnitude of impact: The life cycle CO_2 emissions from hydropower plants are estimated to be very low (about 50 gCO_2e/kWh) on a per unit of electricity produced basis compared to coal (about 1000 gCO_2e/kWh)[261,262]. Consequently, the magnitude of impact for CO_2 reduction from hydropower power plants is expected to be high for replacing coal plants. For certain projects the life cycle emissions may be considerably larger than the value provided above[263]. This may be attributed to the large greenhouse gas emissions from vegetation decomposition in the reservoirs, which can be high depending on the specific conditions related to the project. Such estimations are challenging due to the complexity of the system. Thus, the magnitude of impact for CO_2 reduction will need to be revisited as the understanding of greenhouse gas emissions continues to evolve for different hydropower projects.

Potential for severe environmental impact at scale: Hydropower along with nuclear energy, has been the dominant sources for low carbon electricity for the past several decades[264]. The cumulative amount of energy produced by hydropower plants from 1965 to 2018 has been about *nine times* the energy produced from solar and wind together during that timeframe[265]. However, the cumulative amount of energy produced from hydropower has been lower by more than an order of magnitude compared to fossil fuels[266].

Over the last few decades, several environmental concerns have been recognized related to hydropower technology. Environmental concerns include impacts on the ecology, physical characteristics of the river, water quality, biological diversity, and spread of waterborne diseases[267,268]. Significant efforts have been directed towards developing management strategies to decrease the environmental concerns from hydropower projects. As discussed earlier, although the implementation of hydropower technology has been substantial, there has not yet been a wide enough implementation of hydropower that will ensure a comprehensive understanding of issues related to environmental impacts. As a result, there is still some potential for a severe impact (which is currently not understood) at a much larger scale of implementation of hydropower.

Due to the relatively dilute nature of the energy source, a large amount of flowing water is required per unit of electricity produced. This in turn means that the human activity involved for energy extraction is significant for hydropower (managing river flow, dams, etc.). Based on the overall discussion above, there is a medium potential for severe environmental impact from hydropower at widescale implementation.

Dependence on another new technology: Similar to fossil fueled plants, hydropower plants are also not dependent on any other new technology.

Speed of impact: The main factors which are favorable from a speed of implementation perspective for hydropower are the maturity of the technology and operational flexibility (which could be helpful for supporting intermittent renewable sources)[269]. On the flip side, less favorable characteristics include typically long project lead time and the fact that many suitable sites have already been taken. The above discussion indicates a medium speed of implementation for the next decade, and a gradually reducing speed after that, as fewer and fewer suitable sites remain available.

3.1.11 Power plants with CO_2 Capture and Storage

CO_2 capture and storage involves capture of CO_2 from fuel combustion or other processes, and transport of this CO_2 to a location where it is permanently stored, deep underground in the geological formations. The power (electricity) sector, which is by far the largest direct emitter of CO_2, is responsible for about 40% of the global CO_2 emissions[270]. Therefore, the capture and storage of CO_2 from coal/natural gas power plants can be considered as one of the most important applications for CO_2 capture and storage.

Cost: The CO_2 capture and storage solution for power plants involves three cost components: CO_2 capture cost, transportation cost and storage cost. The cost of CO_2 capture is by far the largest cost component amongst the three[271]; hence most of the cost related discussion herein will revolve around this component. The CO_2 capture component includes the capture of CO_2 from the mixture of byproducts from coal or natural gas power plants, and compression of the CO_2 to enable its transportation. The capital cost and operating and maintenance costs for coal and natural gas plants with CO_2 capture (90% capture) are substantially higher than the corresponding power plants without capture (Table 9)[272].

	Capital Cost ($/kW)	Variable O&M ($/MWh)	Fixed O&M ($/kW-yr)
Coal	3661	4.5	40.4
Natural gas	1079	2.5	14.0
Coal with capture	5997	10.9	59.3
Natural gas with capture	2569	5.8	27.5

Table 9. Capital Cost, operating and maintenance cost (O&M) comparison: fossil-fueled plants without capture and with capture. Data source: U.S. EIA[273]

The capital cost per unit capacity for a coal plant with capture is more than twice that of the natural gas plant with capture. Since the capital cost of a coal power plant without capture is high to begin with, the further cost increase due to CO_2 capture makes the capital cost even more challenging from an initial investment perspective.

The levelized cost of electricity is more than 50% higher for a coal plant with capture plant compared to a natural gas plant with capture[274,275]. For a natural gas plant, the inclusion of CO_2 capture increases the capital cost by more than a factor of two and the levelized cost of electricity production by about 55%. Transportation and storage further increase the levelized cost of electricity by ~5%.

Magnitude of impact: The life cycle CO_2 emissions are estimated to be about 250 gCO_2e/kWh from a coal plant with CO_2 capture and storage and about 170 gCO_2e/kWh for natural gas power plant with CO_2 capture and storage,[276,277] both of which are significantly lower than the corresponding values for plants without capture. Thus, inclusion of CO_2 capture and storage with power plants will result in a medium-to-high reduction in CO_2 emissions.

Potential for severe environmental impact at scale: The CO_2 capture and storage technology for power plant applications has been implemented on an extremely small scale (less than 50 million tons of CO_2 per year)[278]. Thus, the current level of implementation is negligibly small considering that the coal power plants alone generate around 10,000 million tons of CO_2 per year[279]. Based on practical constraints of the *very* limited available data, it is expected that environmental studies undertaken to-date will not be able to anticipate potential severe environmental impact for capture and storage technology that could arise when implemented at a wide scale. Hence, there is a significant possibility for some type of severe environmental impact from the CO_2 capture and storage solution when implemented at the required enormous scale. The potential environmental impact of the CO_2 capture and storage technology at scale can be further discussed by considering the related human activity requirements.

Capture and transportation of CO_2 is an inefficient process due to the inherent characteristics of the power plants (which produce large amounts of difficult-to-capture, relatively inert, byproduct CO_2 gas), and the long distances of separation between power plants and appropriate storage sites. Also, there is significant need for human activity for CO_2 capture and transportation due to large material and energy requirements[280,281]. Therefore, at widescale implementation, there is a high potential for one or more factors related to CO_2 capture and storage technology such as materials (production, disposal/recycling), indirect emissions, long term storage integrity issues, etc., to result in some type of severe environmental impact.

Dependence on another new technology: There is no dependence on any other new technology. However, it is noteworthy that CO_2 capture and storage for power plants consists of two relatively complex technology components (i.e. capture and storage).

Speed of impact: The speed of implementation of CO_2 capture and storage technology for power plants is expected to be slow within the next decade considering the technical challenges for the technology[282] and also practical challenges (such as long distances, appropriate storage locations, etc.) related to transportation and storage of the captured CO_2.

3.2 Key characteristics of the CO_2 reduction solutions for the transportation sector

The transportation sector is responsible for about 25% of the direct global CO_2 emissions[283,284]. This sector includes a wide range of transportation modes: light duty vehicles, buses, two-three wheeled vehicles, rail, trucks, air, and marine vessels. The single largest component in the transportation sector in terms of CO_2 emissions is light duty vehicles (e.g. cars, sport utility vehicles, etc.)[285,286]. Hence, the major focus of CO_2 reduction technology solutions in the transportation sector has been on light duty vehicles. In 2018, the global CO_2 emission from the transportation sector was about 8 billion tons, out of which roughly 3 billion tons of CO_2 emission was from light duty vehicles[287,288]. The two popular light duty vehicle technologies that are being considered for CO_2 reduction (via replacement of conventional vehicles) include hybrid electric vehicles and battery electric vehicles. In the first part of this section, the hybrid electric vehicle and battery electric vehicle technology will be discussed as a replacement for conventional light duty vehicles. Other related replacement solutions such as biofuels and shared transportation will be discussed later in this section.

The light duty vehicles group includes several different types of vehicles and vehicle manufacturers. To facilitate a practical evaluation between technologies, representative vehicles have been selected to represent the *major* light duty vehicle categories. Cars and small/crossover sport utility vehicles (SUV) dominate the light duty vehicle market in the United States and globally[289]; and hence, the conventional, hybrid, and battery electric technologies were specifically compared in these categories. The representative vehicles are selected based on mass affordability (< 40,000 $), similar size, a greater than 200 miles driving range and relative popularity/brand recognition. The selected representative vehicles afford the best possible practical comparison between conventional, hybrid and battery electric vehicle technologies by allowing reasonable representation of the light duty vehicle segment. A majority of the data used in the analysis of the different key characteristics has been obtained from the *official United States Government source for fuel economy information*[290]. The vehicle life has been assumed to be 175000 miles, with 15000 miles driven per year on an average.

3.2.1 Hybrid Electric Vehicles

Conventional light duty vehicles, which are powered by an internal combustion engine (conventional technology), have the majority market share currently. The hybrid electric vehicle technology is based on a relatively *minor modification* to the conventional vehicle technology. In case of hybrid vehicle technology, power is provided by an internal combustion engine and an electric motor. The electric motor uses energy stored in a battery, which is charged by the internal combustion engine and through regenerative braking[291]. *Toyota Prius* and *Toyota Camry hybrid* were selected as the hybrid electric vehicle representatives, and *Honda Civic* and *Toyota Camry* were selected as the conventional vehicle representatives, in the mid-sized car category. In the small/crossover SUV category, *Toyota RAV4 hybrid* was selected as the hybrid representative, and *Toyota RAV4* and *Hyundai Kona* were selected as the conventional vehicle representatives. A basic description of the vehicles is provided in Table 10, which includes the Environmental Protection Agency (EPA) size class and total driving range[292].

	Toyota Camry	Honda Civic	Toyota Camry Hybrid	Toyota Prius Eco	Hyundai Kona	Toyota RAV4	Toyota RAV4 Hybrid
Year	2019	2019	2019	2019	2019	2019	2019
Technology	Conventional	Conventional	Hybrid	Hybrid	Conventional	Conventional	Hybrid
EPA Size Class	Mid-size cars	Mid-size cars	Mid-size cars	Mid-size cars	Small SUV	Small SUV	Small SUV
Total range (Miles) [293]	493	409	676	633	396	406	580

Table 10. Basic information about representative conventional and hybrid electric light duty vehicles. Data source: U.S. DOE, Office of Energy Efficiency and Renewable Energy

Cost: The two cost components of interest for comparing vehicle technology are the retail price and levelized cost of driving. The levelized cost of driving can be considered as the *total* cost per mile driven over the life of the vehicle, and includes retail price, fuel cost, maintenance cost, insurance costs and financial costs. The *summary* cost data comparison between conventional and hybrid electric vehicles obtained by averaging the cost data for the selected representative vehicles is shown in Table 11.

	Conventional	**Hybrid**
Retail price ($)	23190	26970
Fuel cost ($/mile)	0.09	0.06
Maintenance cost ($/mile)	0.063	0.063
Levelized cost ($/mile)	0.37	0.38

Table 11. Cost comparison: conventional and hybrid electric light duty vehicles. Retail price is for base trim.

The retail price and fuel cost per mile for each of the representative vehicles was obtained from the United States fuel economy website[294]. To facilitate a practical comparison, the retail price for the base (*lowest price*) trim[295] was used for each representative vehicle. Table 11 shows that the vehicle cost (retail price) for hybrid electric vehicle technology on an average is about 15% higher than conventional vehicle technology. As a crosscheck, a very good agreement was found between the average cost provided in Table 11 and the cost comparison from the retailer web sites between individual conventional vehicles and hybrid vehicles with the *same trim* (Table 12)[296,297,298,299]; for example, the retail price of *2020 Ford Fusion Hybrid SE* (hybrid technology) was found to be 14% higher (i.e. ratio: 1.14) than the *2020 Ford Fusion SE* (conventional technology).

Model (*TRIM*)	Retail price	Price Ratio
2020 Toyota Camry (*SE*)	26170	
2020 Toyota Camry Hybrid (*SE*)	30130	1.15
2020 Ford Fusion (*SE*)	24500	
2020 Ford Fusion Hybrid (*SE*)	28000	1.14
2020 Honda CRV (*LX*)	25050	
2020 Honda CRV Hybrid (*LX*)	27750	1.11

Table 12. Retail price comparison between conventional and hybrid electric light duty vehicles for the same trims. Retail price ratio (hybrid to conventional) is also provided. Data source: Official retailer websites (accessed June 2020)

The levelized cost per mile was obtained by including the vehicle retail price, sales tax, financial cost, fuel cost, insurance cost and maintenance cost[300,301,302]. The higher retail price for the hybrid technology is compensated to a certain extent by the significantly lower fuel cost for the hybrid vehicle technology. When the levelized costs per mile (which includes retail price, sales tax, financial cost, fuel cost, insurance cost, and maintenance cost) are considered over the vehicle life, the hybrid vehicle technology only has a 1% higher cost than the conventional vehicle technology in the United States. The above discussion on costs is based on the average data applicable to the United States. For other countries around the world, the ratio of the retail prices between hybrid electric and conventional vehicles is expected to be similar to the United States;

however, the levelized cost per mile for the vehicle will be depend on the gasoline price, sales tax, and financing cost for the given country. Please see Appendix for more information about levelized costs per mile estimation.

Magnitude of impact: The life cycle CO_2 emissions from light duty vehicles includes the following components: tail pipe emissions, fuel cycle emissions and vehicle manufacturing emissions. The official United States fuel economy site provides data for the tail pipe emissions and fuel cycle emissions[303]. The vehicle manufacturing emissions are relatively a small component of the total emissions. The differences in vehicle manufacturing emissions between the three technologies arise primarily from battery manufacturing emissions[304]. In case of hybrid vehicle technology, the battery size is only modestly larger than conventional vehicles, and therefore the vehicle manufacturing CO_2 emissions are comparable for hybrid and conventional vehicle technologies. Due to superior fuel economy, the hybrid vehicle technology on an average provides a significant CO_2 reduction over the conventional vehicle technology. As can be seen from Figure 16, hybrid vehicle technology will, on an average, provide a reduction of about 110 gCO_2e per mile when replacing conventional vehicle technology[305]. The above discussion suggests a medium magnitude of impact on CO_2 reduction for hybrid vehicles.

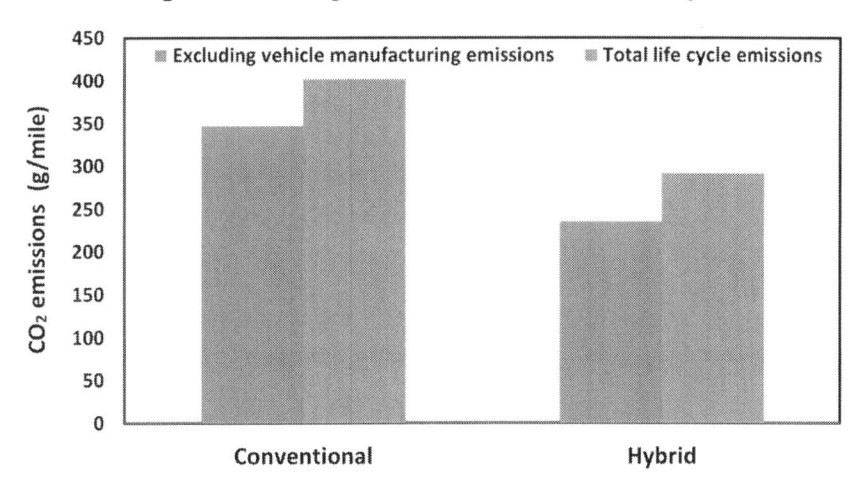

Figure 16. Representative CO_2 emission comparison: conventional and hybrid electric light duty vehicles. Data source: U.S. DOE, Office of Energy Efficiency and Renewable Energy

Potential for severe environmental impact at scale: The conventional light duty vehicle technology has been implemented at an extremely large-scale around the globe, and as such, the environmental impacts are well understood. Considering that the hybrid light duty vehicle technology includes an internal combustion engine, uses regular fuel, and requires no external charging, the modification relative to the conventional vehicle technology[306] is minor. Thus, the environmental impacts, which include tailpipe emissions such as NO_x, particulate matter, etc. from conventional fuel, are well understood in case of hybrid electric vehicles[307]. The environmental regulations that have been introduced over the past several years have considerably decreased the severity of impact from these pollutants from conventional fuel and additional tightening of these regulations is expected to further decrease the impact. Based on the above discussion, there is a low to medium potential for severe unknown environmental impact at wide scale from hybrid vehicle technology, which is not currently understood.

Dependence on another new technology: Similar to conventional vehicles, the hybrid vehicles also use conventional fossil fuel and do not require external battery charging; hence hybrid vehicle technology has no dependence on any other new technology.

Speed of impact: There are several favorable factors from the viewpoint of speed of implementation for the hybrid vehicle technology. These include compatibility with existing infrastructure and fairly mature technology. Therefore, from a technical perspective the speed of widescale implementation of hybrid electric technology is expected to be medium-to-high. Also, it should be noted that an important factor that will eventually determine the speed and extent of implementation of hybrid vehicles will be the messaging about this technology relative to battery electric vehicle technology.

3.2.2 Battery Electric Vehicles

Electric vehicles do not have an internal combustion engine, instead, they are driven by one or more electric motors powered by energy stored in batteries[308]. Unlike hybrid electric vehicles, which do not require external charging, battery electric vehicles need to be plugged into an electric power source for charging the battery after it is depleted. *Tesla Model 3* and *Nissan Leaf*, with a minimum driving range of 200 miles, are selected as the battery electric vehicle representatives in the mid-sized car category, and *Hyundai Kona electric* is selected as the battery electric representative in the small/crossover SUV category[309]. Tesla Model Y is not selected considering that only the expensive versions (cheapest available version was $50,000) were available at the time of writing this book. The same *representative* conventional light duty vehicles that were discussed in the previous section are also used for this comparison. A basic description of the vehicles is provided in Table 13, which includes the EPA size class, and total driving range. The Table shows that the *selected* battery electric vehicles have a significantly inferior performance in terms of driving range[310].

	Toyota Camry	**Honda Civic**	**Tesla Model 3**	**Nissan Leaf**	**Hyundai Kona**	**Toyota RAV4**	**Hyundai Kona Electric**
Year	2019	2019	2019	2019	2019	2019	2019
	Conv-ntional	Conven-tional	Battery Electric	Battery Electric	Conven-tional	Conven-tional	Battery Electric
EPA Size Class	Mid-size cars	Mid-size cars	Mid-size cars	Mid-size cars	Small SUV	Small SUV	Small SUV
Total range (Miles)	493	409	220	226	396	406	258

Table 13. Basic information about representative conventional and battery electric light duty vehicles. Data source: U.S. DOE, Office of Energy Efficiency and Renewable Energy

Cost: The *summary* cost data comparison between conventional and battery electric vehicles obtained by averaging the cost data for the selected representative vehicles is shown in Table 14. The retail price and fuel cost per mile for each of the representative vehicles was obtained from the United States fuel economy website[311]. To facilitate a practical comparison, the retail price for the base (*lowest price*) trim[312] is used for each representative vehicle.

	Conventional	Battery Electric
Retail price ($)	23190	36390
Fuel cost ($/mile)	0.09	0.04
Maintenance cost ($/mile)	0.063	0.028
Levelized cost ($/mile)	0.37	0.40

Table 14. Representative cost comparison: conventional and battery electric light duty vehicles.

On an average, the upfront vehicle cost (retail price) for battery electric vehicle technology is about **60%** higher than conventional vehicle technology, and about **35%** higher[313] than hybrid electric technology. As a crosscheck, a very good agreement was found between the average cost provided in this work and the *direct* cost comparison from the retailer websites between conventional, hybrid and battery electric vehicles with the ***same trim*** (Table 15)[314,315,316].

Model (*TRIM*)	Retail price	Price Ratio
2020 Hyundai Kona (*SEL*)	22100	
2020 Hyundai Kona Electric (*SEL*)	37190	1.68
2020 Hyundai Kona (*Limited*)	26100	
2020 Hyundai Kona Electric (*Limited*)	41800	1.60
2020 Kia Niro Hybrid (*EX-Premium*)	32790	
2020 Kia Niro Electric (*EX-Premium*)	44590	1.36

Table 15. Retail price comparison between *conventional & battery electric light duty vehicles* and *hybrid & battery electric vehicles* for the same trims. Retail price ratio (*battery electric to conventional* and *hybrid to battery electric*) is also provided. Data source: Official retailer websites (accessed June 2020)

The higher retail price for the battery electric technology is compensated to a limited extent by the considerably lower fuel and maintenance cost (Table 14) for the battery electric vehicle technology[317]. When the levelized costs per mile (which includes retail price, sales tax, financial cost, fuel cost, insurance cost, and maintenance cost) [318,319,320,321] are considered over the vehicle life, the battery electric vehicle technology has about 8 % higher cost than the conventional vehicle technology in the United States. This is a lower end estimate considering that factors such as home charger equipment, installation cost, and higher electricity costs at supercharging stations (e.g. ~$0.28 $/kWh at Tesla supercharging stations)[322] have not been included in this analysis. The above discussion on costs is based on the data from the United States. For other countries around the world, the ratio of the retail prices between battery electric and conventional vehicles is expected to be similar to the United States; however, the levelized cost per mile for the vehicle will be depend on the gasoline price, sales tax, and financing cost for the given country. Please see Appendix for more information about levelized costs per mile estimation.

Magnitude of impact: Battery electric vehicles produce zero tail-pipe emissions. However, emissions are produced during electricity production and vehicle manufacturing. The United States fuel economy site provides data for the tail-pipe emissions and electricity production (fuel cycle) emissions[323]. The vehicle manufacturing emissions, which are a relatively small component of the total CO_2 emissions, are comparable for the three different technologies except for battery manufacturing[324]. In case of battery electric vehicle technology, the battery system is large[325]. Correspondingly, the vehicle manufacturing CO_2 emissions are modestly higher for battery electric vehicles. Several recent studies have reported a wide range of CO_2 emission values for battery production[326]. For this study, the lower end battery manufacturing emission of 61 Kg CO_2e/kWh is used[327]. Due to higher efficiency of battery electric vehicles and relatively low amounts of CO_2 emitted during electricity production (for example, average global emissions from electricity grid: ~475 gCO_2/kWh)[328,329,330], the battery electric vehicle technology on an average generates significantly lower CO_2 emissions compared to the conventional vehicle technology. As seen from Figure 17, the battery electric light duty vehicle technology will, on an average, provide a reduction of about 180 gCO_2e per mile when replacing the conventional vehicle technology[331]. The above discussion suggests a medium-to-high magnitude of impact for battery electric vehicles.

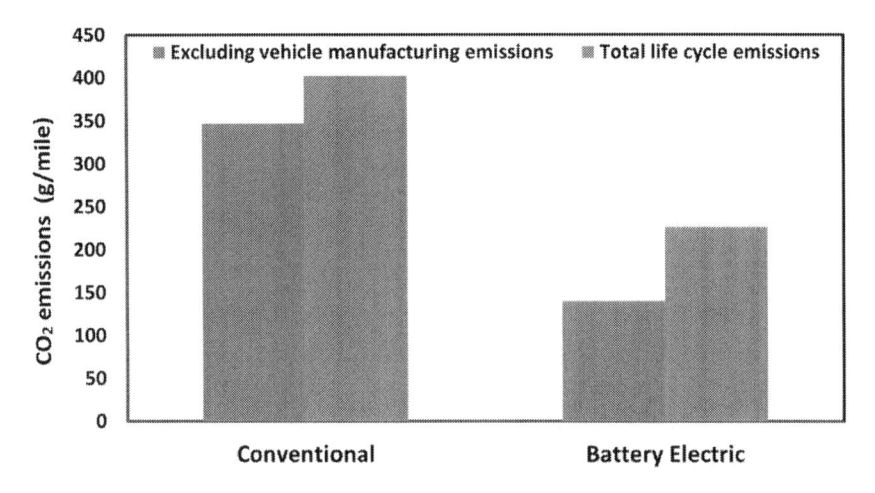

Figure 17. Representative CO_2 emission comparison: conventional and battery electric light duty vehicles. Primary data source: U.S. DOE, Office of Energy Efficiency and Renewable Energy

Potential for severe environmental impact at scale: Battery electric vehicle technology uses large battery systems that are charged by plugging into an electricity source. As a result, there are large differences between conventional vehicle technology and battery electric vehicle technology. Battery electric vehicle technology has been implemented at a relatively tiny scale (e.g. 1 % of the global cars on the road in 2019)[332]. As discussed earlier, a **very low level of implementation** of a technology solution suggests that there could be a potential for a severe environmental impact at scale. Furthermore, the energy storage in case of battery systems is not efficiently supported by nature. An example for efficient support from nature for energy storage is the solar energy stored in the past remains of plants and animals, which has been converted to very high energy density fossil fuels over millions of years by nature via heat and pressure in the earth's crust[333]. Unfortunately, such efficient support from nature is not available for the energy storage in batteries. Instead, battery systems are characterized by **very low energy densities**[334], and therefore require substantial human activity primarily in terms of mining/extracting of raw materials, fabrication of various components, charging, recycling/disposal, etc.[335]. Also, the increase in the *electricity requirements will be substantial* for the widescale implementation of battery electric vehicles. This additional electricity production requirement could also increase the potential for severe environmental impact. On the positive side, battery electric vehicles have a significant advantage from the viewpoint of **zero tail-pipe emissions** (e.g. zero particulate matter, etc.). Based on the overall discussion, for battery electric vehicle technology there is a medium potential for severe environmental impact at widescale implementation.

Dependence on another new technology: Battery electric vehicles require external charging, which presents significant challenges. Charging of battery electric vehicles exclusively at home for the general global population is not possible for practical reasons (e.g. lack of accessibility, range limitations, etc.). Thus, a widescale implementation of battery electric vehicles would require a network of public charging stations comparable to the vast conventional fuel station network available today. Currently, the availability of charging stations is extremely small compared to the conventional fueling stations. Furthermore, the charging rates offered by most of the public charging stations are currently more than an order of magnitude lower than energy transfer rates for gasoline pump for conventional light duty vehicle fueling[336]. Fast charging stations (also known as superchargers), which can currently charge vehicles in about 45 minutes, are expensive (equals much higher electricity cost for the battery electric vehicle owner)[337] and are still *much slower* than conventional fuel pumps. Due to cost issues, majority of the public charging stations currently are slow chargers[338], wherein few hours are required for charging the battery electric vehicle[339]. Thus, a successful widescale implementation of battery electric vehicles is dependent on the widescale implementation of *low-cost fast charging* technology.

There is also some dependence of battery electric vehicle technology on the low carbon electricity generation technologies. For example, the life cycle CO_2 emissions from a battery electric vehicle from the state of Pennsylvania was more than twice that from the same battery electric vehicle in the state of California in 2019[340]. The large difference in life cycle emissions can be attributed to the differences in CO_2 emissions from the electricity production in the two states in 2019 (i.e. it is related to the much higher amounts of low carbon electricity generation in California compared to Pennsylvania)[341]. From a *cost/benefit perspective* it is important that battery electric vehicles have a as big impact as possible on CO_2 reduction. Thus, a widescale implementation of battery electric vehicle technology would also *require widescale implementation of low carbon electricity generation technologies*, several of which are relatively less established.

Speed of impact: Battery electric vehicle technology has some favorable factors from the viewpoint of speed of impact. These include a superior driving experience and zero tail-pipe emissions of environmental pollutants (e.g. particulate matter, etc.). However, it also has significant issues related to compatibility with the existing infrastructure (e.g. lack of *fast charging* infrastructure and need for low-carbon electricity for an improved cost-to-benefit ratio). Considering the above issues, the speed of implementation of battery electric vehicle technology for light duty vehicles is expected to be medium. One of the key factors driving the recent rapid growth in battery electric vehicles has been the highly positive perception of this technology due to the lack of appropriate consideration of the critically important issues, when compared to other CO_2 reduction solutions. These issues will be systematically considered in the next chapter, which focuses on comparing the different technology solutions based on how they meet the critical challenges associated with CO_2 reduction.

3.2.3 Biofuels

A variety of biomass-based feedstocks can be used to produce transportation biofuels. However, it is not practical to use feedstocks (e.g. vegetable oil, corn, etc.) that compete with food to produce biofuels on a wide scale due to the potential for misalignment with the food sustainability of the rapidly growing global population[342]. Therefore, further discussions herein will be restricted to cellulosic biomass feedstocks such as wood, grass, crop residues, forestry residue etc., that do not compete directly with food. The discussion will include key biofuel production processes such as cellulosic ethanol and cellulosic biomass-to-liquids.

Cost: The low energy density and chemical composition of biomass makes every aspect of biomass to biofuels process such as the transportation of biomass, process conversion efficiency etc., quite challenging[343]. The cost of producing biofuels from cellulosic biomass is high due to the challenging chemistry/engineering related to biomass processing and the small size of the biofuel production plants (i.e. poor economy of scale). For example, the production scale of an average cellulosic ethanol plant (~0.05 million gallons per day) is about 100 times smaller than an averaged sized oil refinery (~5 million gallons per day)[344,345]. Due to the factors discussed above, the average capital cost of cellulosic biofuel production on a per gallon basis for the few plants that have been built has been more than 6 times higher than that of conventional fuel production at an oil refinery[346,347,348]. The cellulosic biofuel product, considering all costs (e.g. capital, feedstock, operating costs), is 2 to 3 times more expensive compared to conventional fuel[349,350,351]. The past two decades have shown cellulosic biofuels to be a classic example of overpromising and underdelivering[352,353,354]. In the early 2000s, a large number of reports from different sources (academia and industry) provided a flurry of misleadingly optimistic information on biofuels. Based on poor understanding about costs and operational challenges about cellulosic biofuels, these reports promised very competitive costs for cellulosic biofuels relative to conventional fuels within a few years. This in turn led to a misinformed regulatory action in the United States related to cellulosic biofuels[355,356]. Based on the 2007 Energy Independence and Security Act (2007 EISA), the mandated cellulosic biofuel volume in the United States was supposed to increase from **100 million gallons** in 2010 to **10,500 million gallons** in 2020. The *gross lack of understanding* about cellulosic biofuels was obvious from the fact that there was *negligible to no* production of cellulosic biofuels from 2010 to 2013[357]. Although the hype about the potential for future cost reductions for cellulosic biomass has continued over the years, the *total amount* of liquid cellulose biofuels produced in the United States has been *less than 50 million gallons* at the time of writing this book; i.e. only about **0.1%** of the total premised 2010-2020 volume of cellulosic liquid biofuels has been produced to-date. The remarkably high cost of cellulosic biofuels production has been one of the key challenges for the implementation of the technology.

The track record has been very poor[358,359] and therefore, the continued optimism for potential cost reductions is not reliable.

Magnitude of impact: When replacing conventional fuels, about 95% CO_2 emission reductions are expected based on the life cycle analysis for cellulosic biofuels[360]; thus, indicating a high magnitude of CO_2 reduction impact (reduction of about 330 gCO_2/mile compared to conventional gasoline). However, it is important to note that the life cycle greenhouse gas emissions related to biomass feedstocks are not adequately understood due to the high complexity arising from issues such as *land use and change* impact[361]. The magnitude of impact for CO_2 reduction will need to be revisited as the understanding about the complex issues related to biomass-to-energy at scale continues to evolve.

Potential for severe environmental impact at scale: Implementation of biomass for modern applications such as electricity and transportation has been on an extremely small scale compared to fossil fuels[362]. But even when considering the heating application of traditional biomass, the scale of the application has been an order of magnitude smaller compared to fossil fuels[363]. The current small scale of biomass application indicates the possibility for severe environmental impact when applied at a scale representative of fossil fuel use. Due to the *low energy density of biomass* related to its very high moisture/oxygen content[364], significant human activity is required to grow, transport and covert cellulosic biomass to biofuels. In comparison, the human activity required for the highly energy dense fossil fuels (due to efficient support from nature) is considerably smaller. Based on the very large requirements of water and land for growing biomass and related issues[365,366,367], a high potential for severe environmental impact is expected for a widescale implementation of biomass.

Dependence on another new technology: Similar to fossil fuels, biofuel technologies are also not dependent on any other new technology.

Speed of impact: One positive factor from the viewpoint of speed of implementation of cellulosic biofuels is good compatibility with the existing infrastructure. However, the low maturity of cellulosic biofuels, logistics and the poor technology track record are strongly unfavorable factors for the speed of implementation. Based on the above discussion, the speed of implementation of cellulosic biofuels is expected to be slow-to-medium.

3.2.4 Shared Transportation

For the purpose of this discussion, the *shared transportation* term includes all options such as public transportation (bus, rail, etc.), carpooling (sharing rides), etc., that involves sharing of a transportation vehicle by multiple passengers. This solution involves the considerable expansion of public transportation (bus, rail, etc.) and carpooling (sharing rides). The efficacy of the shared transportation solution is controlled by policy issues[368] rather than technology issues. It has been considered as a potential CO_2 reduction solution herein, as it directly competes with the technology-based light duty vehicle transportation solutions. Since it is not a typical technology solution, the shared transportation solution has been discussed below in a different format compared to the other solutions.

The discussion on the shared transportation solution is facilitated with the help of an example. Consider four passengers traveling between their homes (e.g. suburban neighborhood) and a common work location (e.g. downtown), which are located 15 miles apart. Several different cases are considered in this example.

The *base case* involves the four passengers travelling individually in separate conventional light duty vehicles. As discussed earlier, a conventional light duty vehicle has average CO_2 emissions of ~400 gCO_2 per mile. Based on the above information, the base case will involve the travel of 120 vehicle miles on a roundtrip basis and corresponding release of 48 kg CO_2 per day[369].

The *second case* involves use of carpooling by the four passengers, wherein they share the transportation between their home and the work using a *single* conventional light duty vehicle. In this case, the CO_2 emissions released on a daily basis will only be 12 kg CO_2 (i.e., only **100 gCO_2 per passenger mile**), corresponding to the fact that carpooling will result in about a *fourth* of the total vehicle miles compared to the base case[370]. The *much fewer total vehicle miles* travelled for the *same total passenger miles* will also translate into significant savings based on lower fuel consumption and maintenance cost. Moreover, the significantly increased access to vehicles for other household members might preclude the need for additional vehicle(s) in one or more of the four households.

The *third case* involves these four passengers travelling individually in *separate* battery electric light duty vehicles (this is an example of replacement of private conventional light duty vehicles with private battery electric vehicles). As discussed earlier, a battery electric light duty vehicle has average CO_2 emissions of 226 gCO_2 per mile. From this information it can be estimated that the case involving the use of individual battery electric vehicles for transportation will have a much higher CO_2 emission (27 kg CO_2)[371] compared to the shared transportation case emission of (12 kg CO_2). The battery electric vehicle case will also result in a substantially higher total cost compared to the shared transportation example because of the requirement of *four times* higher total vehicle miles for the same total passenger miles.

The above discussion distinctly shows the powerful ability of shared transportation to reduce CO_2 emissions from the transportation sector in an extremely cost-efficient manner. It is also evident from the above example that the overall impact from the shared transportation solution will be sensitive to the occupancy of the vehicle; i.e. the CO_2 reduction advantage will decrease significantly as the vehicle occupancy decreases. For instance, in the above shared transportation carpooling case, if only two passengers carpooled instead of four, the CO_2 emissions will be 200 gCO_2 per passenger mile instead of 100 gCO_2 per passenger mile. This is because in case of carpooling with an occupancy of only two passengers, the total vehicle miles travelled per day will be reduced by a factor of two as opposed to a factor of four when the carpooling occupancy is four passengers.

The sensitivity to occupancy becomes even more important for public transportation (mass transit). This is related to the higher cost and inferior fuel economy associated with the larger vehicles (e.g. bus, train, etc.) involved in public transportation. Results from a comprehensive 2010 study by the U.S. Department of Transportation provide excellent historical data about the impact of *vehicle occupancy* in buses/trains on the CO_2 emissions[372]. The study showed that for bus transit, the CO_2 emissions decreased from **291 gCO_2 per passenger mile** for the *28%* (actually observed) average historical vehicle occupancy of the bus to **82 gCO_2 per passenger mile** for *100%* (maximum) occupancy of the bus. For commuter train, the CO$_2$ emissions decreased from **150 gCO$_2$ per passenger mile** for the *30%* (actually observed) average historical occupancy of the commuter train to **45 gCO$_2$ per passenger mile** for *100%* (maximum) occupancy. The study also showed an average CO$_2$ emission of 327 gCO$_2$/per passenger mile for private auto trips based on the observed average occupancy of 1.4 passengers per private auto trip for work and other general reasons. Thus, the above study shows that a reasonably high occupancy of 70% for shared transportation will have a large CO$_2$ reduction compared to private auto travel. Maintaining reasonably high occupancy (70% or higher of maximum capacity) for the shared transportation options is a challenge that can be addressed via pragmatic policy decisions. Although the above study was based on data from major cities in the United States, the general conclusions are valid across the globe.

Shared transportation options at 70% occupancy have a value of *120 gCO$_2$ emissions per passenger mile or lower*[373]. Considering that about 3 billion tons of CO$_2$ are emitted from light duty vehicles globally, the magnitude of CO$_2$ reduction impact can be significant for the shared transportation solution. For example, replacement of 60% of private auto use by shared transportation options (for e.g. by using strategic deployment of transportation vans and buses at 70% occupancy) will reduce CO$_2$ emissions by over *1 billion tons per year*.

At high occupancy levels (70% or higher), the cost of the CO$_2$ reduction will also be low due to the significant monetary savings from the drastically reduced total vehicle miles. There would be low-to-no dependency on any other new technology solution. Also, there will be a significantly decreased potential for (yet unknown) severe environmental impact considering that the technology and related components used in shared transportation options have been implemented on a wide scale. Furthermore, considering that the number of total vehicle miles will decrease drastically, there will be lower human activity per passenger mile due to need for fewer vehicles, lower fuel consumption, lower maintenance and so on. Correspondingly, there will be a *low to medium* potential for severe environmental impact from shared transportation. Since shared transportation can leverage mature technology (e.g. *cars, transport vans and buses*), and has good compatibility with the existing infrastructure, the speed of impact should be medium to high. Furthermore, shared transportation provides a key practical advantage of drastically reducing traffic and therefore will help with *decongesting roads* in major cities/regions around the world.

Due to the historically cultivated habit of private travel, there is a low incentive for using shared transportation for a significant fraction of the population. The large expansion of shared transportation will, therefore, require policy decisions targeted towards considerably increasing the *incentives for using shared transportation*. It will also be very important to ensure that there is clear messaging that reminds the global population that incidents such as COVID-19 are rare and most importantly are temporary[374].

3.3 Brief discussion on key characteristics for direct CO_2 capture from air

Considering that the final goal of any CO_2 reduction solution is to prevent the excess accumulation of CO_2 in the atmosphere, the concept of direct capture of CO_2 from air and its storage/utilization is extremely appealing. This section will briefly consider the key issues related to direct CO_2 capture from air technology.

Direct CO_2 capture from air technology has not yet been implemented on a commercially relevant scale. Correspondingly, robust cost estimates are not available for the technology. However, it is possible to use CO_2 capture from fossil fueled power plants as a reference case to discuss the relative cost of the direct capture from air technology.

In case of CO_2 capture from power plants, the concentration of CO_2 in the byproduct stream is typically **above 5%**[375]. In contrast, the amount of CO_2 in the atmosphere is about **0.04%**[376]. Due to this *extremely low concentration of CO_2 in air*[377], the overall efficiency of direct CO_2 capture from air is *substantially lower* than CO_2 capture from power plants. Considering that the CO_2 capture technology from power plants *itself has a high cost* for CO_2 reduction[378,379], it follows that direct CO_2 capture from air *will have even higher costs*.

Based on decades of historical data on new technology commercialization in the energy/chemicals sectors it is well understood that cost numbers are significantly underestimated for a complex new technology[380]. Many of the project and process uncertainties are not well understood for a new complex technology *until several large commercial units are built and operated successfully*. This lack of understanding of project uncertainties, unfortunately leads to unrealistic cost estimates. Incorrect (underestimated) cost estimation due to *unrealistic optimism* was one of the key reasons for the embarrassing cellulosic biofuels-related regulations problem discussed previously in this chapter[381,382]. It is therefore important to be extremely cautious about any initial cost estimations about direct CO_2 capture from air, especially from sources that have financial interest in the project. Due to the many unknowns, it is currently not possible to accurately estimate the cost for direct CO_2 capture from air. However, based on the much lower efficiency for *direct CO_2 capture from air* compared to *CO_2 capture from power plants*, it can be confidently predicted that the cost for direct CO_2 capture is going to be *very high* on a per unit of CO_2 reduced basis relative to other low-carbon technologies. No significant cost improvements or environmental benefits are expected by converting the captured CO_2 into useful products such as chemicals due to extremely poor energetics[383]. This is related to the scientific fact that, while it is easy to convert carbon-based material into CO_2, it is extremely energetically inefficient to convert CO_2 into useful carbon-based products. In summary, the direct air capture and storage/utilization technology solution is extremely challenged by basic laws of nature; therefore, any claims related to major cost breakthroughs in this area will need carefully evaluation based on **at-least a few years of operating data on several large-scale operational units**. This required data is **not expected** to be available for *at-least* the next 10 to 15 years.

Currently, there is no widescale implementation of the direct air CO_2 capture technology. Also, the *very poor efficiency* for direct air CO_2 capture arising due to the very low concentration of CO_2 in the air (*100 to 300 times lower* compared to byproduct from power plants)[384] is indication of very large requirements of human activity (i.e. very large requirements of materials, energy, water, and land). Based on the above discussion, there will be a high potential for yet unknown severe impact from direct CO_2 capture form air and storage/utilization, when implemented at the required scale.

The speed of implementation for direct CO_2 capture from air technology and storage/utilization is expected to be very slow in the next couple of decades considering a) that there are currently no commercial-scale operating units (i.e. there is a very high technology risk) and b) the very high anticipated costs of the substantially challenged technology. Since that the focus of the book is on discussing widescale implementation in the short-to-midterm (within the next decade or so) the direct CO_2 capture from air technology solution will not be further discussed in this book.

Other technologies such as *fuel cells* and *geothermal energy* are also not discussed in this book, because their current applications are very limited, and furthermore, these technologies are not expected to be implemented on a wide scale for at-least a decade due to severe current limitations related to either high cost, and/or technical challenges and/or lack of availability of appropriate infrastructure or locations[385,386,387,388,389,390]. Although these technologies are beyond the scope of this book, they should be *monitored for progress based on credible data* (i.e., adequate commercial-scale data as and when it becomes available over the next decades). This will allow a robust comparison analysis of these potentially promising technologies as soon as adequate data become available.

...§§§-§-§§§...

Chapter 4: Comparison of Technology Solutions

This chapter compares the technology solutions in terms of their key characteristics. The solutions are first compared within the individual sectors they belong to (i.e. electricity generation and transportation). This is followed by a comparison of CO_2 reduction cost effectiveness of the technology solutions across the sectors.

The primary goal of this chapter is to compare the proposed technology solutions in terms of their abilities to address all the critical challenges related to CO_2 reduction. Such a comparison is an essential first step for prioritization of the technologies, which is discussed in the next chapter.

4.1 Comparison of solutions within the electricity generation sector (EGS)

The key characteristics of the technology solutions from the electricity generation sector discussed in the previous chapter are summarized herein to facilitate the comparison.

4.1.1 Comparison of EGS solutions: Cost

The cost comparison discussion below is focused on the United States; discussions related to other regions of the world will be included in the next chapter. The summarized capital cost data per unit capacity for the different electricity generation technologies in the United States is shown in Figure 18[391,392,393]. Natural gas plants, solar-utility and wind-onshore have a low capital cost per unit capacity, while wind-offshore, solar with storage, nuclear, and coal with capture have a high capital cost per unit capacity.

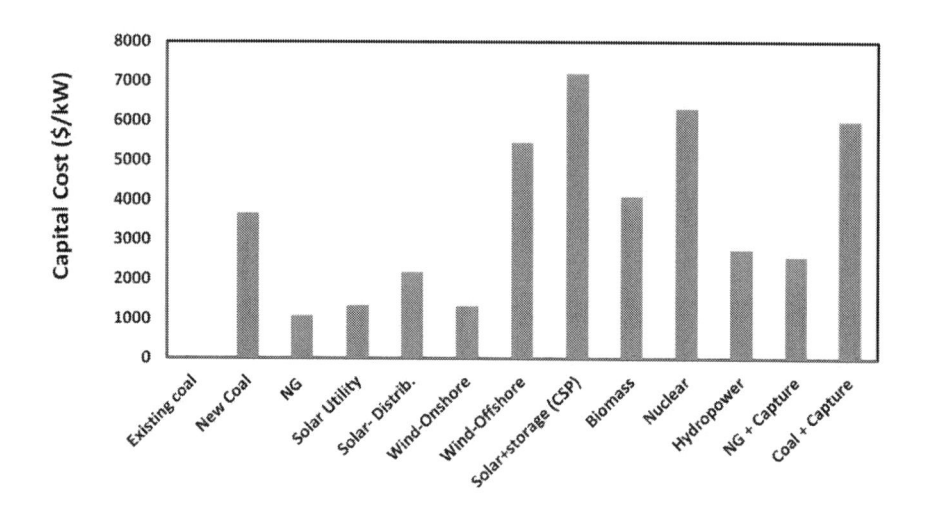

Figure 18. Capital cost per unit capacity for the different technologies in the electricity generation sector (2019$); NG = natural gas. Data sources: U.S. EIA and NREL

Capacity factor[394] data for each technology, which also influences the total initial investment requirement, is shown in Figure 19[395,396,397].

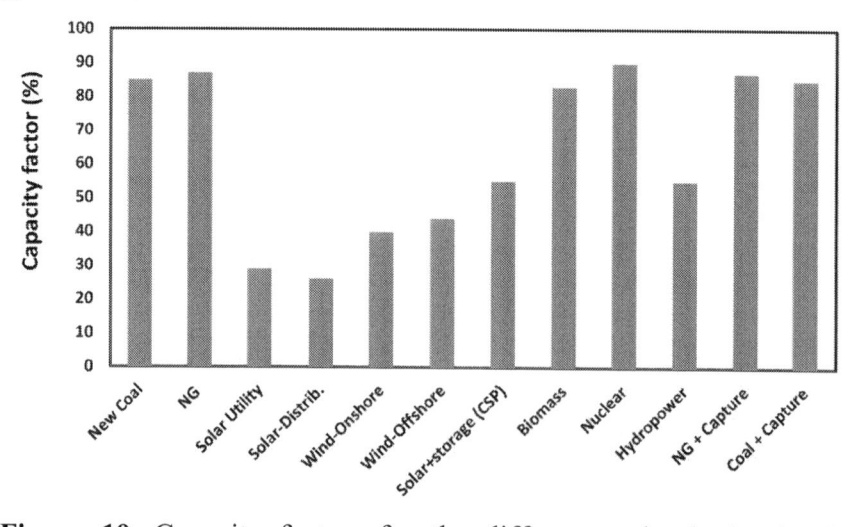

Figure 19. Capacity factors for the different technologies in the electricity generation sector; NG = natural gas. Data sources: U.S. EIA, NREL

The upper end value of the capacity factors is provided for each technology to enable the best possible comparison between the technologies[398].

Nuclear has the highest capacity factor, while solar-utility and solar-distributed technologies have the lowest capacity factors. The summarized levelized cost of electricity for each technology solution, which includes the capital cost per unit capacity, capacity factor and O&M cost data, is presented in Figure 20[399,400,401,402]. Natural gas plants, solar-utility and wind-onshore have a low levelized cost of electricity, while wind-offshore, solar with storage[403], and coal with capture have a high corresponding cost. Since this cost comparison does not consider CO_2 reduction, it does not provide any information about the cost effectiveness of CO_2 reduction for the technology solutions. The cost effectiveness characteristic, which is very important for comparing the technologies, is discussed in a later section.

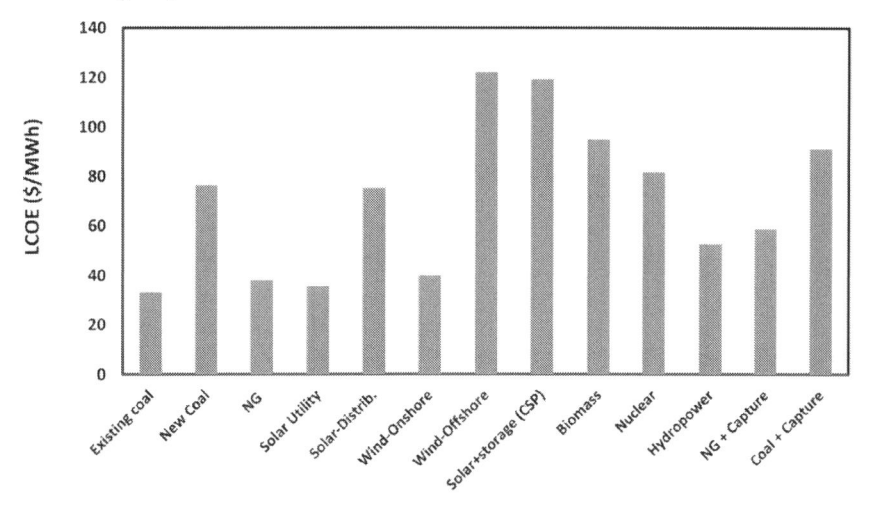

Figure 20. Levelized cost of electricity for the different technologies in the electricity generation sector; NG = natural gas. Data sources: U.S. EIA, NREL and NETL[404]

4.1.2 Comparison of EGS solutions: Magnitude of impact

The *magnitude of impact* comparison is discussed herein in terms of CO_2 emissions avoided relative to the existing coal plants. Existing coal plants are considered as the reference technology to be replaced since these plants generate about 70% of the global CO_2 emissions in the power sector[405,406]. The CO_2 emissions avoided relative to existing coal plants for the different electricity generation technology solutions are summarized in Figure 21[407,408]. In terms of the magnitude of CO_2 reduction impact characteristic, the different proposed technology solutions range from *medium impact* to *high impact*. While natural gas technology has medium impact (reduction of ~500 gCO_2e/kWh), technologies such as solar, wind and nuclear have high impact (reduction of ~950 gCO_2e/kWh) when they replace existing coal plants. As discussed earlier, there is an *enormous advantage* for dispatchable technologies compared to non-dispatchable technologies due to electricity supply/demand issues. Therefore, the characteristics such as costs and magnitude of impact *cannot be used in isolation* to make decisions between dispatchable and non-dispatchable technologies. However, these characteristics can be considered *together* with all the other key characteristics to obtain the necessary *overall effectiveness* information for the different technology solutions (which is provided in the next chapter).

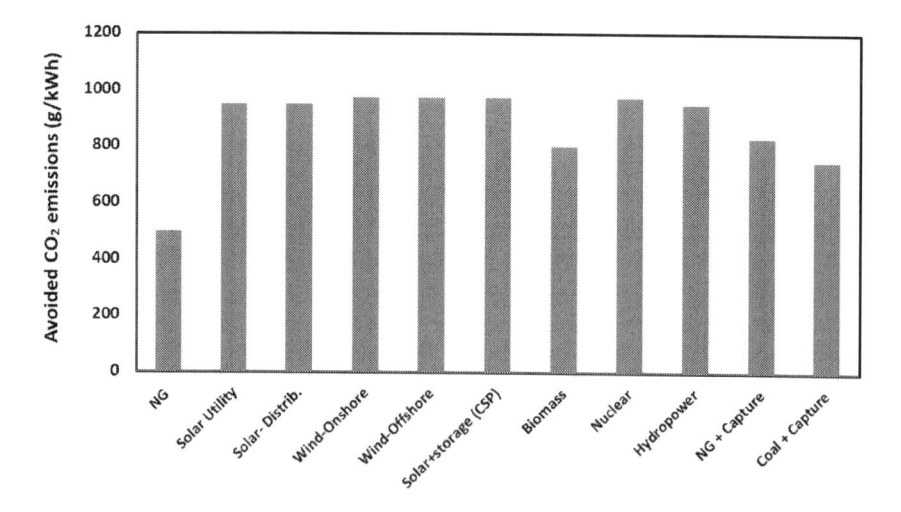

Figure 21. CO_2 emissions avoided per unit of electricity produced (gCO_2e/kWh) for the different technology solutions when used as a replacement for the existing coal plants. Primary data source: U.S. National Energy Technology Laboratory.

4.1.3 Comparison of EGS solutions: Potential for severe environmental impact at the required scale

As detailed previously, the potential for (yet unknown) severe unknown environmental impact at the required scale is an extremely important characteristic, which unfortunately is also the most overlooked. The potential for severe environmental impact at scale of any technology can be evaluated by considering its *current scale of implementation* and *efficiency of assistance provided by nature*. The conclusions from the previous discussions about this characteristic for the different technology solutions are summarized together in Table 16.

Solution	Potential for severe environmental impact at scale
Natural gas	Medium
Solar-Utility	Medium to High
Solar-Distributed	Medium
Wind-Onshore	Medium to High
Wind-Offshore	High
Solar with storage	High
Biomass	High
Nuclear	Medium
Hydropower	Medium
Natural gas with capture/storage	High
Coal with capture/storage	High

Table 16. Comparison of the electricity generation technologies based on the potential for, yet unknown, severe environmental impact.

Expectedly, due to the *relatively tiny* scale of current implementation and *significant requirement* of human activity, several of the proposed CO_2 reduction technologies have either a *medium to high* potential or *high* potential for (yet unknown) severe environmental impact, when considered at a wide scale.

4.1.4 Comparison of EGS solutions: Dependence on another new technology

Dependence on another new solution is an important characteristic since it determines the *extent of self-sufficient penetration* of the technology solution. The conclusions from the previous discussions about this characteristic for the different technology solutions are summarized in Table 17.

Solution	Dependence on another new technology
Natural gas	No
Solar-Utility	Yes
Solar-Distributed	Yes
Wind-Onshore	Yes
Wind-Offshore	Yes
Solar with storage	No
Biomass	No
Nuclear	No
Hydropower	No
Natural gas with capture/storage	No
Coal with capture/storage	No

Table 17. Comparison of the electricity generation technologies based on the dependence on another new technology

The widescale application of non-dispatchable solutions such as solar and wind, additionally requires widescale implementation of energy storage technology. This *mandatory dependence* of solar and wind-based technologies on an another less established technology *limits the independent penetration* of these technologies. The other solutions due to their dispatchable characteristic are not dependent on any other less established solution.

4.1.5 Comparison of EGS solutions: Speed of impact

The speed of impact is an indicator of the ability of the technology to have a rapid impact on CO_2 reduction when considering technical and/or practical issues such as technology maturity, compatibility with existing energy infrastructure, logistics, etc. The conclusions from the previous discussions about this characteristic for the different solutions are summarized in Table 18.

Solution	Speed of Impact
Natural gas	High
Solar-Utility	Medium to High
Solar-Distributed	Medium to High
Wind-Onshore	Medium to High
Wind-Offshore	Medium
Solar with storage	Low to Medium
Biomass	Low to Medium
Nuclear	Medium
Hydropower	Medium
Natural gas with capture/storage	Low
Coal with capture/storage	Low

Table 18. Comparison of the electricity generation technologies based on the speed of impact

Amongst the different proposed solutions, the natural gas technology is the most favorable technology with respect to speed of implementation. On the other hand, the speed of implementation is expected to be the least favorable for technologies such as natural gas with capture/storage and coal with capture/storage.

4.2 Comparison of solutions within the transportation sector (TS)

The key characteristics of the solutions from the light duty vehicle transportation sector are summarized herein to compare the different technology solutions.

4.2.1 Comparison of TS solutions: Cost

The *summarized* retail price (initial investment) for the representative light duty vehicle technologies in the United States is shown in Figure 22. As discussed earlier, the conventional technology serves as a reference.

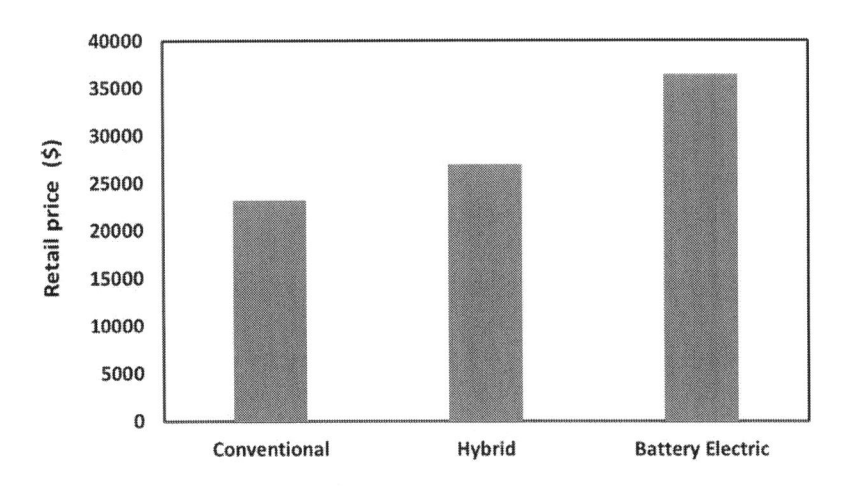

[Bar chart showing Retail price ($) for Conventional (~23000), Hybrid (~27000), and Battery Electric (~36500) vehicles.]

Figure 22. Retail price for the representative light duty vehicles (2019$).

Compared to conventional vehicle technology, the hybrid vehicle technology requires about 15% higher initial investment. The battery electric vehicle technology requires an even higher initial investment (about 60% higher than the conventional vehicle technology). The levelized cost per mile over the vehicle life is also considerably higher for the battery electric vehicle technology. While the total cost for the hybrid electric vehicle technology is only 1% higher than the conventional vehicle technology, the levelized cost for the battery electric vehicle technology is a substantial 8 % higher[409].

In case of the biofuels technology solution, the initial investment of a cellulosic biofuels plant is about 6 times higher compared to a conventional fuels production plant. Also, the cost of the cellulosic biofuels product is 2 to 3 times higher than that of gasoline. In other words, the cost of biofuel technology is considerably higher than the reference technology.

The solution that is most economical from a cost viewpoint in the transportation sector is the shared transportation solution. The shared transportation solution has a much **lower ratio** for *total vehicles miles to total passenger miles* compared to private travel in conventional light duty vehicles (see section 3.2.4). Large cost savings are therefore expected due to significantly lower fuel use, and reduced need for light duty vehicles per household. It should be noted that the large advantage offered by shared transportation can be only leveraged at reasonably high occupancy rates (70% or higher of maximum occupancy). The cost comparison discussion above is focused on the United States; discussions related to other regions of the world are included in the next chapter.

4.2.2 Comparison of TS solutions: Magnitude of impact

The *magnitude of impact* comparison data is discussed herein in terms of the *CO_2 emissions avoided per mile* relative to the reference (conventionally fueled light duty vehicle) technology. The CO_2 emissions avoided by the different solutions in the transportation sector relative to the reference technology are summarized in Figure 23.

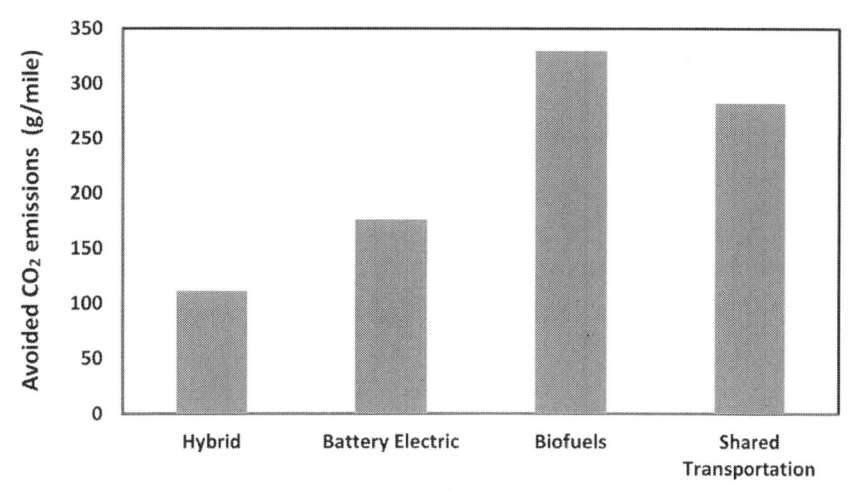

Figure 23. CO_2 emissions avoided per mile travelled (gCO_2e/mile) for the proposed technology solutions when used to replace the conventional light duty vehicle technology.

In terms of the magnitude of impact characteristic, the different proposed solutions range from *medium* impact to *high* impact. While hybrid technology has a medium CO_2 reduction impact, technologies such as biofuels and shared transportation (at high occupancy rates) have a high impact when they replace conventionally fueled light duty vehicles.

4.2.3 Comparison of TS solutions: Potential for severe environmental impact at scale

The conclusions from the previous discussions about the *potential for severe environmental impact* characteristic for the different solutions are summarized in Table 19.

Solution	Potential for severe environmental impact at scale
Hybrid	Low to Medium
Battery Electric	Medium
Biofuels	High
Shared Transportation	Low to Medium

Table 19. Comparison of the transportation sector solutions based on the potential for, yet unknown, severe environmental impact at scale.

Amongst the different proposed solutions, the hybrid and shared transportation solutions are expected to have a low-to-medium potential for (yet unknown) severe environmental impact at scale. On the other hand, the battery electric light duty vehicle technology is expected to have a medium potential and biofuels technology is expected to have a high potential for severe environmental impact, when applied on a wide scale.

4.2.4 Comparison of TS solutions: Dependence on another new technology

The conclusions from the previous chapter about this characteristic for the different solutions are summarized in Table 20. Amongst the solutions considered herein, the only solution that has a dependence on another less established technology is the battery electric vehicle technology.

Solution	Dependence on another new technology
Hybrid	No
Battery Electric	Yes
Biofuels	No
Shared Transportation	No

Table 20. Comparison of the transportation sector solutions based on the dependence on another less established technology.

4.2.5 Comparison of TS solutions: Speed of impact

The conclusions from the previous chapter about the *speed of impact* characteristic for the different solutions are summarized in Table 21. The hybrid electric vehicle technology and shared transportation solution are expected to have a medium-to-high speed of implementation. On the other hand, the speed of implementation is expected to be low-to-medium for the biofuels technology solution.

Solution	Speed of Impact
Hybrid	Medium to High
Battery Electric	Medium
Biofuels	Low to Medium
Shared Transportation	Medium to High

Table 21. Comparison of the transportation sector solutions based on the speed of impact.

4.3 CO_2 Reduction Cost

In the previous sections, the *cost characteristic* of the proposed technology solutions was compared on an absolute basis; i.e. **without any consideration to CO_2 reduction**. A more effective way to compare the cost characteristic of the technology solutions is to use *CO_2 reduction costs* (i.e. costs relative to the avoided CO_2). An important advantage of utilizing CO_2 reduction cost is that it allows for a direct comparison of the **cost effectiveness of CO_2 reduction between technologies**. Another important advantage of using CO_2 reduction cost is that it enables cost comparisons **across sectors**, i.e. it allows comparison between technology solutions from different categories (e.g. power plant technology vs vehicle technology vs fuel technology). Thus, a CO_2 reduction cost characteristic comparison is important for robust prioritization between different technology solutions. From this point onwards, the *CO_2 reduction cost characteristic* will be used for cost comparison between solutions.

The CO_2 reduction cost can be estimated by using the cost and CO_2 emissions data for the proposed solution and the reference (to be replaced) technology. As discussed earlier, the reference technology is existing coal plants for the electricity generation sector and conventionally fueled light duty vehicles for the light duty vehicle transportation sector.

There are **two important components** of the CO_2 reduction cost characteristic: a) *initial investment cost per avoided CO_2 ton per year* and b) *total cost per avoided CO_2 ton*.

The *initial investment cost per avoided CO_2 ton per year* is important from the viewpoint of understanding the efficiency of upfront investment for technology solutions. It essentially provides information related to the **extent of CO_2 emission reductions per year** that can be achieved for a **given upfront investment**. Considering the need for extremely large amounts of CO_2 reduction per year, it is important that the *initial investment cost per avoided CO_2 ton per year* be as low as possible for maximizing the efficiency in budgeting; this is very important considering that there are several competing urgent problems (e.g. poverty, health care, etc.) that also need to be addressed by each country.

The *total cost per avoided CO_2 ton* is important as an indicator of **total cost efficiency** (i.e. lifetime cost efficiency) for the proposed solution.

As shown below, the *initial investment cost per avoided CO_2 unit per year* can be estimated from the initial investment (capital) cost and CO_2 emissions data for the proposed technology solution and the reference (Ref.) technology.

$$\left.\begin{array}{l}\text{Initial Investment cost per}\\ \text{avoided } CO_2 \text{ unit per year}\end{array}\right\}$$
$$= \frac{\text{Initial Investment}_{Solution} - \text{Initial Investment}_{Ref}}{(CO_2 \text{ Emissions}_{Ref} - CO_2 \text{ Emissions}_{Solution})yr}$$

The *total cost per avoided CO₂ unit* can be estimated from the total cost and CO₂ emissions data for the proposed technology solution and the reference (Ref.) technology.

$$\left.\begin{array}{l}\text{Total cost per}\\ \text{avoided } CO_2 \text{ unit}\end{array}\right\} = \frac{\text{Levelized Cost}_{Solution} - \text{Levelized Cost}_{Ref}}{CO_2 \text{ Emissions}_{Ref} - CO_2 \text{ Emissions}_{Solution}}$$

In this sub-section the CO₂ reduction costs of the proposed solutions are first discussed for the electricity generator sector (EGS) and subsequently for the transportation sector (TS).

4.3.1 Comparison of EGS solutions: CO₂ reduction costs

The *initial investment cost per avoided CO₂ ton per year* and the *total cost per avoided CO₂ ton* for the different technology solutions in the electricity generation sector were estimated using the *United States specific* cost data and CO₂ emissions data (provided in earlier sections)[410] based on the above discussed estimation methodology. The results are shown in Figures 24 and 25.

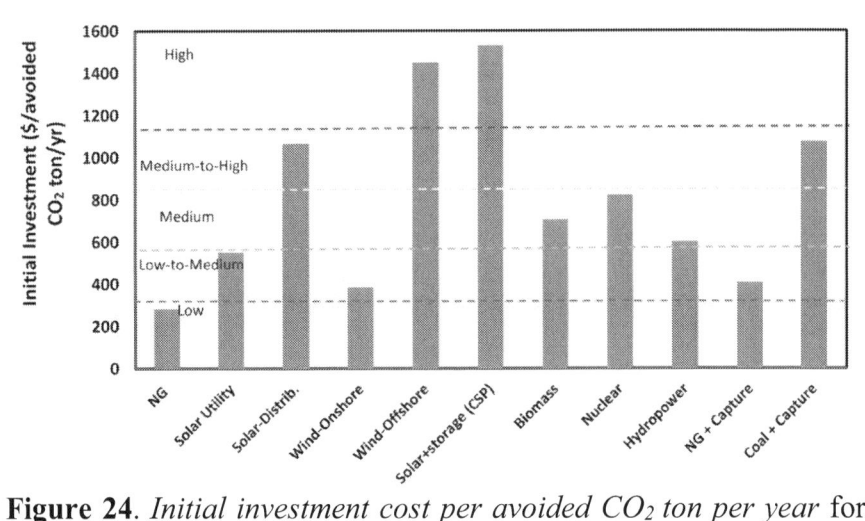

Figure 24. *Initial investment cost per avoided CO₂ ton per year* for the technology solutions for replacing existing coal plants (2019$); NG = natural gas.

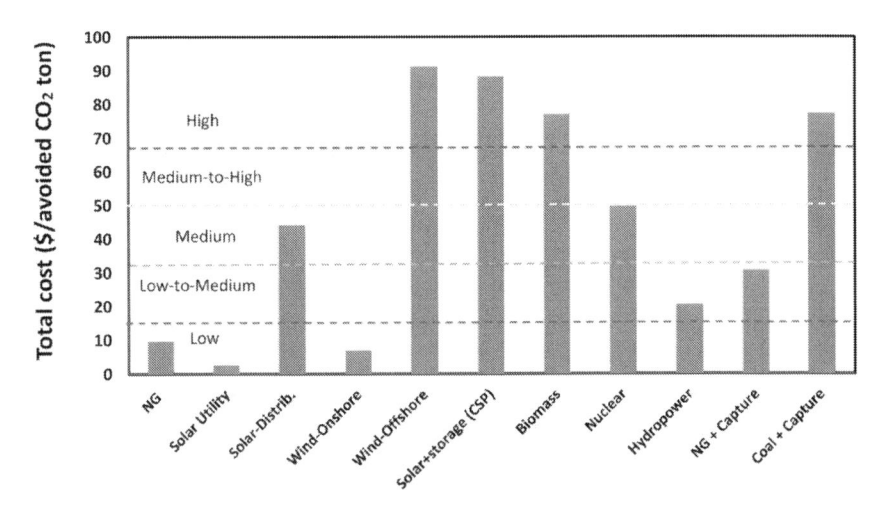

Figure 25. Total cost per avoided CO2 ton for the technology solutions when replacing existing coal units (2019$); NG = natural gas.

Based on the data in the figures, the technology solutions can be broadly classified as either low, low-to-medium, medium, medium-to-high or high cost options. For example, natural gas technology has a low cost, while solar with storage[411] and wind-offshore have a high cost for both the components of the CO_2 reduction cost characteristic. Some technologies such as nuclear energy look significantly more favorable when considered on the basis of cost effectiveness for CO_2 reduction than on an absolute cost basis. This is related to the favorable capacity factors and low CO_2 emissions for nuclear technology. As noted previously, the above discussed results are based on United States cost data. Comparisons related to other regions of the world will be addressed in the next chapter.

4.3.2 Comparison of TS solutions: CO₂ reduction costs

The *initial investment cost per avoided CO₂ ton per year* and the *total cost per avoided CO₂ ton* for different technology solutions in the light duty vehicle transportation sector were estimated using the *United States specific* cost data and CO_2 emissions data[412,413] based on the earlier discussed estimation methodology. The results are shown in Figures 26 and 27.

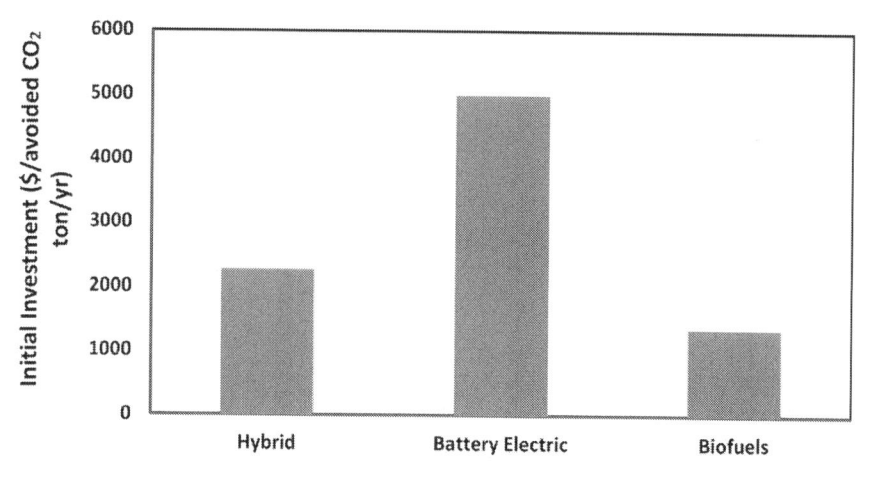

Figure 26. Initial investment cost per avoided CO_2 ton per year for the technology solutions for replacing (reference) conventional light duty vehicle technology.

While the biofuels technology has a low initial investment cost per avoided CO₂ ton per year, it has the highest *total cost per avoided CO₂ ton* amongst the three technology solutions.

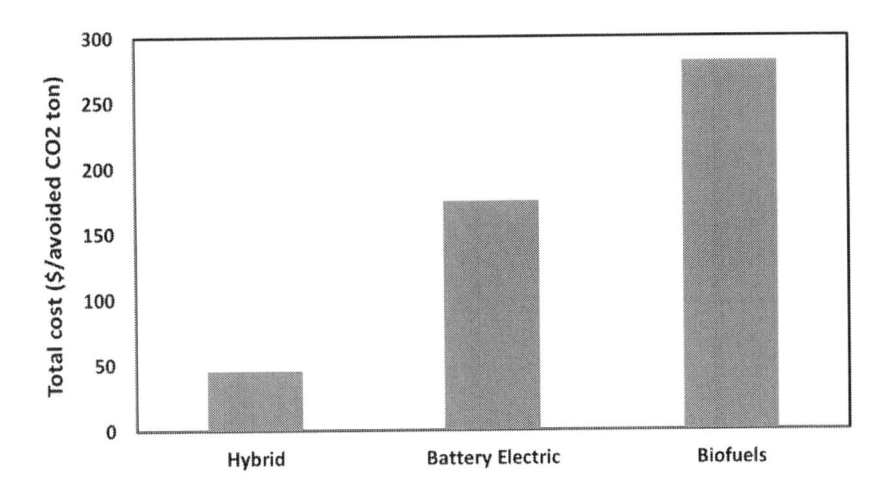

Figure 27. Total cost per avoided CO_2 ton for the technology solutions when replacing (reference) conventional light duty vehicle technology.

The hybrid electric vehicle technology is substantially superior to the battery electric vehicle technology for both the components of the CO_2 reduction cost characteristic. Since the relative initial investment costs for the proposed technology solutions are less sensitive to the country[414], the above discussed relative *initial investment cost per avoided CO₂ ton per year* comparison between the different proposed solutions should be reasonably valid for several countries. However, since the total cost is very sensitive to fuel/electricity prices, information related to *total cost per avoided CO₂ ton* will be region/country specific. Further discussions related to other regions of the world will be included in the next chapter.

Amongst the solutions in this sector, the shared transportation solution, which is more of a policy based solution, is estimated to have the lowest cost for both the *initial investment cost per avoided CO₂ ton per year* (< $500 /ton/yr) and the *total cost per avoided CO₂ ton* (< $1 /ton)[415]. As discussed earlier this can be attributed to the low initial investment cost, low O&M costs, and high CO_2 reduction per passenger mile for the shared transportation solution when the occupancy rate is reasonably high (70% or higher). The above cost information for the shared transportation solution is specific to the United States. However, based on the inherent characteristics of the different solutions, the shared transportation solution is also expected to have the least relative cost globally.

...§§§-§-§§§...

Chapter 5: Prioritization of Technologies for Efficient CO_2 Reduction

In this chapter, the focus will be on prioritizing the different solutions by using the comparison information from the previous chapter. A robust prioritization of technology solutions is essential for maximizing the efficiency of the CO_2 reduction efforts by the global society. This is the *most practical way* to ensure that our limited resources are efficiently utilized for CO_2 reduction. In absence of a robust prioritization of the technology solutions, the *incentives* provided by the local/national governments are expected to be inefficient in terms of reducing CO_2 emissions. *Incentives* for a **less efficient technology would take away resources from a more efficient technology** resulting in overall inefficiencies in the CO_2 reduction efforts. Thus, a robust prioritization analysis is critical for ensuring that incentives/subsidies are efficiently utilized by the global society for CO_2 reduction.

The prioritization analysis would be quite straight forward if the only challenge associated with the CO_2 reduction problem was to achieve a quick and substantial CO_2 reduction. However, as discussed in Chapter 2, there are several other critical challenges associated with CO_2 reduction which increases the complexity of the prioritization analysis. As a result, a **robust prioritization analysis** of the different technology solutions requires a comparison of the solutions based on their abilities to **address all the critical challenges** related to CO_2 reduction. The required prioritization of the technology solutions can be achieved by systematically considering the *relative favorability* of their characteristics in meeting the critical challenges. As detailed earlier, the key characteristics that need to be considered for prioritization of the different technology solutions include CO_2 reduction cost, magnitude of impact on CO_2 reduction, potential for severe environment impact at scale, speed of impact on CO_2 reduction, and dependency on another new solution.

For facilitating the prioritization discussion, the key characteristics for the different technology solutions are *rated* herein in terms of their *relative favorability*[416]. For example, if the CO_2 reduction cost characteristic for a technology solution is high relative to the other solutions, it is rated as *highly unfavorable* and correspondingly, a medium-to-high cost is rated as *unfavorable*, a medium cost is rated as *moderate*, a low-to-medium cost is rated as *favorable* and a low cost is rated as *highly favorable*. Similarly, for the magnitude of impact characteristic, a high CO_2 reduction impact relative to other solutions is rated as highly favorable, a medium-to-high impact is rated as favorable, a medium impact is rated as moderate, a low-to-medium impact is rated as unfavorable and a low impact is rated as highly unfavorable. Since there is no spectrum for the dependency characteristic, a lack of dependency on another new technology is rated as favorable, while a presence of a dependency is rated as unfavorable.

Considering that there are multiple characteristics for each technology solution with a range of potential favorability ratings, a pragmatic methodology to prioritize the solutions is in terms of *Tiers*. Correspondingly, the solutions have been classified into Tiers as following: a) **Tier 1**: solutions that have at least four *favorable to highly favorable* ratings and no highly unfavorable rating for the key characteristics, b) **Tier 2**: solutions that have at least four *moderate to highly favorable* ratings and one or less highly unfavorable rating for the key characteristics, c) **Tier 3**: solutions have at least three *moderate to highly favorable* ratings and two or less highly unfavorable rating for the key characteristics, and d) **Tier 4**: All solutions which do not fit in the top three Tiers. The relative Tier-based prioritization classification framework has been designed such that it is narrow enough to distinctly **distinguish between effective and less effective solutions**, but is also broad enough that any potential changes (e.g. decrease in future cost for certain solutions) will **not substantially impact** the relative prioritization between the solutions *within the next decade or so*.

The prioritization discussion would have been extraordinarily complicated if each of these key characteristics of the technology solutions was sensitive to the country/location, where the technology solution was to be applied. Fortunately, the relative favorability of four of the key characteristics of the technology solutions is not expected to significantly depend on the country of application. This is because characteristics such as magnitude of impact on CO_2 reduction, speed of impact, potential for severe environmental impact, and dependence on another new solution are primarily defined by the **nature of the technology**. On the other hand, the relative favorability of the total cost of CO_2 reduction characteristic is expected to be substantially influenced by the country where the technology is to be applied. This is related to the fact that fuel and electricity prices, which strongly influence the total cost of CO_2 reduction, are country specific.

To facilitate the comparison, a prioritization analysis will be first provided for the United States. A generic global prioritization analysis will be discussed subsequently, which will account for the differences in the cost of fuel, electricity and other factors between countries. It should be noted that the prioritization discussion herein is mainly focused on the **next decade** or so (i.e. for deployment of solutions within the next 10 to 15 years).

5.1 Prioritization discussion for the United States

To facilitate the discussion related to the United States, the prioritization of the solutions is first discussed for the electricity generation sector (EGS), followed by the (light duty vehicle) transportation sector (TS) and finally *considered across the two sectors*.

5.1.1 Prioritization of EGS solutions for the United States

Although coal power plants produce less than 25% of the electricity in the United States, they emit 60% of the CO_2 from the electricity generation sector[417,418]. About 1 billion tons of CO_2 are emitted by existing coal power plants, out of the total ~1.6 billion tons from the sector. Based on annual energy outlook by U.S. EIA, the electricity demand is not expected to grow significantly in the next two decades[419]. This means that the EGS technology solutions can mainly be expected to replace the existing *high CO_2 emitting* coal power plants in the United States in the next decade. Table 22 shows the relative favorability ratings (based directly on data from the last chapter) for the key characteristics of the proposed solutions for CO_2 reduction in the electricity generation sector. The relative favorability ratings are indicative of the ability of the technology solutions to address the critical challenges associated with CO_2 reduction.

	Initial investment per avoided CO_2 ton per year	Total cost per avoided CO_2 ton	Potential for severe environmental impact	Magnitude of impact	Speed of Impact	Dependence on another new technology
Natural gas	Highly Favorable	Highly Favorable	Moderate	Moderate	Highly Favorable	Favorable
Solar Utility	Favorable	Highly Favorable	Unfavorable	Highly Favorable	Favorable	Unfavorable
Solar Distributed	Unfavorable	Moderate	Moderate	Highly Favorable	Favorable	Unfavorable
Wind Onshore	Favorable	Highly Favorable	Unfavorable	Highly Favorable	Favorable	Unfavorable
Wind Offshore	Highly Unfavorable	Highly Unfavorable	Highly Unfavorable	Highly Favorable	Moderate	Unfavorable
Solar with storage	Highly Unfavorable	Highly Unfavorable	Highly Unfavorable	Highly Favorable	Unfavorable	Favorable
Biomass	Moderate	Highly Unfavorable	Highly Unfavorable	Favorable	Unfavorable	Favorable
Nuclear	Moderate	Moderate	Moderate	Highly Favorable	Moderate	Favorable
Hydropower	Moderate	Favorable	Moderate	Favorable	Moderate	Favorable
Natural gas with capture/storage	Favorable	Favorable	Highly Unfavorable	Favorable	Highly Unfavorable	Favorable
Coal with capture/storage	Unfavorable	Highly Unfavorable	Highly Unfavorable	Favorable	Highly Unfavorable	Favorable

Table 22. Favorability ratings of the key characteristics of the technology solutions in the electricity generation sector of the United States.

The previously discussed classification methodology can be used to categorize the solutions into four Tiers for prioritization purposes. Natural gas power plants, solar-utility, and wind-onshore are Tier 1 solutions for the United States, considering that these solutions have at least four *favorable to highly favorable* ratings and no highly unfavorable rating for the key characteristics. Solar-distributed, nuclear and hydropower are Tier 2 solutions, considering that these solutions have at-least four *moderate to highly favorable* ratings and one or less highly unfavorable rating for the key characteristics. Natural gas with capture and biomass technologies are Tier 3 solutions, considering that they have three or more *favorable to highly favorable* ratings and two or less highly unfavorable rating for the key characteristics. Solar with storage[420], wind-offshore, and coal with capture are Tier 4 solutions since these solutions do not fit in the top three tiers.

The above classification can be used effectively for prioritizing the implementation of the different technology solutions within the next decade or so (i.e. phase 1). Tier 1 solutions, such as solar utility and wind-onshore, should be implemented with top prioritization **until they are limited** by their unfavorable dependency rating resulting from their inherent intermittent nature of electricity production. Once the limitation is reached, these solutions *will no longer be Tier 1* solutions due to increase in cost and inferior environmental performance. Although natural gas power plant technology only has a moderate magnitude of impact rating, it has a highly favorable rating for speed of impact and CO_2 reduction investment cost. Furthermore, it also has important practical advantages due to its favorable dependency rating (dispatchable). Hence, *natural gas power plant technology* is also a solution that needs to be *highly prioritized*.

Tier 2 solutions such as solar-distributed, nuclear, and hydropower should be implemented with high priority where they have an advantage over Tier 1 solutions due to specific circumstances. Such circumstances that would increase the priority of Tier 2 solutions are not expected to be very uncommon considering that the United States has very wide variations in the nature of the existing electricity infrastructure, weather conditions, geology, population density etc., across the country. Since natural gas with capture and storage has favorable ratings for several key characteristics, one of the advantages of replacing existing coal plants with natural gas plants technology is the future possibility of retrofitting these plants with CO_2 capture and storage. Therefore, a limited deployment of the Tier 3 natural gas with capture and storage is warranted in phase 1 (to gain the required experience/knowledge) in view of its potential importance in the next phase. The Tier 3 biomass solution should be deployed in a limited manner under special circumstances such as accessibility to very low-cost (waste) biomass feedstock. Tier 4 solutions such as solar with energy storage, wind-offshore and coal with CO_2 capture and storage, due to their several highly unfavorable ratings, should be deployed in a very limited manner in the next decade. Deployment of solar with limited (e.g. 4 to 8) hours of storage might be reasonable for limited projects if the CO_2 reduction cost characteristics becomes favorable due to specific circumstances.

Using the overall prioritization information discussed above, substantial CO_2 reduction can be achieved in the electricity generation sector in the United States in an efficient manner; i.e. in a manner that addresses all the critical challenges related to CO_2 reduction. For example, if the existing coal power plants are replaced by a combination of 35% solar utility/distributed and wind-onshore, 35% natural gas power plants, 15% hydropower and nuclear, and 15% other low-carbon solutions, this would result in a reduction of about **0.8 billion tons per year** of CO_2 emissions from the U.S. electricity generation sector. Based on the favorability ratings for the characteristics of the different technologies, such an approach would be **cost-efficient and implementable at a relatively high speed** within the next decade or so. Also, since the scale of application for individual technologies will be limited due to the use of several different technology solutions, this will **ensure a relatively low potential for severe environmental impact**.

In the next phase (i.e. after a decade or so), the focus can be on increasing the implementation of top tier low-carbon technologies and reducing CO_2 from natural gas plants. The top tier low-carbon technologies for the next phase (after 10 or so years) can be determined by **revisiting** the approach outlined in this book. For example, it is possible that a technology solution that is currently Tier 3 or Tier 4 may achieve a top tier technology status due to major technology breakthroughs in the next decade. Potentially, the CO_2 capture/storage technology for natural gas power plants will achieve a superior level of maturity and improved costs in the next decade or so. Consequently, the newer natural gas plants can be retrofitted with capture/storage technology gradually in the next phase to further reduce CO_2.

5.1.2 Prioritization of TS solutions for the United States

The United States has over 200 million light duty vehicles on the road[421], the vast majority of which are conventional vehicles. Considering that these conventional light duty vehicles have relatively high CO_2 emissions (on an average ~400 g/mile), there is a reasonable potential for reducing CO_2 by replacing these vehicles by using efficient alternative solutions for transportation. Table 23 shows the relative favorability ratings (directly based on data from the last chapter) for the key characteristics of the proposed solutions for CO_2 reduction in the U.S. transportation sector.

	Initial investment per avoided CO_2 ton per year	Total cost per avoided CO_2 ton	Potential for severe environmental impact	Magnitude of impact	Speed of Impact	Dependence on another new technology
Hybrid Electric	Moderate	Favorable	Favorable	Moderate	Favorable	Favorable
Battery Electric	Highly Unfavorable	Unfavorable	Moderate	Favorable	Moderate	Unfavorable
Biofuels	Favorable	Highly Unfavorable	Highly Unfavorable	Highly Favorable	Unfavorable	Favorable
Shared Transportation	Highly Favorable	Highly Favorable	Favorable	Highly Favorable	Favorable	Favorable

Table 23. Favorability ratings of the key characteristics of the solutions in the transportation sector of the United States

The relative favorability, which is based on the key characteristics data provided in the previous chapter, is indicative of the ability of the proposed solutions to address all the critical challenges related to CO_2 reduction. The classification discussed earlier can again be used to categorize the solutions into different Tiers for prioritization purposes. The shared transportation and hybrid solutions are Tier 1 considering that they have four or more *favorable to highly favorable ratings* for the key characteristics and no highly unfavorable rating. Battery electric light duty vehicle and biofuels are Tier 3 solutions, considering that they have three or more *moderate to favorable* ratings and two or less highly unfavorable rating.

The key implications from the above classification are discussed next in terms of implementation of the solutions in the United States in the next decade or so. Since top Tier solutions such as shared transportation and hybrid electric vehicles are considerably superior to solutions such as battery electric vehicles and biofuels in addressing the critical challenges for CO_2 reduction, the top Tier solutions need to be implemented with much higher priority for decreasing the CO_2 emissions from the conventional vehicles (i.e. for decreasing conventional light duty vehicle miles). To further illustrate the advantage offered by the top Tier solutions, the hybrid electric vehicle technology is compared with battery electric vehicle technology using the cost and CO emissions data discussed in the previous chapter. If 200 million existing conventional light duty vehicles in the United States were replaced by hybrid electric vehicles instead of new conventional light duty vehicles, the additional initial investment cost to the society would be about **750 billion dollars**; corresponding there will be a CO_2 reduction of about **0.3 billion tons per year**. Alternatively, if the existing 200 million conventional light duty vehicles were replaced by battery electric vehicles instead of new conventional light duty vehicles, the additional initial investment cost to the society would be about **2600 billion dollars**; corresponding there will be a CO_2 reduction of about **0.5 billion tons per year**. In other words, use of battery electric technology solution will require an additional **1850 billion dollars** of upfront investment for an increase in CO_2 reduction by **0.2 billion tons per year**. As seen from the above example, CO_2 reduction efficiency (i.e. extremely high cost to benefit ratio) of the battery electric vehicle technology is very poor. Moreover, the *total cost per avoided CO_2 ton* over the life of the vehicles, which includes fuel, electricity, maintenance and other costs, is also about 3 times higher for the battery electric vehicles compared to hybrid electric vehicles.

Amongst the top tier solutions, the shared transportation solution has a significant advantage over the hybrid electric solution in several categories. Hence the shared transportation solution needs to be implemented with the highest priority wherever it is practicable. As discussed earlier, the advantages of shared transportation are large only at or above 70% occupancy levels, which could be challenging in regions that are less densely populated. Since the population density of United States is low in several regions, use of a combination of solutions in phase 1 (i.e. within the next decade) will be more practical; i.e. phase 1 would consist of shared transportation as the dominant solution in densely populated areas, and the hybrid electric vehicle solution as the dominant solution in sparsely populated areas. Considering that roughly 1.1 billion tons of CO_2 are produced per year by the conventional light duty vehicles in the United States[422], a combination of 60% shared transportation solution and 40% hybrid electric vehicle solution has the potential to decrease the emissions from the sector by about 0.6 billion tons per year. Alternatively, if a 100% battery electric light duty vehicle solution is used, the potential to decrease the CO_2 emissions from the sector will be slightly lower (about 0.5 billion tons annually), and furthermore will also require **several times** higher initial investment cost and total cost over the ownership life of the vehicles. This is expected considering that the *initial investment cost per avoided ton of CO_2 per year* is more than **two times higher** and the *total cost per avoided ton of CO_2* is more than **three times higher** for battery electric vehicles compared to hybrid electric vehicles. The battery electric vehicle solution is even more cost disadvantaged compared to the shared transportation solution.

From the current retail prices of battery electric vehicles, it is evident that higher driving range equals much higher retail price[423]. The comparison used in this study between battery electric vehicles and the conventional/hybrid vehicles offers undue advantage to the former, considering that typical battery electric vehicles currently have a much lower driving range[424]. From a technology perspective the battery technology will *need to improve substantially* to have a *similar* driving range as a conventional vehicle, while *maintaining a competitive retail price*. Herein, a *significant* benefit of doubt has been given to battery electric vehicle technology; i.e. it has **already been assumed** that battery electric vehicles would *soon* deliver a similar driving range as conventional light duty vehicles at the *current price of a lower range* battery electric vehicle. As an example, it has *already* been assumed in the current analysis that *technology advances in the very near future* will result in a Tesla Model 3 with a retail price of *~$35000 for a driving range of* **400 miles**. For reference, the current cost for a Tesla Model 3 with a driving range of 325 miles is $47,000[425]. In other words, the battery electric light duty vehicles are currently so disadvantaged from a

CO_2 reduction cost effectiveness perspective in the United States, that even assuming aggressive decrease in battery costs, it would be unlikely for it to be a cost competitive solution within the next several years. In phase 2, after large CO_2 reductions are achieved in the electricity generation sector (which will decrease life cycle CO_2 emissions from battery electric vehicles), and if aggressive cost reductions[426] are achieved for battery electric light duty vehicle technology, a combination of shared transportation solution and battery electric light duty vehicle solution could be considered[427].

From a shared transportation viewpoint, battery electric transportation *vans and buses* could be considered with a higher priority for phase 1[428]. This is especially important for cities with very high population densities to minimize local pollution from particulate matter, etc.

5.1.3 Prioritization across the EGS & TS sectors for the United States

An important advantage of the CO_2 reduction cost characteristic is that it allows a reasonable cost comparison of the different solutions across the sectors. The CO_2 reduction costs (in terms of *initial investment cost per avoided ton of CO_2 per year* and *total costs per avoided ton of CO_2*) in the United States for the different technology solutions across the two sectors are compared in Figures 28 and 29.

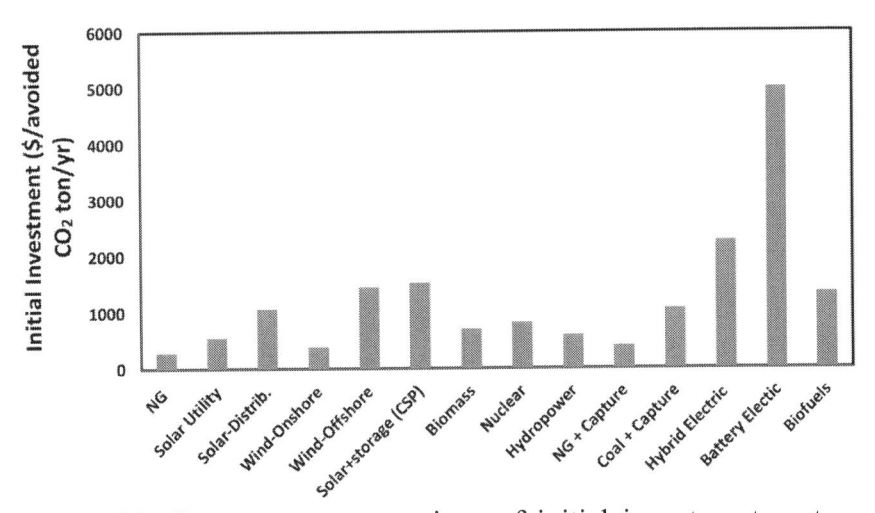

Figure 28. Cross sector comparison of initial investment cost per avoided CO_2 ton per year for the technology solutions, when replacing the reference technology. Reference technology = coal power plants for the electricity generation sector and conventionally fueled light duty vehicles for the transportation sector.

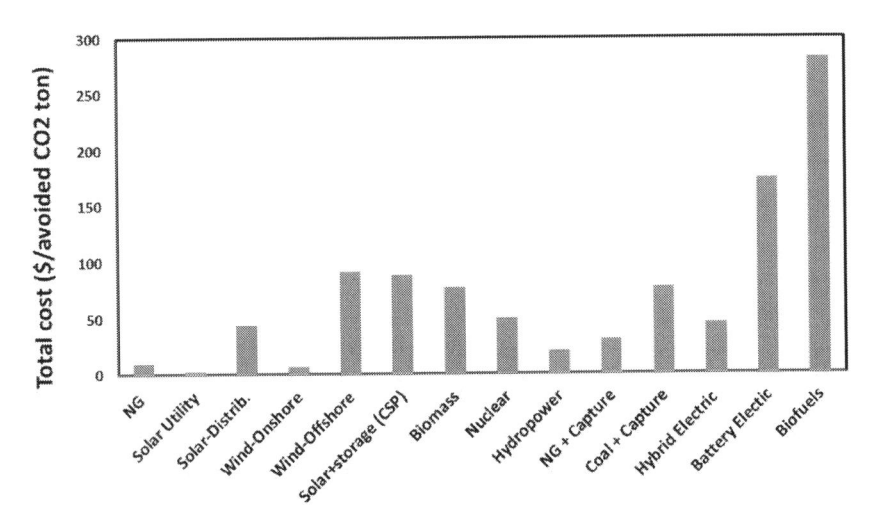

Figure 29. Cross sector comparison of total cost per avoided ton of CO_2 for the technology solutions, when replacing the reference technology. Reference technology = coal power plants for the electricity generation sector and conventionally fueled light duty vehicles for the transportation sector.

In general, the technology solutions from the electricity generation sector have much lower costs than the solutions from the transportation sector. From the figures 28 and 29, it is apparent that the technology solutions such as battery electric vehicles and biofuels, which are proposed for the transportation sector, have extremely high CO_2 reduction costs for either the initial investment or total costs. The battery electric vehicle and biofuels technology solutions are, in general, extremely cost inefficient from the viewpoint of CO_2 reduction. On the other hand, technology solutions such as natural gas power plants, solar-utility and wind-onshore have low costs for both the CO_2 reduction cost components and therefore are cost efficient from the viewpoint of CO_2 cost reduction. As discussed earlier, the most cost-efficient solution in the transportation sector is shared transportation assuming that reasonably high occupancy rates (at or above 70%) are achieved via policy decisions.

Battery electric light duty vehicles are currently **assumed** to be one of the more efficient CO_2 reduction solutions in the United States. However, this assumption is inaccurate. For example, the natural gas plant technology solution for replacing existing coal plants is more than 10 times more efficient from the viewpoint of *initial investment cost per avoided ton of CO_2 per year* as compared to battery electric light duty vehicles replacing conventional light duty vehicles. Even on a *total cost basis per avoided ton of CO_2* over the life of the technology, the natural gas technology is much more efficient than battery electric vehicles. In fact, even the costliest solution within the electricity generation sector is considerably more cost efficient than the battery electricity light duty vehicle solution. The inaccuracy of the current misleading assumptions about battery electric light duty vehicles in the society can be further illustrated by considering the required investment cost and annual CO_2 emissions that could be avoided in the United States. As mentioned earlier, if 200 million conventional light duty vehicles were replaced by battery electric light duty vehicles instead of new conventional light duty vehicles, the additional initial investment cost to the society would be about **2600 billion dollars** and there will be a CO_2 reduction of about **0.5 billion tons per year**. For comparison, if all the existing coal plants were replaced with natural gas plants in the United States, the additional cost to the society would only be **about 220 billion dollars** and correspondingly there would also be a reduction of about **0.5 billion tons of CO_2 per year**. Based on the above prioritization discussion, it would be very inefficient for the United States to significantly incentivize (e.g. subsidies etc.) battery electric vehicle technology in the next decade or so. On the other hand, significantly incentivizing shared transportation and hybrid electric vehicles would be an efficient approach for CO_2 reduction in the transportation sector of the United States.

In summary, there is an excellent opportunity within the next few years in the electricity generation sector of the United States to reduce 0.8 billion tons per year of CO_2 using Tier 1 solutions such as solar-utility, wind-onshore and natural gas coupled with Tier 2 solutions such as solar-distributed, hydropower, and nuclear. An efficient opportunity for CO_2 reduction also exists in the transportation sector for decreasing about 0.6 billion tons of CO_2 per year using a combination of shared transportation and hybrid electric vehicles. However, in the event that there are very stringent budgeting issues (e.g. potentially uncontrollable large budget deficit due to after-effects of COVID-19), the implementation of the solutions in the electricity generation sector need to be prioritized (incentivized) in the United States compared to the transportation sector, considering the higher cost effectiveness and magnitude of impact of the solutions in the electricity generation sector.

5.2 Global Prioritization Discussion

As discussed previously, other than the CO_2 cost reduction characteristic, the relative favorability rating of the other key characteristics for the different solutions is expected to be *less sensitive* to the country of implementation. In other words, the United States related discussion on four key characteristics (magnitude of impact, potential for severe environmental impact, speed of impact, and dependence on another new solution) should be reasonably applicable to other countries/regions for prioritization of the CO_2 reduction technologies in most cases.

However, the relative favorability rating of the CO_2 cost reduction characteristic is expected to be sensitive to the country of implementation. This is related to the fact that the fuel costs for certain technologies depend on the specific country. For example, unlike United States, natural gas price is highly disadvantaged compared to coal price in China. This section discusses prioritization of the solutions in countries around the globe by providing generic favorability ratings for the CO_2 cost reduction characteristic between the proposed technology solutions using representative regions (*European Union* and *Asia*) as examples. This section includes a) a prioritization discussion for the electricity generation sector (EGS), b) a prioritization discussion for the transportation sector (TS), and c) a generic summary discussion on global prioritization.

5.2.1 Global prioritization of EGS solutions

The global electric power sector, which is by far the largest direct emitter of CO_2, is responsible for about 40% of the direct global CO_2 emissions[429,430]. The majority of the CO_2 (~10 billion tons annually) from this sector is emitted from coal fueled power plants[431]. Thus, there is significant world-wide potential for CO_2 emission reductions by replacing existing coal plants. As discussed earlier, typically only the cost characteristic is substantially dependent on the country of implementation. Herein, the relative favorability rating of the CO_2 cost reduction characteristic is considered for two representative regions, European Union and Asia. The relative natural gas price is the main difference between the countries. For example, the relative natural gas price is low in the United States, medium in the European Union and high in Asia[432]. Thus, the whole spectrum is covered by the representative countries/regions considered herein. Information related to the relative favorability ratings of the CO_2 cost reduction characteristic for European Union and Asia regions was developed using credible data from several available sources[433,434,435,436].

European Union: Table 24 shows the relative favorability ratings for the key characteristics of the proposed CO_2 reduction solutions in the electricity generation sector of the European Union. Natural gas power plants, solar utility, and wind-onshore are Tier 1 solutions for the European Union region, considering that these solutions have at-least four *favorable to highly favorable* ratings and no highly unfavorable rating for the key characteristics. Solar-distributed, nuclear, biomass and hydropower are Tier 2 solutions considering that these solutions have at-least four *moderate to highly favorable* ratings and one or less highly unfavorable rating for the key characteristics. Natural gas with capture/storage and wind-offshore technologies are Tier 3 solutions considering that they have at-least three *moderate to highly favorable* ratings and two or less highly unfavorable rating for the key characteristics. Solar with storage, and coal with capture are Tier 4 solutions for the European Union since these solutions do not fit in the top three Tiers.

	Initial investment per avoided CO_2 ton per year	Total cost per avoided CO_2 ton	Potential for severe environmental impact	Magnitude of impact	Speed of Impact	Dependence on another new technology
Natural gas	Highly Favorable	Favorable	Moderate	Moderate	Favorable	Favorable
Solar Utility	Favorable	Highly Favorable	Unfavorable	Highly Favorable	Favorable	Unfavorable
Solar Distributed	Moderate	Moderate	Moderate	Highly Favorable	Favorable	Unfavorable
Wind Onshore	Favorable	Highly Favorable	Unfavorable	Highly Favorable	Favorable	Unfavorable
Wind Offshore	Unfavorable	Moderate	Highly Unfavorable	Highly Favorable	Moderate	Unfavorable
Solar with storage	Highly Unfavorable	Highly Unfavorable	Highly Unfavorable	Highly Favorable	Unfavorable	Favorable
Biomass	Moderate	Moderate	Highly Unfavorable	Favorable	Unfavorable	Favorable
Nuclear	Moderate	Unfavorable	Moderate	Highly Favorable	Moderate	Favorable
Hydropower	Favorable	Moderate	Moderate	Favorable	Moderate	Favorable
Natural gas with capture/storage	Favorable	Moderate	Highly Unfavorable	Favorable	Highly Unfavorable	Favorable
Coal with capture/storage	Unfavorable	Highly Unfavorable	Highly Unfavorable	Favorable	Highly Unfavorable	Favorable

Table 24. Favorability ratings for the key characteristics of the technology solutions in the electricity generation sector of the European Union region

Asia: Table 25 shows the relative favorability ratings for the key characteristics of the proposed CO_2 reduction solutions in the electricity generation sector of the Asian region. Solar-utility, wind-onshore, and hydropower are Tier 1 (Top Tier) solutions for Asia considering that these solutions have at-least four *favorable to highly* *favorable* ratings and **no** highly unfavorable rating for the key characteristics.

	Initial investment per avoided CO₂ ton per year	Total cost per avoided CO₂ ton	Potential for severe environmental impact	Magnitude of impact	Speed of Impact	Dependence on another new technology
Natural gas	Highly Favorable	Moderate	Moderate	Moderate	Moderate	Favorable
Solar Utility	Favorable	Highly Favorable	Unfavorable	Highly Favorable	Favorable	Unfavorable
Solar Distributed	Unfavorable	Moderate	Moderate	Highly Favorable	Favorable	Unfavorable
Wind Onshore	Favorable	Highly Favorable	Unfavorable	Highly Favorable	Favorable	Unfavorable
Wind Offshore	Unfavorable	Unfavorable	Highly Unfavorable	Highly Favorable	Moderate	Unfavorable
Solar with storage	Highly Unfavorable	Highly Unfavorable	Highly Unfavorable	Highly Favorable	Unfavorable	Favorable
Biomass	Highly Favorable	Favorable	Highly Unfavorable	Favorable	Unfavorable	Favorable
Nuclear	Moderate	Favorable	Moderate	Highly Favorable	Moderate	Favorable
Hydropower	Favorable	Favorable	Moderate	Favorable	Moderate	Favorable
Natural gas with capture/storage	Favorable	Unfavorable	Highly Unfavorable	Favorable	Highly Unfavorable	Favorable
Coal with capture/storage	Unfavorable	Moderate	Highly Unfavorable	Favorable	Highly Unfavorable	Favorable

Table 25. Favorability ratings for the key characteristics of the technology solutions in the electricity generation sector of the Asian region

Natural gas power plants, solar distributed, nuclear and biomass are Tier 2 solutions considering that these solutions have at-least four *moderate to highly favorable* ratings and one or less highly unfavorable rating for the key characteristics. Natural gas with capture and coal with capture technology are Tier 3 solutions considering that they have at-least three *moderate to highly favorable* ratings and two or less highly unfavorable rating for the key characteristics. Solar with storage and wind-offshore are Tier 4 solutions for Asia since these solutions have less than three *moderate to highly favorable* ratings or three or more highly unfavorable rating for the key characteristics.

5.2.2 Global prioritization of TS solutions

The transportation sector is responsible for about 25% of the direct global CO_2 emissions[437,438], with the light duty vehicles component being the largest single contributor[439]. There are about 1 billion light duty vehicles on the road in the world currently[440]. In 2018, the global CO_2 emission from the transportation sector was about 8 billion tons, out of which roughly 3 billion tons of CO_2 emission was from light duty vehicles[441]. As discussed earlier, amongst the key characteristics of the proposed technology solutions, typically only the CO_2 cost reduction characteristic is substantially dependent on the country of implementation. Herein, the relative favorability rating of the cost characteristic is considered for two representative regions, the European Union and Asia. The relative gasoline and electricity prices are the main difference between the countries. For example, United States has *low* liquid petroleum fuel prices and *medium* electricity prices, the European Union has *high* liquid petroleum fuel prices and a *high* electricity price and Asia has *medium* liquid petroleum fuel prices and a *low* electricity price[442,443]. Thus, a wide spectrum is covered by the representative countries/regions discussed herein. The relative favorability ratings of the CO_2 cost reduction characteristic for the European Union and Asia regions was developed using a similar methodology discussed earlier for the United States.

European Union: Table 25 shows the relative favorability ratings for the key characteristics of the proposed CO_2 reduction solutions in the transportation sector for the European Union region. The shared transportation and hybrid electric vehicle solutions are the Tier 1 options for the European Union, considering that these solutions have four or more *favorable to highly favorable* ratings and no *highly unfavorable* ratings for the key characteristics. The main difference in the comparison of the key characteristics between the European region and the United States, is the relatively improved economics for *total cost per avoided ton of CO_2* for the battery electric vehicles in case of the European Union region due to higher fuel prices and lower CO_2 emissions from electricity generation due to the cleaner grid. This results in battery electric vehicle technology being a Tier 2 solution in the European Union region (four *moderate to highly favorable* ratings with one highly unfavorable rating for the key characteristics). Biofuels is a Tier 3 solution since it has three *favorable to highly favorable* ratings and one highly unfavorable rating for the key characteristics.

	Initial investment per avoided CO_2 ton per year	Total cost per avoided CO_2 ton	Potential for severe environmental impact	Magnitude of impact	Speed of Impact	Dependence on another new technology
Hybrid Electric	Moderate	Favorable	Favorable	Moderate	Favorable	Favorable
Battery Electric	Highly Unfavorable	Moderate	Moderate	Favorable	Moderate	Unfavorable
Biofuels	Favorable	Unfavorable	Highly Unfavorable	Highly Favorable	Unfavorable	Favorable
Shared Transportation	Highly Favorable	Highly Favorable	Favorable	Highly Favorable	Favorable	Favorable

Table 26. Favorability ratings for the characteristics of the technology solutions in the transportation sector of the European Union region.

Asia: Table 27 shows the relative favorability ratings for the key characteristics of the proposed CO_2 reduction solutions in the transportation sector for the Asian region. The solutions fall in the same Tiers (overall prioritization ranking) for the Asian region as in case of the European Union region.

	Initial investment per avoided CO₂ ton per year	Total cost per avoided CO₂ ton	Potential for severe environmental impact	Magnitude of impact	Speed of Impact	Dependence on another new technology
Hybrid Electric	Moderate	Favorable	Favorable	Moderate	Favorable	Favorable
Battery Electric	Highly Unfavorable	Favorable	Moderate	Favorable	Moderate	Unfavorable
Biofuels	Favorable	Unfavorable	Highly Unfavorable	Highly Favorable	Unfavorable	Favorable
Shared Transportation	Highly Favorable	Highly Favorable	Favorable	Highly Favorable	Favorable	Favorable

Table 27. Favorability ratings for the characteristics of the technology solutions in the transportation sector of the Asian region.

5.2.3 Summary discussion on global implementation of technology solutions

The information from the previous sections on the representative countries/regions has been used herein to develop a discussion on the global implementation of technology solutions based on their overall abilities to address the critical challenges associated with CO_2 reduction. Since even advanced economies are constrained by resources due to competition from other extremely important problems, a prioritization discussion is critical for ensuring that the limited resources of each country are optimally used by deploying the most effective technology solutions for CO_2 reduction. In other words, it is critical that potential **incentives/subsidies** from regional or national governments **should be aligned with a robust prioritization analysis** for efficient CO_2 reduction around the globe.

Electricity generation sector: Based on the analysis, solar-utility and wind-onshore technology solutions have been globally identified as having the highest deployment priority for all the countries within the next decade or so (phase 1). However due to the inherent intermittent nature (non-dispatchable) of these solutions, they should be deployed *only to the extent* that there is a reasonable compatibility with the local electricity generation and distribution infrastructure. For example, these intermittent solutions should only be implemented to the extent to which no significant electricity curtailment is required. The optimum level of implementation of the technology solutions is expected to be unique for each country/region since it will depend on the specific nature of the electricity generation and distribution infrastructure in that country/region. Implementation beyond the optimum levels will result in significant reduction in the effectiveness of these solutions due to inferior economics and environmental performance; i.e. these solutions will lose their top prioritization after a certain level of implementation is reached. The other solution, which has been identified as a higher priority solution for several countries around the world is the natural gas power plant technology. However, its priority ranking (Tier 1 or 2) for a given country depends on the price of natural gas. Thus, the different countries can be generically divided based on the price of natural gas.

For countries that have a *low or moderate natural gas price* (e.g. EU countries, United States), natural gas power plant technology is a Tier 1 solution and should be deployed with the highest priority along with solar-utility and wind-onshore technologies. Tier 2 solutions such as hydropower, nuclear and solar-distributed should mainly be deployed in locations where they are preferred over Tier 1 solutions due to specific circumstances for these countries. Tier 3 and Tier 4 solutions such as natural gas with storage, biomass, wind-offshore, solar with storage and coal with storage should be limited to few special strategic cases (e.g. gain experience, special circumstances etc.) within the next decade or so.

For countries with *high natural gas prices* (e.g. China, India), along with solar-utility and wind-onshore, hydropower is also a Tier 1 solution. Tier 2 solutions for these countries include natural gas power plant technology, solar-distributed, nuclear and biomass. The optimum implementation levels of solar-utility, wind-onshore, and hydropower can be used to determine the extent of deployment of Tier 2 technologies that will be required for these countries to ensure robust electricity generation. The relative extent of deployment of Tier 2 solutions will depend on specific constraints for the different locations in the country. Tier 3 and Tier 4 solutions such as natural gas with storage, wind-offshore, solar with storage and coal with storage should be limited to few special strategic cases (e.g. gain experience, special circumstances etc.) within the next decade or so.

In the next phase (i.e. after a decade or so), the global focus can be on increasing the implementation of the top tier low-carbon technologies and reducing CO_2 from natural gas plants. As the older natural gas plants reach end of life, these can be replaced by a combination of top tier low-carbon technologies in the next phase. Potentially, the CO_2 capture/storage technology for natural gas power plants will have achieved a superior level of maturity and improved costs in the next decade or so. Consequently, the newer (constructed within 15 years) natural gas plants can be retrofitted with capture/storage technology gradually in the next phase to further reduce CO_2. A key takeaway from the previous chapter is that there is an **especially important** environmental advantage related to **using as many solutions as possible**. Use of multiple solutions *ensures* that the application of the technologies will remain on a relatively small scale for the next several decades and will consequently *delay the onset* of any severe, yet unknown, environmental impact.

Light duty vehicle transportation sector: Based on the previous analysis of the representative countries/regions, hybrid electric vehicle technology and shared transportation solutions have been globally identified as having higher deployment priority for all the countries within the next decade (phase 1) for the replacement of the conventionally fueled light duty vehicles. Based on the overall analysis, a potential path forward for implementation is proposed herewith.

For countries with *low gasoline prices* (such as United States), an implementation of roughly 80% shared transportation solution and 20% hybrid electric vehicle solution in regions of high population density, and an implementation of roughly 40% shared transportation solutions and 60% hybrid electric vehicles in regions with low population density, is suggested. Due to the lower overall effectiveness for CO_2 reduction compared to hybrid electric vehicles, the deployment of battery electric light duty vehicle technology should *mainly be limited to strategic reasons* (special circumstances) in countries with low gasoline price.

For countries with *medium to high gasoline price*, battery electric vehicles are relatively less inferior to hybrid electric vehicles. For these countries the relative percentage share of implementation of the shared transportation solution could remain the same as that described for the United States (i.e. 80% for regions with high population density and 40% for regions with low population density). However, the distribution of the remainder of the share of the transportation could be divided between hybrid electric vehicles and battery electric vehicles *depending on the budget* availability.

Hybrid electric vehicles are expected to be significantly advantaged from an upfront budget viewpoint compared to battery electric vehicles on a global basis at-least for the next decade. For the shared transportation solution, electric powered transportation vans and buses could be considered globally with higher priority within the next few years. The corresponding level of implementation could be decided on budget constraints (based on expected occupancy levels). Biofuels technology appears to be a low priority option for all the countries and should only be considered for strategic reasons (only under very special circumstances) within the next decade.

In the next phase (i.e. after a decade or so), after large CO_2 reductions are achieved in the electricity generation sector (which will further decrease life cycle CO_2 emissions from battery electric vehicles), and **assuming** aggressive cost reductions are achieved for battery electric light duty vehicle technology, a combination of shared transportation solution and light duty vehicle battery electric vehicle solutions could be considered. Also, the prioritization framework should be revisited to identify any other potential top tier technologies.

5.2.4 General comments on robustness of the prioritization methodology

The proposed methodology has *built in robustness* owing to prioritization based on several characteristics that take into account *all critical challenges* associated with CO_2 reduction. There is no overwhelming dependence on any single characteristic of the technology solutions which ensures excellent robustness for the methodology.

A challenging case study is discussed to illustrate the robustness of the methodology. For this case study, the introduction of a new characteristic of the technology solutions in the prioritization analysis such as the *currently known environmental impact* is considered. This characteristic **has not been** included in the original analysis as it does not fit the requirements of critical characteristic since, as discussed earlier, current information on environmental impact is inadequate for technologies implemented at low scale. However, for testing purposes, introducing this characteristic to the prioritization methodology is a **good evaluation of robustness**. This characteristic includes all *currently known* life cycle environmental impacts from the technology solutions in terms of air pollutants, water pollutants, impact on wild-life, land, and so on. For the electricity generation sector, coal plants will have a highly unfavorable rating, while natural gas plants will have an unfavorable rating due to their respective extent of pollutant emissions[444,445]. The remainder of the technology solutions in the electricity generation sector can be categorized either as moderate (e.g. nuclear, hydropower) or favorable (e.g. solar, wind) for the *currently known environmental impact* characteristic[446,447,448,449]. For the light duty vehicle transportation sector, hybrid vehicles can be classified as unfavorable, shared transportation as moderate (due to much lower vehicle miles), battery electric vehicles as favorable, and biofuels as moderate[450,451,452]. It is important to note that *even when this new characteristic is introduced* in the analysis, there will be **little-to-no impact** on the overall global prioritization analysis for the different technologies (i.e. *original tier rankings of the different technologies will be maintained*).

As discussed previously, the relative Tier-based prioritization classification framework has been designed such that it is narrow enough to distinctly distinguish between effective and less effective solutions, but broad enough that any potential changes (e.g. decrease in future cost for solutions such as solar with storage, batteries, use of different assumptions, etc.) will not substantially impact the relative prioritization between the solutions within the next decade or so[453].

The *generic framework* proposed for technology prioritization herein is evergreen and, therefore, *could be applicable* for several decades to come. In other words, the prioritization framework discussed in this chapter *could be revisited every decade or so* to refine the implementation strategy for the different low-carbon technologies (based on updated data related to their abilities in addressing the critical challenges related to CO_2 reduction).

...§§§-§-§§§...

Chapter 6: Executive Summary Plus

Along with summary discussions related to the different technology solutions, this final chapter also includes a brief discussion on some aspects that have not been mentioned so far.

6.1 Challenges Associated with CO_2 Reduction

Over the last couple of decades, the global scientific community has repeatedly emphasized the seriousness of climate change consequences if corrective actions related to greenhouse gas emissions are not taken rapidly [454]. In response, significant efforts are being taken by the global society to reduce CO_2 emissions. Based on the considerable momentum around this issue, it is apparent that the deployment rate of the low-carbon technologies will increase rapidly in the coming years. Widescale implementation of low-carbon technologies is an enormous and extremely challenging undertaking and is expected to have a significant impact on the global community. Unfortunately, there is significant potential for the related policy decisions to be affected by emotion driven bias due to lack of pertinent information. This can lead to significant overall inefficiencies for the global society. Thus, irrespective of the individual beliefs about climate change, it is important that everybody is involved in constructive discussions to ensure robust policy decisions and thereby efficient deployment of CO_2 reduction technologies (i.e. efficient use of our limited resources).

In order to understand the effectiveness of CO_2 reduction technologies it is important to consider all the critical challenges associated with CO_2 reduction. Apart from the obvious requirements of high speed and magnitude of CO_2 reduction impact, there are other critical challenges associated with CO_2 reduction that must also be considered when evaluating the overall practical efficiency of the technologies. These critical challenges include the following: CO_2 reduction cost, the potential for (yet unknown) severe environmental impact at scale, and dependence on another new technology/solution.

Cost control is a critical challenge because a) the CO_2 reduction problem is extraordinarily enormous, and b) there are several other extremely important problems such as poverty, healthcare, education, aging infrastructure, etc., that compete for the limited resources that are available to the global society. The cost control challenge is not limited to developing economies. Even advanced economies such as the United States have a substantial budgetary deficit challenge[455] and several critical problems that still need to be resolved. Most importantly, it is critical to respect the overwhelming fact that *over 40% of the global population does not have the luxury to worry about future problems because they are presently struggling to meet their basic everyday needs*[456]. Thus, considering the limited amount of resources, **highly cost-efficient technologies** should be given favorable consideration.

Perhaps the most important challenge is the potential for these technology solutions to have a (yet unknown) severe environmental impact when implemented at a wide scale (i.e. at a scale similar to fossil fuels). This is evident from historical data, which shows that the severity of the CO_2 impact itself was not well understood until several hundred billion tons of CO_2 had been released. This may be related to the unavailability of appropriate data until a **certain threshold level of implementation** of fossil fueled technologies was reached[457,458].

Similarly, the current understanding of the severity of impact from the proposed low-carbon technologies at the relevant widescale implementation is expected to be inadequate due to the unavailability of data. The unavailability of appropriate data for the proposed technologies is, in turn, related to their current **very low levels** of implementation. Thus, the cumulative level of implementation can be considered as one of the potential indicators for, yet unknown, severe environmental impact; i.e. lower the cumulative level of implementation of a technology, greater the possibility of the existence of a severe environmental impact for the widescale implementation of the technology. This challenge is currently not high on the radar of the global scientific community. However, not considering this challenge appropriately could result in an enormous setback to the global society, recovery from which would be extremely difficult. For example, it could potentially result in other severe local or global environmental problem(s) being generated due to an injudicious implementation of one or more CO_2 reduction technology solutions at a wide scale. Considering the associated enormous cost, this will also be a massive setback to the credibility of global environmental efforts.

From historical data, it is obvious that environmental impact is sensitive to the amount of human activity, that is, more the human activity more is the impact on the environment. Thus, in absence of direct data, the potential for severe environmental impact from the proposed technology solutions can be further evaluated based on the requirement of human activity for a given technology solution. Fundamentally, the amount of required human activity depends on the efficiency of support provided by nature; i.e. lesser the efficiency of the support by nature for the technology solution, more would be the required activity. Clearly, this is a fundamental characteristic inherent to the technology solution and cannot be altered by technology innovation; i.e. even after maximum efforts, the technology that is less efficiently supported by nature will, by definition, lose out to a technology that is more efficiently supported by nature. It is, therefore, important to favor technologies that are **efficiently supported by nature** from the viewpoint of a) *access to the energy source* and b) *process efficiency of energy extraction from the energy source*.

There is another critical challenge, which is important from a practical viewpoint for comparing technologies. This challenge is related to the forced interdependency between certain technology solutions. If widescale implementation of a low-carbon technology requires the widescale implementation of another less established technology, this significantly increases the difficulty of implementation. For example, there is increased project risk, increased uncertainty in defining and meeting timelines, and increased potential for severe environmental impact for two less established technologies. Thus, a technology solution **without any dependency** is significantly more favorable.

A highly effective solution for CO_2 reduction will, thus, have the following characteristics: a) low CO_2 reduction cost, b) low potential for yet unknown environmental impact at scale, c) high magnitude of CO_2 reduction impact, d) no dependence on another new solution and e) high speed of CO_2 reduction impact. **In other words, a highly effective solution will be best positioned to meet *all* the critical challenges associated with CO_2 reduction.**

6.2 Prioritization of CO₂ Reduction Technologies

An efficient approach to tackle CO_2 reduction is to systematically prioritize the technologies based on their abilities to address all related critical challenges. Specifically, this requires the prioritization of the technology solutions based on the favorability ratings of their key characteristics. The key characteristics that need to be considered for prioritizing the different technology solutions include CO_2 reduction cost, magnitude of impact on CO_2 reduction, potential for (yet unknown) severe environment impact at scale, dependency on another new solution and speed of impact. The prioritization analysis, wherein the solutions have been classified into four Tiers (Tier 1= highest priority, Tier 4= lowest priority), is separately summarized below for two key sectors. The classification has been designed such that it is narrow enough to distinctly distinguish between effective and less effective solutions, but is broad enough that even relatively large changes (e.g. decrease in future cost for certain solutions) will not substantially change the relative prioritization between the solutions within the next decade or so (i.e. 10 to 15 years).

6.2.1 Prioritization of technology solutions within the electricity generation sector

The global electric power sector, which is by far the largest direct emitter of CO_2, is responsible for about 40% of the CO_2 emissions[459,460]. The majority of this CO_2 (~10 billion tons per year) is emitted from coal fueled power plants[461]. Thus, there is significant potential for CO_2 emission reductions by replacing existing coal plants by the CO_2 reduction technologies selected via a systematic prioritization analysis.

Based on the analysis involving credible data from available sources, solar-utility and wind-onshore technology solutions have been identified as having the highest deployment priority (Tier 1 solutions) for all the countries within the next decade or so. However, due to the inherent intermittent nature (non-dispatchable) of these solutions, they should be deployed only to the extent that there is a reasonable compatibility with the local electricity generation and distribution infrastructure. This is because poor compatibility (after a certain optimum level of implementation has been exceeded) will result in an inferior economics and environmental performance. In other words, after the optimum threshold level has been exceeded, these solutions will **no longer** be top tier. The optimum level of implementation of these technology solutions is expected to be unique for each country/region, since it will depend on the electricity generation mix, resource availability etc., in that country/region.

The other solution, which has been identified as a higher priority solution for most countries around the world is the natural gas power plant technology. However, its priority ranking (either Tier 1 or Tier 2) for a given country depends on the price of natural gas. Thus, the different countries can be generically divided based on the price of natural gas. For countries that have a low or moderate natural gas price (e.g. United States, European Union), natural gas power plant technology is a Tier 1 solution and should be deployed with the highest priority along with solar-utility and wind-onshore technologies. Tier 2 solution solutions such as hydropower, nuclear and solar-distributed should be deployed mainly in locations where they are preferred over Tier 1 solutions due to location/project specific circumstances for these countries.

For countries with high natural gas prices (e.g. India, China), the natural gas technology is Tier 2 solution for electricity generation. Along with natural gas technology, other Tier 2 solutions for countries with high natural gas price include solar-distributed, nuclear and biomass. Tier 1 solutions for countries with high natural gas prices include solar-utility, wind-onshore, and hydropower. The optimum implementation levels of these Tier 1 solutions can be used to determine the extent of deployment of Tier 2 technologies for these countries to meet the total demand for electricity. Thus, the relative extent of deployment of Tier 2 solutions will depend on specific constraints/issues for the different locations in the country.

Globally (for all the countries), Tier 3 and Tier 4 solutions such as natural gas with CO_2 capture/storage, wind-offshore, solar/wind with energy storage and coal with CO_2 capture & storage should be limited to few special strategic cases (e.g. to gain experience, special circumstances, etc.) within the next decade or so. Deployment of solar/wind with *limited* (e.g. 4 to 8) hours of storage might be reasonable for certain projects if the CO_2 reduction cost becomes favorable due to specific circumstances.

In the next phase (i.e. after a decade or so), the focus should be on increasing the implementation of top tier low-carbon technologies and reducing CO_2 from natural gas plants. As the older natural gas plants reach end of life, these could be replaced by a combination of top tier technologies. Potentially, the CO_2 capture/storage technology for natural gas power plants will have achieved a superior level of maturity and improved costs in the next 10 to 15 years. Consequently, the newer natural gas plants can be retrofitted with capture/storage technology gradually in the next phase to further reduce CO_2. Use of multiple solutions ensures that the application of the technologies will remain on a relatively small scale for the next several decades and will consequently delay the onset of any severe, yet unknown, environmental impact.

6.2.2 Prioritization of technology solutions within the light duty vehicle transportation sector

The transportation sector is responsible for about 25% of the direct global CO_2 emissions, with the light duty vehicles component being the single largest contributor[462]. There are about 1 billion conventional light duty vehicles on the road in the world currently[463] and responsible for roughly 3 billion tons per year of CO_2 emissions[464,465]. Thus, although the potential for CO_2 reduction by replacing conventional light duty vehicles is significant, it is *much smaller* than that from the replacement of coal plants in the electricity generation sector.

Based on the prioritization analysis involving credible data from available sources, shared transportation and hybrid electric vehicle solutions have been globally identified as having superior deployment priority within the next decade for decreasing CO_2 emissions from conventionally fueled light duty vehicles. Shared transportation solutions such as car-pools, transportation vans and buses are especially attractive solutions for densely populated regions. Globally for each country, shared transportation should be used as the main solution in densely populated locations, while hybrid electric vehicles should be used primarily in locations with low population density. In general, for countries/regions with relatively high population density, a roughly 80/20% overall implementation of the shared transportation solutions and hybrid electric vehicles is suggested. While, for countries/regions with relatively low population density, a roughly 40/60% overall implementation of the shared transportation solutions and hybrid electric vehicles is suggested.

Battery electric light duty vehicle technology is Tier 2 option for countries with medium or high gasoline prices and Tier 3 option for countries with low gasoline prices. Therefore, deployment of battery electric light duty vehicles should be considered for CO_2 reduction within the next decade **only** if there are significant advantages due to certain specific circumstances. Biofuels is a low priority option for all the countries and should be only considered for strategic reasons (under very special circumstances) within the next decade. Based on the budget availability, it could be worthwhile to consider battery electric powered transportation vans and buses for the shared transportation solution within the next few years. In the following decade (next phase), the focus could be on shared transportation solutions primarily powered by electricity or some other clean fuel source.

6.2.3 General comments about prioritization of technology solutions within the next decade

Currently there are some proposals that are recommending extremely rapid and complete overhaul of the fossil-fuel based technologies with CO_2 reduction technologies such as solar, wind, energy storage, biofuels, battery electric light duty vehicles and so on. The successful transitioning of a major fraction of the Indian population directly to mobile phones bypassing telephone land lines is an often-used analogy for supporting such rapid/drastic changes in technology[466]. However, given that the energy problem has *several orders of magnitude higher cost and complexity* compared to the communication problem, this is *not* an appropriate analogy. Such proposals are inefficient, because they are not based on an appropriate holistic analysis of the CO_2 reduction problem (i.e. they do not consider all the critical challenges). Correspondingly, a rapid and indiscriminate overhaul of the fossil fueled technologies would result in a significant wastage of our limited resources by subsidizing several inefficient technologies. Instead, all decisions related to incentives, subsidies and regulations/taxes should be based on a robust prioritization analysis. This will ensure that a holistic analysis that considers all the CO_2 reduction challenges is employed as opposed to the *inefficient emotion and bias driven approach* that is often used.

The systematic prioritization analysis undertaken in this book clearly shows that apart from the top tier non-fossil electricity generation technologies, natural gas power plants should also be considered as an important part of the global CO_2 reduction solution in the short to mid-term. In case of the transportation sector, an enormous emphasis must be placed on exponentially expanding the use of shared transportation (e.g. car-pool, transportation vans, buses, etc.) by using a wide range of incentives. Lack of appropriate understanding about solutions such as battery electric light duty vehicles, which are significantly inferior in terms of cost effectiveness of CO_2 reduction, is expected to be a deterrent for the quick leveraging of shared transportation; this needs to be addressed quickly. Hybrid electric vehicle technology, which is a significantly more effective CO_2 reduction solution, should be emphasized over battery electric vehicle technology for replacement of conventional light duty vehicles. Battery electric vehicles and biofuels technology solutions are *cost inefficient* for CO_2 reduction, and therefore, are not expected to be practical solutions for replacement of conventional light duty vehicle sector for at-least a decade or so. Correspondingly, these solutions warrant implementation only for special circumstances/regions. On the other hand, battery electric buses and transportation vans could be considered with a higher priority for shared transportation applications globally for regions with very high population densities (assuming high occupancy levels for shared transportation solutions will result in an acceptable CO_2 reduction cost).

In the event that there are very stringent budgeting issues for a given year, the implementation of the solutions in the electricity generation sector need to be prioritized compared to the transportation sector; this stems from the higher cost effectiveness and magnitude of impact of the solutions in the electricity generation sector.

In general, there is a significant advantage for using multiple high priority solutions globally. This is because the use of multiple technology solutions will limit the required scale of implementation of individual technology solutions, thus ensuring that there will be a dilution of any given specific type of environmental impact from the individual solutions. For example, if the above strategy had been followed in the past few decades, the use of fossil fuels could have been limited to around 40% of the total energy production. Under these hypothetical circumstances, the climate change impact from fossil fuel-based technologies would have been substantially smaller to date. In other words, if a mix of fossil and non-fossil energy technologies had been used over the past several decades instead of predominantly fossil-based technologies, the specific CO_2-related environmental impact from fossil-fuels would have been correspondingly diluted due to much lower CO_2 emissions. Consequently, this would have placed us in a much better position in terms of the CO_2 related climate change problem.

The prioritization discussion primarily relates to policy decisions; i.e. for efficient use of tax money by governing bodies globally[467]. However, individuals and corporations, *who desire so and can afford it*, should be encouraged to use a variety of solutions[468].

6.3 Other critical aspects

Since, the primary goal of this book was to compare the common CO_2 reduction technology solutions, the discussions to this point have been purposefully restricted to the corresponding relevant issues. However, CO_2 reduction technologies represent only one of the multiple strategies[469] that will be required to address the ultra-complex climate change problem. Consequently, there are several other practical aspects that need to be considered for addressing the climate change problem. Some such key practical aspects are briefly discussed in this section.

6.3.1 Implications of the global nature of the problem

Most of the environmental pollutants typically cause a local environmental impact (e.g. local pollution of air/water/soil). In contrast, greenhouse gases cause a global impact, which is independent of the location of the source of emissions[470]. Since every country in the world is currently emitting greenhouse gases to some extent or the other, climate change mitigation will require a disciplined contribution from all countries to decrease global emissions. There are enormous challenges in appropriately determining the quantitative greenhouse gas burden for each country and correspondingly the required contribution towards emission reduction. This is related to the fact that the greenhouse gas emissions are dependent on the economic state and population of the country, which is always in flux. Over the years, different countries in the world have emitted greenhouse gases at different rates depending on their population, economic state, available resources etc. For the most part of the twentieth century, the European Union countries and the United States were the dominant greenhouse gas emitters, consistent with their large economic advancement. However, their emissions have been controlled in recent years with efficiency improvements, limited population growth and increasing use of lower carbon intensity energy sources. On the other hand, emissions from countries such as China and India have been increasing rapidly in recent decades due to their rapid economic progress and increasing population (which results in more energy consumption, more agriculture and so on). In fact, the annual greenhouse gas emissions from China are so high currently, that they exceed the combined annual emissions from the European Union and the United States[471].

Until recently, the distribution of energy sources (e.g. natural gas, coal, gasoline, nuclear, wind, biomass etc.,) used by countries around the world has primarily been driven by cost. The above is expected since low energy cost has historically been one of the key drivers for economic progress. Thus, for the vast majority of the countries the existing distribution of energy sources is as cost effective as it can practically be[472]. In other words, replacement of the existing energy infrastructure even with relatively cost-efficient CO_2 reducing alternatives is going to result in substantial increase in the overall cost of energy. Energy costs are one of the factors, which determine the economic competitiveness of the country. For example, the manufacturing/transportation cost of goods is favorable in countries with low energy costs. Since energy is a critical requirement for routine daily activities (heating, cooling, transportation, powering devices), low energy costs are especially important for ensuring access to basic needs for the economically deprived population. Thus, there is a challenging cost/benefit dilemma faced by economically disadvantaged countries when considering climate change mitigation.

The more affluent countries are expected to be relatively more shielded from the higher energy costs related to replacing traditional energy sources with CO_2 reducing alternatives. Unfortunately, greenhouse gas reductions from *only* the affluent countries will be grossly inadequate in resolving the climate change problem.

Furthermore, this can also have a significant detrimental impact on the affluent countries as discussed in the example below.

Let us assume for this example that only the European Union and the United States take on the responsibility of rapidly and drastically reducing their greenhouse emissions; i.e. this example assumes a relatively modest and gradual change for other countries, but a rapid and radical change for European Union and the United States. Such a rapid and drastic CO_2 reduction will force the inclusion of significantly cost inefficient technologies in their energy mix[473]. The resulting tens of trillions of dollars price tag will significantly increase the overall cost of energy for the European Union and the United States. The increase in energy costs will cause an unjustifiable burden on the tens of millions of people, who are still living in poverty in these advanced economies. Furthermore, this will greatly increase the budgetary challenges and take away from the several other critically important issues (poverty, healthcare, education, basic infrastructure, and so on) that these countries still need to address[474].

Higher energy costs will also cause a further acceleration of the manufacturing industry moving to countries with lower overall costs. Consequently, this will erode the competitiveness of the European Union and the United States. The increase in the shift of the manufacturing industry to countries such as China etc., wherein energy production is much dirtier (due to significantly larger use of coal) than the European Union and the United States, will further increase greenhouse gas emissions. This will be counter-productive from the viewpoint of reducing overall greenhouse gas emissions[475].

Moreover, there will be no competitive advantage in terms of *net job creation* for the European Union and the United States. Net job creation is one of the popular misconceptions forwarded by the proponents for a rapid and drastic change in energy technologies. The one critical requirement for *net job* creation by replacing an existing technology is the need to replace it with a superior technology in terms of **net value and/or efficiency**. Clearly, net job creation is fundamentally impossible in case of a rapid change, considering that drastic and rapid CO_2 reduction will force the inclusion of highly inefficient (Tier 3 & 4 solutions) technologies in the European Union and the United States. For example, a widescale deployment of *highly cost inefficient energy storage* will be needed for high penetration of solar and wind; widescale deployment of highly cost inefficient battery electric vehicles will also be needed and so on. In fact, such an approach will likely result in a competitive disadvantage (net job losses) with respect to the other countries, who will have a much smaller implementation of such inefficient technologies[476].

Perhaps most importantly, complete elimination of greenhouse gases from the European Union and the United States will result in a **relatively small** (at most only about 20%) global reduction in greenhouse gases[477]. Note, that this 20% reduction number is extremely optimistic considering that the greenhouse gas emissions are expected to increase significantly in the countries that have developing economies due to anticipated increase in standard of living of the growing population in these countries[478]. Since climate change is a *global phenomenon*, there will be **no special local benefit** (i.e. from lower *environmental damage*) to the European Union and the United States from a climate change impact perspective[479]. Thus, for the example considered above, overall there will be an extremely limited benefit to the global society with an *unjustifiable cost* for the European Union and the United States.

The above example was not discussed to suggest that greenhouse gas emission reduction efforts should not be aggressively taken by these countries. Instead, it was discussed to ensure that the path forward is selected strategically, instead of emotionally. It is abundantly clear that the efficient addressing of this problem will require a globally coordinated effort. The Paris Agreement has been a good starting point for this effort. It is important to understand that sustainability of the climate change mitigation related efforts can be hindered by either some countries not keeping up with their fair share of contribution to greenhouse gas emission reductions, **or** by some countries attempting an extremely rapid change away from fossil fuels. The second point, which might sound surprising, is based on very simple logic that CO_2 cost reduction efforts that have a very *poor cost to benefit ratio* will not be supported on a long term by the general population of any country. In fact, such an approach will very likely have the very unfortunate consequence of that country **not** participating in future efforts.

6.3.2 Strategic importance of climate change adaptation

Climate change adaptation involves anticipation of the adverse effects of climate change and taking appropriate action to minimize the corresponding damage and/or taking advantages of the opportunities that can arise[480]. Some examples of climate change adaption are building flood defenses, developing drought tolerant crops, efficient use of water, and adapting buildings designs to accommodate future extreme weather conditions. It is universally accepted by experts that a global coordinated effort is the best solution to addressing climate change mitigation. Unfortunately, given the extraordinarily challenging nature of the climate change problem, even a well-coordinated global response is expected to fall short in addressing the problem in a timely manner. In other words, it is quite unlikely that climate change mitigation will be adequately addressed in the next several decades. Thus, if the consensus from the global climate experts is to be believed, the local impact from climate change on each country can be expected to be significant in the decades to come (e.g. larger number of floods, droughts, extreme weather incidents, etc.). This clearly suggests that each country would benefit significantly by strategic investments in climate change adaption. A key advantage of climate change adaptation is that it is **primarily a local issue** that can be dealt with unilaterally by each country. In other words, while no single country has control on climate change mitigation, *each country has substantial control on its ability to adapt to climate change.*

Thus, a two-pronged global approach for each country seems to be most practical for addressing the climate change problem: a) climate change mitigation contributions based on a fair assessment of the burden and cost impact on the population of each country and b) strategic investments in climate change adaption, specifically designed to minimize the anticipated local impacts from climate change for the given country.

...§§§-§-§§§...

Glossary & Units

1 trillion = 1000 billion; **1 billion** = 1000 million; **1 million** = 1000000
1 billion ton = 1 gigaton = 1,000,000,000 tons
1 MW = 1000 kW; **1 kW** = 1000 W
Assistance from nature: Support or help provided by nature; e.g. tail-wind assistance for air travel.
Capacity factor: The ratio of the electrical energy produced by an electricity generating unit for the period of time considered to the electrical energy that could have been produced at continuous full power operation during the same period.
Capacity output: The maximum rated output of an electricity generation unit.
Climate change: A term used to refer to significant change from one prevailing climatic condition to another. In some cases, "climate change" has been used synonymously with the term "global warming".
Climate resilience: Ability to prepare for, recover from and adapt to detrimental impacts from climate change.
Crude oil: A mixture of hydrocarbons that exists in liquid phase in natural underground reservoirs.
ppm: part per million (10^{-6})
Dispatchable: Electricity generation units whose output can be varied to follow demand.
Economy of scale: The principle that larger production facilities have lower costs per unit produced than smaller facilities.
Energy density of the source: Amount of energy per appropriate unit (e.g. volume, mass etc.). Provides a measure of the process efficiency for extracting usable energy from the energy source.
Environmental impact: For the purpose of this book, this term includes a collective impact to health, safety and the environment.
Feedstock: Raw material to fuel a machine or industrial process.
Human activity: Actions taken or driven by humans; e.g. clearing of land, production of fertilizers, mining of minerals and so on.
Natural gas: A gaseous mixture of hydrocarbon compounds, the primary one being methane.

Order of magnitude: One order of magnitude higher cost = about 10 times higher cost

Ozone: Inorganic molecule with chemical formula O_3.

Plastics: Polymer (large number of similar chemical units bonded together) compounds with high molecular mass.

Reference technology: The dominant conventional technology that has been the major contributor to CO_2 emissions.

Refinery: An installation that primarily converts crude oil to finished products such as gasoline, heating oil/diesel, propane, butane, etc.

Stratosphere: Second major layer of earth's atmosphere.

Ton: Specifically used in this book as substitute for *metric ton* (i.e. herein, 1 Ton = 1000 kg)

Tons of oil equivalent: Unit of energy; defined as amount of energy released from burning 1 ton of crude oil.

Total driving range: The total distance that can be travelled by the vehicle after it is fully fueled or charged.

Watt (W): Unit of electrical power (e.g. a typical incandescent light bulb: 60-80 W)

Watt hour (Wh): The electrical energy unit of measure equal to one watt of power supplied to, or taken from, an electric circuit steadily for one hour. Example: an average U.S. home uses ~30,000 Wh (30 kWh) per day

Appendix

Chapter 2

Section 2.1.2
Calculation of weight of population vs. CO_2 emitted in 2017

World population (2017): 7.5 billion
Average weight *assumption* per human (adult + child): 50 Kgs
Weight of human population (2017): 0.4 billion tons

CO_2 emissions (2017): 37 billion tons
CO_2 emitted in 4 days (2017): 0.4 billion tons

Section 2.2.2
Incremental cost for replacing 1 billion light vehicles with new battery electric light vehicles instead of with new conventional vehicles

Assumptions:
Average retail price for conventional new vehicle (Table 14): $23000

Relative cost of electric vehicle for same trim compare to conventional vehicle: 60% higher
60% higher cost is directly based on retail prices directly from retailer websites (See Table 15, section 3.2.2)

Corresponding Retail price for same trim: 23,000 * 1.6: $36,800

Estimation:
Incremental cost for replacing 1 billion cars with new electric cars instead of new conventional cars: 13.8 trillion dollars (@60% higher cost of electric car)

Chapter 3

Section 3.1.4
Stand-alone Capital Cost comparison (small town example): Natural gas plant vs. utility scale solar + Li ion battery energy storage

Assumptions:
For Current case
Electricity consumption: 10,000 MWh/day

Natural gas plant capital cost per unit capacity output: 1079 $/kW
Capacity factor: 87%

Solar utility plant capital cost per unit capacity output: 1331 $/kW
Capacity factor: 29%

Li ion battery cost: 380 $/kWh
Storage duration: 12 hours

Estimations:
Natural gas plant cost: 520 MM$
Solar plus energy storage cost: 3810 MM$
Solar + energy storage capital cost to Natural gas plant capital cost ratio: 7

For Future case: 50% reduction in battery cost and 20% reduction in solar plant cost
Electricity consumption: 10,000 MWh/day

Natural gas plant capital cost per unit capacity output: 1079 $/kW
Capacity factor: 87%

Solar utility plant capital cost per unit capacity output: 1065 $/kW
Capacity factor: 29%

Li ion battery cost: 190 $/kWh
Storage duration: 12 hours

Estimations:
Natural gas plant cost: 520 MM$
Solar plus energy storage cost: 2480 MM$
Solar + energy storage capital cost to Natural gas plant capital cost ratio: 5

Section 3.2.1 & 3.2.2

Levelized cost of driving: conventional vs. hybrid vs. battery electric vehicles

Assumptions:
Conventional vehicle
Retail price: $23190
Sales tax: 7%
Fuel cost: $0.09/mile
Maintenance cost: $0.063/mile
Insurance cost: $500/year
Interest rate: 5%
Vehicle lifetime: 175000 miles

Hybrid electric vehicle
Retail price: $26970
Sales tax: 7%
Fuel cost: $0.06/mile
Maintenance cost: $0.063/mile
Insurance cost: $560/year
Interest rate: 5%
Vehicle lifetime: 175000 miles

Battery electric vehicle
Retail price: $36390
Sales tax: 7%
Fuel cost: $0.04/mile
Maintenance cost: $0.028/mile
Insurance cost: $740/year
Interest rate: 5%
Vehicle lifetime: 175000 miles

Estimations-Levelized cost of driving:
Levelized cost of driving estimated (in terms of $/mile) is essentially the distributed upfront cost (using capital recovery factor) plus the per mile costs of fuel, maintenance, and insurance.
Conventional vehicle: $0.373/mile
Hybrid electric vehicle: $0.378/mile
Battery electric vehicle: $0.404/mile

Section 3.2.1 & 3.2.2

Vehicle manufacturing emissions: conventional vs. hybrid vs. battery electric vehicles

Assumptions:
Battery manufacturing emissions: 61 Kg CO_2e/kWh

Estimations:
Total Vehicle manufacturing emissions = Rest of the vehicle manufacturing emissions + battery manufacturing emissions
Conventional vehicle: 55 gCO_2e/mile
Hybrid electric vehicle: 56 gCO_2e/mile
Battery electric vehicle: 86 gCO_2e/mile

Section 3.2.4

Emissions per passenger mile @70% occupancy:

From U.S. Department of transportation report (large historical database)

Bus Transit emissions: 291 gCO_2 per passenger mile for the 28%
Commuter train emissions: 150 gCO_2 per passenger mile for the 30%

Estimations: Emissions per passenger mile @70% occupancy
Bus Transit: = 291 * 28/70 = 116 gCO_2 per passenger mile
Commuter train: 150 * 30/70 = 64 gCO_2 per passenger mile

Chapter 4

Section 4.3

CO₂ reduction cost estimations

The *initial investment cost per avoided CO₂ unit per year* can be estimated from the initial investment (capital) cost and CO_2 emissions data for the proposed technology solution and the reference (Ref.) technology.

$$\left. \begin{array}{l} \text{Initial Investment cost per} \\ \text{avoided } CO_2 \text{ unit per year} \end{array} \right\} = \frac{\text{Initial Investment}_{Solution} - \text{Initial Investment}_{Ref}}{(CO_2 \text{ Emissions}_{Ref} - CO_2 \text{ Emissions}_{Solution}) yr}$$

The *total cost per avoided CO₂ unit* can be estimated from the total cost and CO_2 emissions data for the proposed technology solution and the reference (Ref.) technology.

$$\left. \begin{array}{l} \text{Total cost per} \\ \text{avoided } CO_2 \text{ unit} \end{array} \right\} = \frac{\text{Levelized Cost}_{Solution} - \text{Levelized Cost}_R}{CO_2 \text{ Emissions}_{Ref} - CO_2 \text{ Emissions}_{Soluti}}$$

For electricity generation sector:

The initial investment cost per avoided CO_2 ton per year for the proposed technology solution was estimated from the a) capital cost data (Figure 18), b) capacity factor data (Figure 19) for the proposed technology solution and the reference technology and c) avoided CO_2 emissions data (Figure 21) for the proposed technology solution with respect to the reference technology. For this calculation, the avoided CO_2 emissions data is considered on an annual basis.

Example for natural gas technology
From Figure 18
Capital cost for natural gas plant = 1079 $/ kW; capital cost for existing gas plant = 0 $/ kW

From Figure 19
Capacity factor for natural gas plant = 87% (0.87)
From Figure 21
CO_2 emissions from natural gas plant = 500 gCO_2e/kWh
CO_2 emissions from existing coal plant = 1000 gCO_2e/kWh

Initial investment cost per avoided CO_2 ton per year = [(1079/0.87) – 0]/ [(1000 – 500) * 365 * 24] * 1000000 = 283 $ per avoided CO_2 ton per year

The total cost per avoided ton of CO_2 was estimated from the levelized cost of electricity data (Figure 20) for the proposed technology solution and the reference technology and avoided CO_2 emissions data (Figure 21) for the proposed technology solution with respect to the reference technology.

Example: for natural gas technology
From Figure 20
Levelized cost (LCOE) for natural gas plant = 38.1 $/MWh
Levelized cost (LCOE) for coal plant = 33.2 $/MWh
From Figure 21
CO_2 emissions from natural gas plant = 500 gCO_2e/kWh
CO_2 emissions from existing coal plant = 1000 gCO_2e/kWh

Total cost per avoided ton of CO_2 = (38.1-33.2)/ (1000 – 500) * (1000000/1000) = 10 $/ton of avoided CO_2

For light duty vehicle transportation sector:
Conventional vs hybrid vs battery electric vehicles
The initial investment cost per avoided CO_2 ton per year for hybrid and battery electric vehicles was estimated using the a) vehicle retail price data (Figure 22) for the proposed technology solution & the conventional vehicle technology and b) avoided CO_2 emissions data (Figure 23). For this calculation, the avoided CO_2 emissions data is considered on an annual basis.

The total cost per avoided ton of CO_2 was estimated using the levelized cost data (Tables 11 & 14) for the proposed technology solution & conventional vehicle technology and avoided CO_2 emissions data (Figure 23).

Conventional fuel vs biofuels

The initial investment cost per annual ton of CO_2 avoided for biofuels was estimated using a) the capital investment costs for a cellulosic biofuels plant & conventional oil refinery (data from sections 3.2.3 & 4.2.1) and b) CO_2 emissions difference between biofuels and conventional fuel per year (Figure 23).

The total cost per ton of CO_2 avoided for biofuels was estimated by using a 2 times higher product price for biofuel compared to a conventional fuel (average gasoline price over 10 years = 2.9 $/gallon) and the corresponding avoided CO_2 emissions for biofuels (Figure 23).

Conventional light duty vehicle vs Shared Transportation

Assumptions:

70% occupancy for Transport Van (15 passenger capacity) and Transit Bus (70 passenger capacity), with both using conventional fuel.

The total distance travelled every day on an average was assumed to be 30 miles.

Only 40% of the passengers using shared transportation were (conservatively) assumed to have a decreased need of a light duty vehicle in their household (this results in corresponding cost savings from fewer light duty vehicles purchases).

The conventional private light duty average vehicle occupancy was assumed to be 1.4 per vehicle.

The mileage of the Transport Van and Transit Bus was assumed to be 12 miles/gallon and 2.5 miles/gallon respectively.

Driver salary: 15$/hour

Estimations - Transit Bus and Transport van:

Initial investment cost per avoided CO_2 ton per year @ 70% vehicle occupancy = < $500 per avoided CO_2 ton per year

Total cost per avoided CO_2 ton @ 70% vehicle occupancy: < $ 1 per avoided CO_2 ton.

Estimates *actually* indicate a cost savings for the shared transportation solution (for replacing private conventional light duty vehicles), when the total cost over the life of the vehicles is considered.

It is noteworthy that any set of reasonable assumptions will show the shared transportation (70% occupancy) to be, by far, the lowest amongst all the other options.

About the Author

Tushar Choudhary has twenty-five years of R&D experience in addressing environmental issues in the energy field. His experience covers a wide spectrum from *fundamental research* to *technology development & commercialization* to *technology analysis*. He has been granted *40 U.S. & International patents* and has an excellent track record in commercially applying his cutting-edge research. Prior to retiring from the energy industry, he served in a dual role as the Director of Technology Analysis & Advancement and Sr. Principal Scientist at a multinational energy company. For the last several years of employment, his primary role was to provide research direction to multiple R&D programs.

He has received numerous prestigious awards and honors within and external to the energy industry for his impactful technology contributions. Some of his external awards include the *Oklahoma Chemist of the Year Award* (American Chemical Society), *Global Indus Technovator Award* (MIT) and South-West *Industrial Innovation Award* (American Chemical Society). He has given keynote lectures at several International Symposiums and his work has been highlighted in trade/scientific magazines, such as Chemical & Engineering News and Science.

Tushar received his Ph.D. in Physical Chemistry from Texas A&M University, College Station; following which he joined the energy industry as a R&D scientist. One of his greatest joys during his time in the energy industry was receiving and sharing knowledge related to all aspects of technology innovation. Following retirement, his goal is to continue sharing knowledge by writing books in areas that he is passionate about.

Author Website: https://www.tushar-choudhary.com

Request: The author would appreciate any comments/reviews (either on the retailer web-site or his personal website).

References and Notes

1. Note: The co-recipients of the first award included Steve Jobs for the development and the introduction of the personal computer. National medal of Technology and Innovation Recipients. https://www.uspto.gov/learning-and-resources/ip-programs-and-awards/national-medal-technology-and-innovation/recipients.
2. World Bank Database. https://data.worldbank.org/indicator/EN.ATM.CO$_2$E.KT
3. Netherlands Environmental Assessment Energy report "Trends in global CO$_2$ and total greenhouse gas emissions; 2018 report", December 2018, *PBL report 3125*. https://www.pbl.nl/en/publications/trends-in-global-co2-and-total-greenhouse-gas-emissions-2018-report
4. U.S. National Oceanic and Atmospheric Administration: Earth System Research Laboratory. https://research.noaa.gov/article/ArtMID/587/ArticleID/2636/Rise-of-carbon-dioxide-unabated
5. NASA Global Climate Change. https://climate.nasa.gov/climate_resources/24/graphic-the-relentless-rise-of-carbon-dioxide/
6. NASA Earth Observatory: Climate & Earth's energy budget. https://earthobservatory.nasa.gov/features/EnergyBalance
7. NASA Global Climate Change: The causes of climate change. https://climate.nasa.gov/causes/
8. European Environment Agency. https://www.eea.europa.eu/data-and-maps/indicators/atmospheric-greenhouse-gas-concentrations-6/assessment-1/
9. IPCC: About the IPCC. https://www.ipcc.ch/about/
10. IPCC, 2014: *Climate Change 2014: Synthesis Report. Contribution of Working Groups I, II and III to the Fifth Assessment Report of the Intergovernmental Panel on Climate Change.* https://www.ipcc.ch/site/assets/uploads/2018/02/SYR_AR5_FINAL_full.pdf

11. Paris Agreement, Status of ratification (accessed: June 2020). https://unfccc.int/process/the-paris-agreement/status-of-ratification
12. Paris Agreement, United Nations 2015. https://unfccc.int/process-and-meetings/the-paris-agreement/the-paris-agreement
13. United Nations, Paris agreement and NDCs. https://unfccc.int/process-and-meetings/the-paris-agreement/the-paris-agreement/nationally-determined-contributions-ndcs
14. Pew Research center, November 2015 Report. "Global concern about climate change. Broad support for limiting emissions". https://www.pewresearch.org/global/2015/11/05/global-concern-about-climate-change-broad-support-for-limiting-emissions/
15. Pew Research center, April 2019. "A look at how people around the world view climate change". https://www.pewresearch.org/fact-tank/2019/04/18/a-look-at-how-people-around-the-world-view-climate-change/
16. Statement from the Commonwealth Academy. https://rsc-src.ca/sites/default/files/Commonwealth%20Academies%20Consensus%20Statement%20on%20Climate%20Change%20-%2012%20March%202018%20-%202.pdf
17. Statement from the National Academies. https://sites.nationalacademies.org/sites/climate/index.htm
18. Statement from the American Association for Advancement of Science. https://whatweknow.aaas.org/get-the-facts/
19. Statement from the American Meteorological society. https://www.ametsoc.org/index.cfm/ams/about-ams/ams-statements/statements-of-the-ams-in-force/climate-change1/
20. Statement from the Joint Science Academies, https://sites.nationalacademies.org/cs/groups/internationalsite/documents/webpage/international_080877.pdf
21. Statement from the Geology Society of America. https://www.geosociety.org/gsa/positions/position10.aspx
22. Statement from the Advancing Earth and Space Science (AGU). https://www.agu.org/Share-and-Advocate/Share/Policymakers/Position-Statements/Position_Climate

23. Statement from the American Chemical Society. https://www.acs.org/content/acs/en/policy/publicpolicies/sustainability/globalclimatechange.html
24. List of (>150) supporting scientific organizations. http://www.opr.ca.gov/facts/list-of-scientific-organizations.html
25. U.S. Department of Energy: Science & Innovation- Energy sources and clean energy.
26. European Commission: Directorate-General for Climate Action.
27. Paris Agreement, United Nations 2015. https://unfccc.int/process-and-meetings/the-paris-agreement/the-paris-agreement
28. IPCC, 2018: *Global Warming of 1.5°C. An IPCC Special Report on the impacts of global warming of 1.5°C above pre-industrial levels and related global greenhouse gas emission pathways, in the context of strengthening the global response to the threat of climate change, sustainable development, and efforts to eradicate poverty.* https://www.ipcc.ch/sr15/chapter/spm/
29. Netherlands Environmental Assessment Energy report "Trends in global CO_2 and total greenhouse gas emissions; 2018 report", December 2018, *PBL report 3125*. https://www.pbl.nl/en/publications/trends-in-global-co2-and-total-greenhouse-gas-emissions-2018-report
30. The World Bank: https://data.worldbank.org/indicator/SP.POP.TOTL 2017 world population= 7.5 Billion.; average human weight (adults + children) assumed = 50 kgs.
31. U.S. Energy Information Administration data: International energy outlook 2019. https://www.eia.gov/outlooks/ieo/
32. The World Bank: https://data.worldbank.org/indicator/SP.POP.TOTL
33. The World Bank: https://data.worldbank.org/indicator/NY.GDP.MKTP.KD?locations=1W (constant 2010 US $)
34. BP statistical review of world energy 2019. https://www.bp.com/content/dam/bp/business-sites/en/global/corporate/pdfs/energy-economics/statistical-review/bp-stats-review-2019-full-report.pdf
35. U.S. Energy Information Administration data: International energy outlook 2019. https://www.eia.gov/outlooks/ieo/

36. IPCC; https://archive.ipcc.ch/ipccreports/tar/wg1/016.htm
37. U.S. Environmental Protection Agency; https://www.epa.gov/ghgemissions/overview-greenhouse-gases
38. World Bank Database. https://data.worldbank.org/indicator/EN.ATM.CO$_2$E.KT
39. United Nations. Statistics Division. https://unstats.un.org/sdgs/report/2019/goal-01/
40. UN Sustainable development goals. https://www.un.org/sustainabledevelopment/sustainable-development-goals/
41. Food and Agriculture Organization of the United Nations (2020). http://www.fao.org/3/ca8800en/ca8800en.pdf
42. World Health Organization: Children- improving survival and well-being (2020). https://www.who.int/en/news-room/fact-sheets/detail/children-reducing-mortality
43. UN Sustainable development goals (Goal 3).https://www.un.org/sustainabledevelopment/wp-content/uploads/2019/07/E_Infographic_03.pdf
44. U.S. Census Bureau. https://www.census.gov/library/publications/2019/demo/p60-266.html
45. Note: Data for the Figure was developed from the different references provided in the text on this topic.
46. Climate change history. https://www.history.com/topics/natural-disasters-and-environment/history-of-climate-change
47. Data from "Carbon Dioxide Information Analysis Center". T. Boden, D. Andres, Oakridge National Laboratory. https://cdiac.ess-dive.lbl.gov/ftp/ndp030/global.1751_2014.ems
48. UN Environment. Global Chemicals Outlook II, From Legacies to Innovative solutions (2019). https://wedocs.unep.org/bitstream/handle/20.500.11822/27651/GCOII_synth.pdf?sequence=1&isAllowed=y
49. American Institute of Physics. https://history.aip.org/climate/summary.htm
50. United States President's Science Advisory Committee (1965), Restoring the quality of our environment. https://www.worldcat.org/title/restoring-the-quality-of-our-environment-report-of-the-environmental-pollution-panel-of-the-presidents-science-advisory-committee/oclc/562799 Note: The

only future recommendation in this report by the esteemed panel of scientists related to this topic was to continue the precise measurements of CO_2 and temperature at different heights in the stratosphere (Page 26). The level of understanding of severity can be most practically evaluated by the set of recommendations in this study. The lack of recommendation of any stringent action to reduce CO_2 is the best evidence for absence of appropriate understanding about the severity of the effect from CO_2.

51 Data from "Carbon Dioxide Information Analysis Center". T. Boden, D. Andres, Oakridge National Laboratory. https://cdiac.ess-dive.lbl.gov/ftp/ndp030/global.1751_2014.ems

52 U.S. National Science Foundation Report: Science and the Challenges ahead (1974)- See Pages: 24-25. https://archive.org/details/sciencechallenge00nati/mode/2up

53 U.S. National Academy of Science Report: Understanding Climate Change (1975). https://archive.org/details/understandingcli00unit/mode/2up

54 Data from "Carbon Dioxide Information Analysis Center". T. Boden, D. Andres, Oakridge National Laboratory. https://cdiac.ess-dive.lbl.gov/ftp/ndp030/global.1751_2014.ems

55 IPCC history. https://www.ipcc.ch/about/history/

56 IPCC Report. https://www.ipcc.ch/report/climate-change-the-ipcc-1990-and-1992-assessments/

57 IPCC reports. https://www.ipcc.ch/reports/

58 NASA global climate change. https://climate.nasa.gov/scientific-consensus/

59 IPCC, 2018: *Global Warming of 1.5°C. An IPCC Special Report on the impacts of global warming of 1.5°C above pre-industrial levels and related global greenhouse gas emission pathways, in the context of strengthening the global response to the threat of climate change, sustainable development, and efforts to eradicate poverty.* https://www.ipcc.ch/sr15/chapter/spm/

60 International organization of motor vehicle manufacturers. Vehicles in use. http://www.oica.net/category/vehicles-in-use/

61 https://www.worldometers.info/cars/; Note U.S. alone has over ~200 million registered light duty vehicles. https://www.bts.gov/content/number-us-aircraft-vehicles-vessels-and-other-conveyances

62 U.S. Office of transport and air quality: Vehicle prices are provided for different vehicles. https://www.fueleconomy.gov/feg/Find.do?action=sbs&id=40242&id=40812 The 2020 retail price from vehicle manufacturers also show that battery electric light duty vehicles are about 60% more expensive than conventional light duty vehicles for the same trim.

63 Note: This is a straight-forward estimation involving the following calculation: Additional cost to the society equals 1 billion multiplied by the cost difference between electric car technology and conventional fossil fuel-based technology.

64 IEA: Tracking Transport, Tracking Report 2019. https://www.iea.org/reports/tracking-transport-2019 Global CO_2 emission from passenger light duty vehicles was about 3.5 billion tons in 2018, while total global CO_2 emission was about 37 billion tons.

65 World Bank GDP 2019 data for India (constant 2010 U.S. $). https://data.worldbank.org/indicator/NY.GDP.MKTP.KD?locations=IN

66 United Nations: No poverty. Why it matters? https://www.un.org/sustainabledevelopment/wp-content/uploads/2016/08/1.pdf (via economist Jeffry Sachs)

67 United Nations Sustainability Development Goal #1: https://www.un.org/sustainabledevelopment/poverty/

68 World Bank Poverty database. http://iresearch.worldbank.org/PovcalNet/povDuplicateWB.aspx Total global population living under 5.5$/day (2017): ~3.3 billion.

69 United Nations: Water, Sanitation and Hygiene. https://www.unwater.org/water-facts/water-sanitation-and-hygiene/ . Four billion people do not have access to safe sanitation.

70 United Nations Sustainability Development Goal #7: Affordable and clean energy. https://www.un.org/sustainabledevelopment/energy/ Three billion people rely on wood, charcoal or animal waste for heating and cooking.

71 U.N.: Energy for a sustainable future. https://www.un.org/millenniumgoals/pdf/AGECCsummaryreport[1].pdf
72 United Nations Development program: Human Development Index. http://hdr.undp.org/en/content/human-development-index-hdi Human development index provides a summary assessment of average length of life/health, education and standard of living for a country.
73 United Nations Development program: Energizing Human Development. http://hdr.undp.org/en/content/energising-human-development The correlation between human development index and energy consumption capita is strong until a certain threshold value of energy consumption per capita is reached. Thus, the cost of energy is especially important for economically challenged countries, which currently have very low to low energy consumption per capita.
74 U.S. Census Bureau. https://www.census.gov/library/publications/2019/demo/p60-266.html
75 U.S. Congressional Budget office. The budget and economic outlook: 2020 to 2030. https://www.cbo.gov/publication/56020
76 U.S. Congressional Budget office. CBO releases new economic projections. http://www.crfb.org/blogs/cbo-releases-new-economic-projections-0
77 World Bank Poverty database. Select economies and aggregations. http://iresearch.worldbank.org/PovcalNet/povOnDemand.aspx
78 Data from "Carbon Dioxide Information Analysis Center". T. Boden, D. Andres, Oakridge National Laboratory. https://cdiac.ess-dive.lbl.gov/ftp/ndp030/global.1751_2014.ems
79 NASA. July 20, 1969, One giant leap for mankind. https://www.nasa.gov/mission_pages/apollo/apollo11.html
80 IPCC, 2001: Climate Change 2001: Synthesis Report. Third Assessment Report of the Integovernmental Panel on Climate Change. https://www.ipcc.ch/site/assets/uploads/2018/05/SYR_TAR_full_report.pdf

[81] Data from "Carbon Dioxide Information Analysis Center". T. Boden, D. Andres, Oakridge National Laboratory. https://cdiac.ess-dive.lbl.gov/ftp/ndp030/global.1751_2014.ems

[82] BP Statistical review of World energy 2020. https://www.bp.com/content/dam/bp/business-sites/en/global/corporate/pdfs/energy-economics/statistical-review/bp-stats-review-2020-full-report.pdf Please refer to this report for further information.

[83] Note: Calculation is based on the relationship between fossil fuel combustion and energy consumption, using data from "Carbon Dioxide Information Analysis Center" and BP statistical review of world energy, 2020.

[84] American Institute of Physics website. https://history.aip.org/climate/co2.htm

[85] BBC News online. https://www.bbc.com/news/uk-england-norfolk-22283372

[86] Climate Change: The 1990 and 1992 IPCC Assessments. https://www.ipcc.ch/site/assets/uploads/2018/05/ipcc_90_92_assessments_far_overview.pdf

[87] American Chemical Society, Chlorofluorocarbons and ozone depletion. https://www.acs.org/content/acs/en/education/whatischemistry/landmarks/cfcs-ozone.html

[88] The Washington Post. https://www.washingtonpost.com/archive/politics/1988/04/10/cfcs-rise-and-fall-of-chemical-miracle/9dc7f67b-8ba9-4e11-b247-a36337d5a87b/ ; The Ozone hole: http://www.theozonehole.com/cfc.htm

[89] Ministry of Economy, trade and Industry, https://www.meti.go.jp/policy/chemical_management/ozone/files/pamplet/panel/08e_basic.pdf

[90] UN Environment program. https://ozone.unep.org/ozone-timeline

[91] US Department of State. https://www.state.gov/key-topics-office-of-environmental-quality-and-transboundary-issues/the-montreal-protocol-on-substances-that-deplete-the-ozone-layer/

[92] U.S. Environmental Protection Energy, https://www.epa.gov/ozone-layer-protection/international-actions-montreal-protocol-substances-deplete-ozone-layer

[93] UN Environment Program. https://ozone.unep.org/ozone-and-you#the-kigali

[94] US Department of State. https://www.state.gov/key-topics-office-of-environmental-quality-and-transboundary-issues/the-montreal-protocol-on-substances-that-deplete-the-ozone-layer/

[95] World Economic forum. https://www.weforum.org/agenda/2018/08/the-world-of-plastics-in-numbers

[96] Our World in Data. Plastic Pollution. https://ourworldindata.org/plastic-pollution

[97] UN Environment. Global Chemicals Outlook II, From Legacies to Innovative solutions (2019). https://wedocs.unep.org/bitstream/handle/20.500.11822/27651/GCOII_synth.pdf?sequence=1&isAllowed=y

[98] UN Environment. The state of plastics. World Environment Day outlook (2018). https://wedocs.unep.org/bitstream/handle/20.500.11822/25513/state_plastics_WED.pdf?sequence=1&isAllowed=y

[99] Note: It might appear that it was a human fault that led to the current plastics problem and not that of plastics directly. But it is important to note that irrespective of that argument, it is clear that the currently observed severe impact from plastics was missed. In other words, if the severity of impact from the plastics dumping problem had been appropriately understood, we would not have caused the problem. Furthermore, the dumping of plastics can be related to the inefficiency of the recycling process. It is the overall inefficiency that also prevents the recycling of CO_2; i.e. if recycling CO_2 was efficient than it would have been an excellent solution for fossil fuels. As discussed in detail later, inefficient processes are expected to have a significant detrimental impact on the environment.

[100] UN Environment. The state of plastics. World Environment Day outlook (2018). https://wedocs.unep.org/bitstream/handle/20.500.11822/25513/state_plastics_WED.pdf?sequence=1&isAllowed=y

[101] Directive 2003/30/EC of the European Parliament on the promotion of biofuels or other renewable fuels for transport. https://eur-lex.europa.eu/legal-

[102] content/EN/TXT/?qid=1586459020405&uri=CELEX:32003L0030

[102] Technical report for EU commission: The impact of EU consumption on deforestation. https://ec.europa.eu/environment/forests/pdf/1.%20Report%20analysis%20of%20impact.pdf

[103] Technical report for EU commission: Study on the environmental impact of palm oil consumption. https://ec.europa.eu/environment/forests/pdf/palm_oil_study_kh0218208enn_new.pdf

[104] The Rainforest Foundation Norway: The impact of continued expansion of palm and soy oil demand through biofuel policy. https://d5i6is0eze552.cloudfront.net/documents/RF_report_biofuel_0320_eng_SP.pdf?mtime=20200310101137

[105] Directive 2009/28/EC of the European Parliament on the promotion of the use of energy from renewable sources and amending and subsequently repealing Directives 2001/77/EC and 2003/30/EC. https://eur-lex.europa.eu/legal-content/EN/ALL/?uri=CELEX:32009L0028

[106] European Parliament resolution of 4 April 2017 on palm oil and deforestation of rainforests. https://www.europarl.europa.eu/doceo/document/TA-8-2017-0098_EN.html?redirect

[107] Transport and Environment: Why is palm oil biodiesel bad? https://www.transportenvironment.org/what-we-do/biofuels/why-palm-oil-biodiesel-bad

[108] U.S. EPA: Environmental topics. https://www.epa.gov/environmental-topics

[109] European Environment agency- a) Health and environment and b) Human activities https://www.eea.europa.eu/soer/2015/europe/health-and-environment; https://www.eea.europa.eu/publications/92-827-5122-8/page011.html

[110] Wikipedia: Human impact on the environment. https://en.wikipedia.org/wiki/Human_impact_on_the_environment

[111] U.S. Census Bureau. https://www.census.gov/library/publications/2019/demo/p60-266.html

[112] Annual Energy outlook 2020. https://www.eia.gov/outlooks/aeo/electricity_generation.php

[113] Federal reserve bank of Minneapolis: Inflation calculator. https://www.minneapolisfed.org/about-us/monetary-policy/inflation-calculator

[114] Annex II: Metrics & Methodology. Climate Change 2014: Mitigation of Climate Change. Contribution of Working Group III to the Fifth Assessment Report of the Intergovernmental Panel on Climate Change. https://www.ipcc.ch/site/assets/uploads/2018/02/ipcc_wg3_ar5_annex-ii.pdf

[115] U.S. EPA: Understanding of global warming potential. https://www.epa.gov/ghgemissions/understanding-global-warming-potentials The global warming potential for methane is 28-36 times that of CO_2 for a 100-year timescale.

[116] Note: Some simple examples are discussed herewith to illustrate the impact of support from nature: a) Lower activity is required to swim with the water flow than against the water flow, b) A tailwind results in lower activity for an air travel as compared to a headwind and c) For places with cooler summers, there is a lower requirement of air conditioning activity.

[117] Note: Although several new materials have been proposed for solar technology over the past several decades, the original material (Si) is still by far the most dominant from a commercial applications viewpoint. Most of the proposed new materials continue to remain either in the pilot stage or at very low levels of implementation. In fact, several start-up companies with new materials have become bankrupt over the past two decades.

[118] IRENA 2018. Renewable power generation costs in 2017. International Renewable Energy Agency. https://www.irena.org/-/media/Files/IRENA/Agency/Publication/2018/Jan/IRENA_2017_Power_Costs_2018.pdf

[119] U.S. EIA: Cost and performance characteristics of new generating technologies (2020). https://www.eia.gov/outlooks/aeo/assumptions/pdf/table_8.2.pdf

[120] IEA: Role of gas in today's energy transition. https://www.iea.org/reports/the-role-of-gas-in-todays-energy-transitions#key-findings

[121] Note: Although, natural gas is not a long-term solution for electricity generation, nevertheless it would be impractical to not consider its potential as an intermediate term solution.

[122] IEA: Global Energy and CO_2 status report 2019. https://www.iea.org/reports/global-energy-co2-status-report-2019/emissions

[123] Annual Energy outlook 2020. https://www.eia.gov/outlooks/aeo/electricity_generation.php

[124] U.S. EIA: Cost and performance characteristics of new generating technologies (2020). https://www.eia.gov/outlooks/aeo/assumptions/pdf/table_8.2.pdf

[125] U.S. EIA: Levelized cost and levelized avoided cost of new generation resources (2020). https://www.eia.gov/outlooks/aeo/pdf/electricity_generation.pdf

[126] U.S. EIA: Capital cost and performance characteristic estimates for utility scale electric power generating technologies. https://www.eia.gov/analysis/studies/powerplants/capitalcost/pdf/capital_cost_AEO2020.pdf

[127] U.S. EIA: Levelized cost and levelized avoided cost of new generation resources (2020). https://www.eia.gov/outlooks/aeo/pdf/electricity_generation.pdf

[128] U.S. National Energy technology Laboratory: Life cycle greenhouse gas emissions. Natural gas and power production. https://www.eia.gov/conference/2015/pdf/presentations/skone.pdf

[129] Annex III: Technology specific cost and performance parameters. Climate Change 2014: Mitigation of Climate Change. Contribution of Working Group III to the Fifth Assessment Report of the Intergovernmental Panel on Climate Change. https://www.ipcc.ch/site/assets/uploads/2018/02/ipcc_wg3_ar5_annex-iii.pdf#page=7

[130] U.S. EIA: https://www.eia.gov/todayinenergy/detail.php?id=31052

[131] U.S. EIA: Levelized cost and levelized avoided cost of new generation resources (2020). https://www.eia.gov/outlooks/aeo/pdf/electricity_generation.pdf

[132] General Electric (GE) Company: How a combined cycle plant works. https://www.ge.com/power/resources/knowledge-base/combined-cycle-power-plant-how-it-works

[133] U.S. EIA: Cost and performance characteristics of new generating technologies (2020). https://www.eia.gov/outlooks/aeo/assumptions/pdf/table_8.2.pdf

[134] Note: Please refer to the reference provided in the text corresponding to this Table, if more detailed information is needed.

[135] U.S. EIA: Levelized cost and levelized avoided cost of new generation resources (2020). Note: data is from Table 1b: unweighted LCOE excluding tax credit for new generation resources in 2019 $/MWh. All major assumptions for the estimations may be found in this report (e.g. capacity factors, WACC, etc.). https://www.eia.gov/outlooks/aeo/pdf/electricity_generation.pdf

[136] Note: The LCOE of existing coal plants has been estimated from the LCOE of the state-of the-art new coal plants (2019$ EIA data) by excluding the capital cost. Existing plants on an average are expected to be less efficient than new plants. Correspondingly, a factor of +15% has been added to the O&M costs to obtain an average LCOE value for the existing fleet of coal plants. The derived average LCOE value reported for existing coal plants herein (based on the above calculation) is in excellent agreement with other reported values for existing coal plants recently reported in literature (e.g. Lazard Version 13.0).

[137] Note: Please refer to the reference provided in the text corresponding to this Figure for detailed information related to assumptions used by U.S. EIA.

[138] Our World in Data. Natural gas prices. https://ourworldindata.org/grapher/natural-gas-prices

[139] IEA: The role of gas in today's energy transitions. https://www.iea.org/reports/the-role-of-gas-in-todays-energy-transitions

[140] U.S. National Energy Technology Laboratory: Life cycle greenhouse gas emissions. Natural gas and power production. https://www.eia.gov/conference/2015/pdf/presentations/skone.pdf

[141] Annex III: Technology specific cost and performance parameters. Climate Change 2014: Mitigation of Climate Change. Contribution of Working Group III to the Fifth Assessment Report of the Intergovernmental Panel on Climate Change.

https://www.ipcc.ch/site/assets/uploads/2018/02/ipcc_wg3_ar5_annex-iii.pdf#page=7
[142] IEA: Global energy and CO_2 status report (2019). https://www.iea.org/reports/global-energy-co2-status-report-2019/emissions
[143] IEA: Natural Gas. https://www.iea.org/fuels-and-technologies/gas
[144] U.S. EIA: Use of natural gas. https://www.eia.gov/energyexplained/natural-gas/use-of-natural-gas.php
[145] U.S. EIA: Natural gas and the environment. https://www.eia.gov/energyexplained/natural-gas/natural-gas-and-the-environment.php
[146] U.S. EIA: Hydraulic fractured wells provide two thirds of natural gas production. https://www.eia.gov/todayinenergy/detail.php?id=26112
[147] U.S. EIA: Natural gas and the environment. https://www.eia.gov/energyexplained/natural-gas/natural-gas-and-the-environment.php
[148] IEA: Natural Gas. https://www.iea.org/fuels-and-technologies/gas
[149] U.S. EIA: Photovoltaics and electricity. https://www.eia.gov/energyexplained/solar/photovoltaics-and-electricity.php
[150] Note: The term large-scale refers to the size (production capacity) of the electricity generating unit.
[151] National Renewable Energy Laboratory. Solar photovoltaics technology basics. https://www.nrel.gov/research/re-photovoltaics.html
[152] Photovoltaics report. Fraunhofer Institute for solar energy systems (2020). https://www.ise.fraunhofer.de/content/dam/ise/de/documents/publications/studies/Photovoltaics-Report.pdf
[153] Annual Energy outlook 2020. https://www.eia.gov/outlooks/aeo/electricity_generation.php
[154] U.S. EIA: Cost and performance characteristics of new generating technologies (2020). https://www.eia.gov/outlooks/aeo/assumptions/pdf/table_8.2.pdf
[155] Note: Please refer to the reference provided in the text corresponding to this Table, if more detailed information is needed.

[156] U.S. EIA: Levelized cost and levelized avoided cost of new generation resources (2020). Note: data is from Table 1b: unweighted LCOE excluding tax credit for new generation resources in 2019 $/MWh. All major assumptions for the estimations may be found in this report (e.g. capacity factors, WACC, etc.). https://www.eia.gov/outlooks/aeo/pdf/electricity_generation.pdf

[157] Note: Please refer to the reference provided in the text corresponding to this Figure for detailed information related to assumptions used by U.S. EIA.

[158] U.S. National Energy technology Laboratory: Life cycle greenhouse gas emissions. Natural gas and power production. https://www.eia.gov/conference/2015/pdf/presentations/skone.pdf

[159] Annex III: Technology specific cost and performance parameters. Climate Change 2014: Mitigation of Climate Change. Contribution of Working Group III to the Fifth Assessment Report of the Intergovernmental Panel on Climate Change. https://www.ipcc.ch/site/assets/uploads/2018/02/ipcc_wg3_ar5_annex-iii.pdf#page=7

[160] National Renewable Energy Laboratory: Solar power and the electric grid. https://www.nrel.gov/docs/fy10osti/45653.pdf

[161] IRENA (2019), Future of Solar Photovoltaic: Deployment, investment, technology, grid integration and socio-economic aspects (A Global Energy Transformation: paper), International Renewable Energy Agency, Abu Dhabi. https://www.irena.org/-/media/Files/IRENA/Agency/Publication/2019/Nov/IRENA_Future_of_Solar_PV_2019.pdf

[162] Note: This has been estimated from the data provided in the BP Statistical review of World energy 2020. https://www.bp.com/en/global/corporate/energy-economics/statistical-review-of-world-energy.html Cumulative solar data includes the total solar energy consumed for all years- i.e. from technology commercialization until 2019. The average amount of fossil fuels consumed per year has been ~11 billion tons of oil equivalent based on the average of last 10 years.

[163] American Institute of Physics web site: The discovery of global warming. https://history.aip.org/climate/index.htm

[164] Carbon Dioxide Information Analysis Center. T. Boden, D. Andres, Oakridge National Laboratory. https://cdiac.ess-dive.lbl.gov/ftp/ndp030/global.1751_2014.ems

[165] BP Statistical review of World energy 2020. https://www.bp.com/content/dam/bp/business-sites/en/global/corporate/pdfs/energy-economics/statistical-review/bp-stats-review-2020-full-report.pdf Please refer to the report for further information and assumptions used for unit conversions.

[166] U.S. EIA: Solar explained. https://www.eia.gov/energyexplained/solar/

[167] IPCC report: Renewable energy sources and Climate change mitigation (Section 3.6). https://www.ipcc.ch/site/assets/uploads/2018/03/SRREN_Full_Report-1.pdf This reference is provided mainly to give a feel for the type of activities involved. At orders of magnitude larger scale, issues related to one or more of these activities could be amplified (i.e. become severe). The severity of the impact is only expected to be revealed after a certain threshold level of implementation has been crossed.

[168] National Renewable Energy Laboratory (2015): Overgeneration from solar energy in California. https://www.nrel.gov/docs/fy16osti/65023.pdf

[169] National Renewable Energy Laboratory: Ten years of analyzing the duck chart. https://www.nrel.gov/news/program/2018/10-years-duck-curve.html

[170] California ISO: Managing Oversupply. http://www.caiso.com/informed/Pages/ManagingOversupply.aspx

[171] Oakridge National Laboratory (2017): Environmental quality and U.S. power sector- air quality, water quality, land use and environmental justice. https://www.energy.gov/sites/prod/files/2017/01/f34/Environment%20Baseline%20Vol.%202--Environmental%20Quality%20and%20the%20U.S.%20Power%20Sector--Air%20Quality%2C%20Water%20Quality%2C%20Land%20Use%2C%20and%20Environmental%20Justice.pdf

[172] Note: This comparison for land requirements is specifically for the power plants (i.e. box is drawn around the power plants for this purpose), given that the discussion is about localized land constraints for certain regions (e.g. high population urban cities).

[173] National Renewable Energy Laboratory (2018): U.S. Solar photovoltaic system cost benchmark. https://www.nrel.gov/docs/fy19osti/72399.pdf

[174] U.S. EPA: Distributed generation of electricity and its environmental impact. https://www.epa.gov/energy/distributed-generation-electricity-and-its-environmental-impacts

[175] National Renewable Energy Laboratory (2012): Renewable electricity futures study. https://www.nrel.gov/docs/fy12osti/52409-2.pdf

[176] U.S. Department of Energy: Concentrating solar power thermal storage system basics. https://www.energy.gov/eere/solar/articles/concentrating-solar-power-thermal-storage-system-basics

[177] U.S. DOE, Solar-plus-storage 101. https://www.energy.gov/eere/solar/articles/solar-plus-storage-101

[178] U.S. EIA: Solar thermal power plants. https://www.eia.gov/energyexplained/solar/solar-thermal-power-plants.php

[179] U.S. EIA: Levelized cost and levelized avoided cost of new generation resources (2019). https://www.eia.gov/outlooks/archive/aeo19/pdf/electricity_generation.pdf

[180] IRENA (2019): Renewable generation costs in 2018. International Renewable Energy Agency. https://www.irena.org/-/media/Files/IRENA/Agency/Publication/2019/May/IRENA_Renewable-Power-Generations-Costs-in-2018.pdf

[181] U.S. EIA: Cost and performance characteristics of new generating technologies (2020). https://www.eia.gov/outlooks/aeo/assumptions/pdf/table_8.2.pdf

[182] Note: Please refer to the reference provided in the text corresponding to this Table if more detailed information is needed.

[183] Note: Concentrated solar power with 8 hours storage (CSP) is used as a representative of solar plus energy storage technology

throughout this book, unless mentioned otherwise. Considering that 8 hours storage is not adequate storage for stand-alone operations (for dispatchable supply), the use of CSP provides a lower end cost estimate for solar plus storage technology. CSP has been used herein since a) there is good quality data available regarding this technology (directly comparable with other technologies) and b) there is value in considering an optimistic case for a relatively less established technology.

[184] U.S. EIA: Capital costs and performance characteristic estimates for utility scale electric power generation technologies (2020). https://www.eia.gov/analysis/studies/powerplants/capitalcost/pdf/capital_cost_AEO2020.pdf

[185] U.S. Department of Energy, Concentrating solar power. https://www.energy.gov/eere/solar/concentrating-solar-power

[186] Note: Higher cost is related to increased requirement of storage and related electricity generation.

[187] U.S. EIA: Cost and performance characteristics of new generating technologies (2020). https://www.eia.gov/outlooks/aeo/assumptions/pdf/table_8.2.pdf

[188] U.S. Department of Energy: Energy storage technology and cost characterization report (2019). https://www.energy.gov/sites/prod/files/2019/07/f65/Storage%20Cost%20and%20Performance%20Characterization%20Report_Final.pdf

[189] U.S. National Energy Technology Laboratory: 2018 U.S. Utility-scale photovoltaics plus energy storage system cost benchmark (2018). https://www.nrel.gov/docs/fy19osti/71714.pdf

[190] U.S. Department of Energy: Energy storage technology and cost characterization report (2019). https://www.energy.gov/sites/prod/files/2019/07/f65/Storage%20Cost%20and%20Performance%20Characterization%20Report_Final.pdf

[191] U.S. National Energy Technology Laboratory: Life cycle greenhouse gas emissions. Natural gas and power production. https://www.eia.gov/conference/2015/pdf/presentations/skone.pdf

[192] Swedish Energy Agency: Li ion vehicle battery production (2019).

https://www.ivl.se/download/18.14d7b12e16e3c5c36271070/1574923989017/C444.pdf

[193] U.S. Department of Energy: Energy storage technology and cost characterization report (2019). https://www.energy.gov/sites/prod/files/2019/07/f65/Storage%20Cost%20and%20Performance%20Characterization%20Report_Final.pdf

[194] Note: Due to the extremely low implementation levels and the many resulting unknowns, it is not possible to focus on any single issue. That is the reason why several potential possibilities that can lead to possible severe environmental concerns are listed herein. Based on historical data it is evident that a much higher level of implementation will be required before the *exact* nature of issues that will lead to a severe environmental impact are clearly understood.

[195] U.S. EIA: Few fuels surpass the energy densities of gasoline and diesel. https://www.eia.gov/todayinenergy/detail.php?id=9991

[196] U.S. Department of Energy: How do wind turbines work? https://www.energy.gov/eere/wind/how-do-wind-turbines-work

[197] U.S. EIA: Types of Wind turbines. https://www.eia.gov/energyexplained/wind/types-of-wind-turbines.php

[198] U.S. EIA: Cost and performance characteristics of new generating technologies (2020). https://www.eia.gov/outlooks/aeo/assumptions/pdf/table_8.2.pdf

[199] Note: Please refer to the reference provided in the text corresponding to this Table if more detailed information is needed.

[200] U.S. EIA: Levelized cost and levelized avoided cost of new generation resources (2020). Note: data is from Table 1b: unweighted LCOE excluding tax credit for new generation resources in 2019 $/MWh. All major assumptions for the estimations may be found in this report (e.g. capacity factors, WACC, etc.). https://www.eia.gov/outlooks/aeo/pdf/electricity_generation.pdf

[201] Note: Please refer to the reference provided in the text corresponding to this Figure for detailed information related to assumptions used by U.S. EIA.

[202] U.S. National Energy technology Laboratory: Life cycle greenhouse gas emissions. Natural gas and power production. https://www.eia.gov/conference/2015/pdf/presentations/skone.pdf

[203] Annex III: Technology specific cost and performance parameters. Climate Change 2014: Mitigation of Climate Change. Contribution of Working Group III to the Fifth Assessment Report of the Intergovernmental Panel on Climate Change. https://www.ipcc.ch/site/assets/uploads/2018/02/ipcc_wg3_ar5_annex-iii.pdf#page=7

[204] BP Statistical review of World energy 2020. https://www.bp.com/content/dam/bp/business-sites/en/global/corporate/pdfs/energy-economics/statistical-review/bp-stats-review-2020-full-report.pdf

[205] Average energy produced from fossil fuels since last 10 years has been ~11 billion tons of oil equivalent per year. BP Statistical review of World energy 2020.

[206] Note: While the exact values for energy densities between different resources are debatable, it is well established that wind and sunlight are *at-least* 10 times more dilute than fossil fuels.

[207] International journal of Green Energy, 5,438, 2008. https://www.researchgate.net/publication/233231163_A_Comparison_of_Energy_Densities_of_Prevalent_Energy_Sources_in_Units_of_Joules_Per_Cubic_Meter

[208] Energy policy, 123, 83, 2018. https://www.researchgate.net/publication/327239302_The_spatial_extent_of_renewable_and_non-renewable_power_generation_A_review_and_meta-analysis_of_power_densities_and_their_application_in_the_US

[209] U.S. DOE: 2016 U.S. Renewable Energy Grid Integration data book. https://www.nrel.gov/docs/fy18osti/71151.pdf

[210] California ISO: Managing Oversupply. http://www.caiso.com/informed/Pages/ManagingOversupply.aspx

[211] Oakridge National Laboratory (2017): Environmental quality and U.S. power sector- air quality, water quality, land use and environmental justice. https://www.energy.gov/sites/prod/files/2017/01/f34/Environment%20Baseline%20Vol.%202--

Environmental%20Quality%20and%20the%20U.S.%20Power%20Sector--Air%20Quality%2C%20Water%20Quality%2C%20Land%20Use%2C%20and%20Environmental%20Justice.pdf

[212] Note: Even though only about 5% of the total land is directly required for the wind farms (i.e. wind turbines), the entire land area needs to be available from a new project planning perspective.

[213] U.S. Bureau of Ocean Energy Management: Renewable energy on the outer continental shelf. https://www.boem.gov/renewable-energy/renewable-energy-program-overview

[214] U.S. EIA: Cost and performance characteristics of new generating technologies (2020). https://www.eia.gov/outlooks/aeo/assumptions/pdf/table_8.2.pdf

[215] Note: Please refer to the reference provided in the text corresponding to this Table if more detailed information is needed.

[216] U.S. EIA: Levelized cost and levelized avoided cost of new generation resources (2020). Note: data is from Table 1b: unweighted LCOE excluding tax credit for new generation resources in 2019 $/MWh. All major assumptions for the estimations may be found in this report (e.g. capacity factors, WACC, etc.). https://www.eia.gov/outlooks/aeo/pdf/electricity_generation.pdf

[217] U.S. Department of energy: https://www.energy.gov/eere/wind/offshore-wind-research-and-development

[218] Note: Please refer to the reference provided in the text corresponding to this Figure for detailed information related to assumptions used by U.S. EIA.

[219] U.S. EIA: Biomass explained. https://www.eia.gov/energyexplained/biomass/

[220] IEA Bioenergy: Bioenergy's role in balancing the electricity grid and providing storage options. https://www.ieabioenergy.com/wp-content/uploads/2017/02/IEA-Bioenergy-bio-in-balancing-grid_master-FINAL.pdf

[221] U.S. EIA: Biomass- wood and wood waste. https://www.eia.gov/energyexplained/biomass/wood-and-wood-waste.php

[222] U.S. EIA: Cost and performance characteristics of new generating technologies (2020). https://www.eia.gov/outlooks/aeo/assumptions/pdf/table_8.2.pdf

[223] Note: Please refer to the reference provided in the text corresponding to this Table if more detailed information is needed.

[224] U.S. EIA: Levelized cost and levelized avoided cost of new generation resources (2020). Note: data is from Table 1b: unweighted LCOE excluding tax credit for new generation resources in 2019 $/MWh. All major assumptions for the estimations may be found in this report (e.g. capacity factors, WACC, etc.). https://www.eia.gov/outlooks/aeo/pdf/electricity_generation.pdf

[225] Note: Please refer to the reference provided in the text corresponding to this Figure for detailed information related to assumptions used by U.S. EIA.

[226] National Renewable Energy Laboratory: Biomass energy basics. https://www.nrel.gov/research/re-biomass.html

[227] Note: The small net emissions are due to other life cycle emission components such as fertilizer production, transportation of biomass, etc.

[228] IPCC Fifth Assessment Report: Life cycle emissions. Figure 7. https://www.ipcc.ch/report/ar5/wg3/energy-systems/06_figure_7-6/

[229] Annex III: Technology specific cost and performance parameters. Climate Change 2014: Mitigation of Climate Change. Contribution of Working Group III to the Fifth Assessment Report of the Intergovernmental Panel on Climate Change. https://www.ipcc.ch/site/assets/uploads/2018/02/ipcc_wg3_ar5_annex-iii.pdf#page=7

[230] IPCC (2019): Special report on climate change and land. https://www.ipcc.ch/srccl/chapter/summary-for-policymakers/

[231] BP statistical review of world energy 2019. https://www.bp.com/content/dam/bp/business-sites/en/global/corporate/pdfs/energy-economics/statistical-review/bp-stats-review-2019-full-report.pdf

[232] Our World in Data: Energy. https://ourworldindata.org/energy
[233] European Biomass Industry Association. Challenges related to biomass. https://www.eubia.org/cms/wiki-biomass/biomass-resources/challenges-related-to-biomass/
[234] IPCC report: Renewable energy sources and Climate change mitigation. https://www.ipcc.ch/site/assets/uploads/2018/03/SRREN_Full_Report-1.pdf
[235] IPCC (2019): Special report on climate change and land. https://www.ipcc.ch/srccl/chapter/summary-for-policymakers/
[236] European Academies Science Advisory Council: Multi-sustainability and functionality in the European Union's forests (2017). https://easac.eu/fileadmin/PDF_s/reports_statements/Forests/EASAC_Forests_web_complete.pdf
[237] U.S. EIA: Nuclear explained. https://www.eia.gov/energyexplained/nuclear/
[238] U.S. EIA: Nuclear power plants. https://www.eia.gov/energyexplained/nuclear/nuclear-power-plants.php
[239] U.S. EIA: Capital cost and performance characteristic estimates for utility scale electric power generating technologies. https://www.eia.gov/analysis/studies/powerplants/capitalcost/pdf/capital_cost_AEO2020.pdf
[240] U.S. EIA: Cost and performance characteristics of new generating technologies (2020). https://www.eia.gov/outlooks/aeo/assumptions/pdf/table_8.2.pdf
[241] U.S. EIA: Levelized cost and levelized avoided cost of new generation resources (2020). Note: data is from Table 1b: unweighted LCOE excluding tax credit for new generation resources in 2019 $/MWh. All major assumptions for the estimations may be found in this report (e.g. capacity factors, WACC, etc.). https://www.eia.gov/outlooks/aeo/pdf/electricity_generation.pdf
[242] Note: Please refer to the reference provided in the text corresponding to this Table if more detailed information is needed.

[243] Note: Please refer to the reference provided in the text corresponding to this Figure for detailed information related to assumptions used by U.S. EIA.
[244] U.S. National Energy technology Laboratory: Life cycle greenhouse gas emissions. Natural gas and power production. https://www.eia.gov/conference/2015/pdf/presentations/skone.pdf
[245] Annex III: Technology specific cost and performance parameters. Climate Change 2014: Mitigation of Climate Change. Contribution of Working Group III to the Fifth Assessment Report of the Intergovernmental Panel on Climate Change. https://www.ipcc.ch/site/assets/uploads/2018/02/ipcc_wg3_ar5_annex-iii.pdf#page=7
[246] IEA Report: Nuclear power in a clean energy system (2019). https://www.iea.org/reports/nuclear-power-in-a-clean-energy-system
[247] Note: This is based on data from the BP statistical review of world energy 2019. https://www.bp.com/content/dam/bp/business-sites/en/global/corporate/pdfs/energy-economics/statistical-review/bp-stats-review-2019-full-report.pdf
[248] BP statistical review of world energy 2019. https://www.bp.com/content/dam/bp/business-sites/en/global/corporate/pdfs/energy-economics/statistical-review/bp-stats-review-2019-full-report.pdf
[249] U.S. EIA: Nuclear power and the environment. https://www.eia.gov/energyexplained/nuclear/nuclear-power-and-the-environment.php
[250] Nuclear Energy Institute: Nuclear fuel. https://www.nei.org/fundamentals/nuclear-fuel
[251] U.S. EIA: Nuclear fuel cycle. https://www.eia.gov/energyexplained/nuclear/the-nuclear-fuel-cycle.php
[252] U.S. DOE-Office of nuclear energy: Advantages and Challenges of nuclear energy. https://www.energy.gov/ne/articles/advantages-and-challenges-nuclear-energy

[253] U.S. DOE: Water Power Technologies Office. Types of Hydropower plants. https://www.energy.gov/eere/water/types-hydropower-plants

[254] U.S. EIA: Hydropower explained. https://www.eia.gov/energyexplained/hydropower/

[255] IEA: Hydropower. https://www.iea.org/fuels-and-technologies/hydropower

[256] IRENA (2019): Renewable generation costs in 2018. International Renewable Energy Agency. https://www.irena.org/-/media/Files/IRENA/Agency/Publication/2019/May/IRENA_Renewable-Power-Generations-Costs-in-2018.pdf

[257] U.S. EIA: Cost and performance characteristics of new generating technologies (2020). https://www.eia.gov/outlooks/aeo/assumptions/pdf/table_8.2.pdf

[258] U.S. EIA: Levelized cost and levelized avoided cost of new generation resources (2020). Note: data is from Table 1b: unweighted LCOE excluding tax credit for new generation resources in 2019 $/MWh. All major assumptions for the estimations may be found in this report (e.g. capacity factors, WACC, etc.). https://www.eia.gov/outlooks/aeo/pdf/electricity_generation.pdf

[259] Note: Please refer to the reference provided in the text corresponding to this Table if more detailed information is needed.

[260] Note: Please refer to the reference provided in the text corresponding to this Figure for detailed information related to assumptions used by U.S. EIA.

[261] U.S. National Energy technology Laboratory: Life cycle greenhouse gas emissions. Natural gas and power production. https://www.eia.gov/conference/2015/pdf/presentations/skone.pdf

[262] Annex III: Technology specific cost and performance parameters. Climate Change 2014: Mitigation of Climate Change. Contribution of Working Group III to the Fifth Assessment Report of the Intergovernmental Panel on Climate Change. https://www.ipcc.ch/site/assets/uploads/2018/02/ipcc_wg3_ar5_annex-iii.pdf#page=7

[263] IPCC AR5 Report: Chapter 7 and Hydropower section. https://www.ipcc.ch/site/assets/uploads/2018/03/Chapter-5-Hydropower-1.pdf

[264] IEA Tracking Report: Hydropower. https://www.iea.org/reports/tracking-power-2019/hydropower

[265] Note: This estimate is based on data from the BP statistical review of world energy 2019. https://www.bp.com/content/dam/bp/business-sites/en/global/corporate/pdfs/energy-economics/statistical-review/bp-stats-review-2019-full-report.pdf

[266] BP statistical review of world energy 2019. https://www.bp.com/content/dam/bp/business-sites/en/global/corporate/pdfs/energy-economics/statistical-review/bp-stats-review-2019-full-report.pdf

[267] IPCC report: Renewable energy sources and Climate change mitigation. https://www.ipcc.ch/site/assets/uploads/2018/03/SRREN_Full_Report-1.pdf

[268] U.S. EIA: Hydropower and the environment. https://www.eia.gov/energyexplained/hydropower/hydropower-and-the-environment.php

[269] U.S. Department of the Interior-USGS: Hydroelectric power: Advantages of production and usage. https://www.usgs.gov/special-topic/water-science-school/science/hydroelectric-power-advantages-production-and-usage?qt-science_center_objects=0#qt-science_center_objects

[270] IEA Technology Report. Transforming industry through CCUS (2019). https://www.iea.org/reports/transforming-industry-through-ccus

[271] IPCC special report: CO_2 capture and storage (2005). https://www.ipcc.ch/site/assets/uploads/2018/03/srccs_wholereport-1.pdf

[272] U.S. EIA: Cost and performance characteristics of new generating technologies (2020). https://www.eia.gov/outlooks/aeo/assumptions/pdf/table_8.2.pdf

[273] Note: Please refer to the reference provided in the text corresponding to this Table if more detailed information is needed.

[274] National Energy technology Laboratory: Cost and performance baseline for fossil energy plants (2015). https://www.netl.doe.gov/projects/files/CostandPerformanceBaselineforFossilEnergyPlantsVolume1aBitCoalPCandNaturalGastoElectRev3_070615.pdf

[275] U.S. EIA: Levelized cost and levelized avoided cost of new generation resources (2019). https://www.eia.gov/outlooks/archive/aeo19/pdf/electricity_generation.pdf

[276] U.S. National Energy technology Laboratory: Life cycle greenhouse gas emissions. Natural gas and power production. https://www.eia.gov/conference/2015/pdf/presentations/skone.pdf

[277] Annex III: Technology specific cost and performance parameters. Climate Change 2014: Mitigation of Climate Change. Contribution of Working Group III to the Fifth Assessment Report of the Intergovernmental Panel on Climate Change. https://www.ipcc.ch/site/assets/uploads/2018/02/ipcc_wg3_ar5_annex-iii.pdf#page=7

[278] IEA Report: 20 years of carbon capture and storage (2016). https://webstore.iea.org/download/direct/316

[279] IEA: Global energy and CO_2 status report (2019). https://www.iea.org/reports/global-energy-co2-status-report-2019/emissions

[280] IPCC special report: CO_2 capture and storage (2005). https://www.ipcc.ch/site/assets/uploads/2018/03/srccs_wholereport-1.pdf

[281] European Environment Agency: Carbon capture and storage could also impact air pollution. https://www.eea.europa.eu/highlights/carbon-capture-and-storage-could

[282] IEA Tracking report: CCUS in power (2019). https://www.iea.org/reports/tracking-power-2019/ccus-in-power#abstract

[283] U.S. EIA: International Energy Outlook 2019. https://www.eia.gov/outlooks/aeo/data/browser/#/?id=15-IEO2019&region=4-0&cases=Reference&f=A

[284] IEA Technology Report. Transforming industry through CCUS (2019). https://www.iea.org/reports/transforming-industry-through-ccus

[285] U.S. EIA: International Energy Outlook 2016. https://www.eia.gov/outlooks/ieo/pdf/transportation.pdf

[286] U.S. Bureau of Transportation statistics: https://www.bts.gov/content/number-us-aircraft-vehicles-vessels-and-other-conveyances

[287] IEA: Transport. https://www.iea.org/topics/transport

[288] IEA: Tracking Transport (2020). https://www.iea.org/reports/tracking-transport-2020

[289] U.S and Global car sales analysis 2018. https://carsalesbase.com/us-car-sales-analysis-2019-compact-suv/; https://carsalesbase.com/global-car-sales-2018/

[290] U.S. DOE, Office of Energy Efficiency and Renewable Energy, Compare cars side by side. https://www.fueleconomy.gov/feg/Find.do?action=sbsSelect

[291] U.S. DOE, Office of Energy Efficiency and Renewable Energy, Electric-drive vehicles, 2017, https://afdc.energy.gov/files/u/publication/electric_vehicles.pdf

[292] U.S. DOE, Office of Energy Efficiency and Renewable Energy, Compare cars side by side. https://www.fueleconomy.gov/feg/Find.do?action=sbsSelect

[293] Note: Total range refers to the number of miles that can be driven following a full tank or 100% charging of the vehicle.

[294] U.S. DOE, Office of Energy Efficiency and Renewable Energy, Compare cars side by side. https://www.fueleconomy.gov/feg/Find.do?action=sbsSelect

[295] Note: "Trim" is also sometimes referred to as "model". For e.g. Three popular trims for 2020 Toyota Camry are L, LE and XLE. L is the base (cheapest) trim for Toyota Camry.

[296] Note: The best possible (apples-to-apples) comparison between two different vehicle technologies can be done by comparing within the same trim. "Trim" is also sometimes referred to as "model".

[297] Toyota web site: https://www.toyota.com

[298] Honda web site: https://www.honda.com

[299] Ford web site: https://www.ford.com

[300] Note: A recent detailed MIT study was used for the assumptions for sales tax (7%), nominal interest (5%), insurance cost (2% of vehicle price). MIT Energy Initiative, Insights into Future Mobility (2019): http://energy.mit.edu/wp-content/uploads/2019/11/Insights-into-Future-Mobility.pdf

[301] Note: The average gasoline price from the last decade ($2.9/gallon) was used as the fuel cost. U.S. EIA, Retail motor gasoline and on highway diesel prices: https://www.eia.gov/totalenergy/data/monthly/pdf/sec9_6.pdf

[302] Note: The maintenance cost per mile was obtained from a recent report from the International Council on Clean Transportation. Update on electric vehicle costs in the U.S. through 2030. https://theicct.org/sites/default/files/publications/EV_cost_2020_2030_20190401.pdf

[303] U.S. DOE, Office of Energy Efficiency and Renewable Energy, Compare cars side by side. https://www.fueleconomy.gov/feg/Find.do?action=sbsSelect The site directly provides the vast majority of the required information (only vehicle manufacturing emissions, which are a smaller component, are not provided).

[304] The International Council on Clean Transportation. The effects of battery manufacturing on electric vehicle life cycle GHG emissions (2018). https://theicct.org/sites/default/files/publications/EV-life-cycle-GHG_ICCT-Briefing_09022018_vF.pdf

[305] U.S. DOE, Office of Energy Efficiency and Renewable Energy, Compare cars side by side. https://www.fueleconomy.gov/feg/Find.do?action=sbsSelect

[306] U.S. DOE, Office of Energy Efficiency and Renewable Energy, Electric-drive vehicles, 2017, https://afdc.energy.gov/files/u/publication/electric_vehicles.pdf

[307] U.S. EPA, Smog, soot and other air pollution from transportation. https://www.epa.gov/transportation-air-pollution-and-climate-change/smog-soot-and-local-air-pollution

[308] U.S. DOE, Office of Energy Efficiency and Renewable Energy, Electric-drive vehicles, 2017, https://afdc.energy.gov/files/u/publication/electric_vehicles.pdf

[309] Note: The base models were selected such that the vehicles satisfied the condition of having a minimum driving range of 200 miles.

[310] Note: Tesla Model 3 (long range) with a 325 miles of driving range was priced at $47,000. Tesla Model 3 with a standard range of 220 miles was selected in this analysis to ensure that the maximum allowed price requirements were met (i.e. to allow qualification based on the selection criteria discussed in section 3.2). Further discussion related to this topic is included in Chapter 5.

[311] U.S. DOE, Office of Energy Efficiency and Renewable Energy, Compare cars side by side. https://www.fueleconomy.gov/feg/Find.do?action=sbsSelect

[312] Note: "Trim" is also sometimes referred to as "model". For e.g. Three popular trims for 2020 Toyota Camry are L, LE and XLE. L is the base (cheapest) trim for Toyota Camry.

[313] Note: Based on price comparison between hybrid and battery electric technology from Table 11 and Table 14.

[314] Note: The best possible (apples-to-apples) comparison between different vehicle technologies can be done by comparing within the same trim/model.

[315] Hyundai Web site: https://www.hyundaiusa.com/us/en/home

[316] Kia web site: https://www.kia.com/us/en

[317] The International Council on Clean Transportation. Update on electric vehicle costs in the U.S. through 2030. https://theicct.org/sites/default/files/publications/EV_cost_2020_2030_20190401.pdf

[318] Note: A recent detailed MIT study was used for the assumptions for sales tax (7%), nominal interest (5%), insurance cost (2% of vehicle price). MIT Energy Initiative, Insights into Future Mobility (2019): http://energy.mit.edu/wp-content/uploads/2019/11/Insights-into-Future-Mobility.pdf

[319] Note: The average gasoline price from the last decade ($2.9/gallon) was used as the fuel cost. U.S. EIA, Retail motor gasoline and on highway diesel prices: https://www.eia.gov/totalenergy/data/monthly/pdf/sec9_6.pdf

[320] Note: The maintenance cost per mile was obtained from a recent report from the International Council on Clean Transportation. Update on electric vehicle costs in the U.S. through 2030.

[320 cont.] https://theicct.org/sites/default/files/publications/EV_cost_2020_2030_20190401.pdf

[321] Note: The 2019 electricity price of 0.13 $/kWh was used as the electricity cost. U.S. EIA, Electricity Power Monthly: https://www.eia.gov/electricity/monthly/epm_table_grapher.php?t=epmt_5_03 The 2019 price was used for electricity as electricity price has been steady over time. This is unlike gasoline price, which has been volatile, and therefore required consideration over the decade.

[322] Tesla Supercharging Support web site: https://www.tesla.com/support/supercharging (website last accessed September 20, 2020)

[323] U.S. DOE, Office of Energy Efficiency and Renewable Energy, Compare cars side by side. https://www.fueleconomy.gov/feg/Find.do?action=sbsSelect Fortunately, the site directly provides the vast majority of the required information (only vehicle manufacturing emissions, which are a smaller component, are not provided).

[324] The International Council on Clean Transportation. The effects of battery manufacturing on electric vehicle life cycle GHG emissions (2018). https://theicct.org/sites/default/files/publications/EV-life-cycle-GHG_ICCT-Briefing_09022018_vF.pdf

[325] NREL: Battery requirements for plug-in hybrid electric vehicles (slide 9). https://www.nrel.gov/docs/fy08osti/42469.pdf

[326] The International Council on Clean Transportation. The effects of battery manufacturing on electric vehicle life cycle GHG emissions (2018). https://theicct.org/sites/default/files/publications/EV-life-cycle-GHG_ICCT-Briefing_09022018_vF.pdf

[327] IVL in cooperation with the Swedish Energy Agency: Li ion vehicle battery production (2019). https://www.ivl.se/download/18.14d7b12e16e3c5c36271070/1574923989017/C444.pdf Please see Appendix for more information.

[328] IEA, Global Energy and CO_2 report 2019. https://www.iea.org/reports/global-energy-co2-status-report-2019/emissions

[329] IEA, Tracking the decoupling of electricity demand and associated CO_2 emissions. https://www.iea.org/commentaries/tracking-the-decoupling-of-electricity-demand-and-associated-co2-emissions

[330] U.S. EIA: How much CO_2 is produced per kWh of U.S. electricity generation (2018). https://www.eia.gov/tools/faqs/faq.php?id=74&t=11

[331] U.S. DOE, Office of Energy Efficiency and Renewable Energy, Compare cars side by side. https://www.fueleconomy.gov/feg/Find.do?action=sbsSelect

[332] IEA: Tracking Transport, Electric Vehicles, Tracking Report 2020. https://www.iea.org/reports/electric-vehicles

[333] U.S. EIA: Natural gas explained. https://www.eia.gov/energyexplained/natural-gas/

[334] U.S. EIA: Few fuels surpass the energy densities of gasoline and diesel. https://www.eia.gov/todayinenergy/detail.php?id=9991

[335] National Renewable Laboratory: Annual technology baseline-electricity. https://atb.nrel.gov/electricity/2019/index.html?t=st

[336] MIT Energy Initiative, Insights into Future Mobility: http://energy.mit.edu/wp-content/uploads/2019/11/Insights-into-Future-Mobility.pdf

[337] Tesla website: Supercharging. https://www.tesla.com/support/supercharging

[338] IEA: Global EV Outlook 2019. https://www.iea.org/reports/global-ev-outlook-2019

[339] U.S. DOE, Office of Energy Efficiency and Renewable Energy, Vehicle charging. https://www.energy.gov/eere/electricvehicles/vehicle-charging

[340] U.S. DOE, Office of Energy Efficiency and Renewable Energy, Compare cars side by side. https://www.fueleconomy.gov/feg/Find.do?action=sbsSelect

[341] Note: The CO_2 reduction impact from battery electric vehicles is primarily dependent on the CO_2 emissions produced during electricity generation (i.e. the fuel cycle emissions component).

[342] UN Sustainable Development Goal # 2. https://www.un.org/sustainabledevelopment/hunger/

[343] IEA: Technology roadmap delivering sustainable bioenergy. Bioenergy technologies, Annex II.

https://webstore.iea.org/Content/Images/uploaded/Bioenergy_2017_Annex2.pdf

[344] IEA Bioenergy: Advanced Biofuels- Potential for Cost reduction (2020). https://www.ieabioenergy.com/wp-content/uploads/2020/02/T41_CostReductionBiofuels-11_02_19-final.pdf

[345] U.S. EIA: Number and capacity of U.S. Refineries. https://www.eia.gov/dnav/pet/pet_pnp_cap1_dcu_nus_a.htm

[346] Cellulosic Ethanol: Status and Innovation. https://www.osti.gov/servlets/purl/1364156

[347] IEA Energy Technology Network. Oil Refineries. https://iea-etsap.org/E-TechDS/PDF/P04_Oil%20Ref_KV_Apr2014_GSOK.pdf

[348] Hydrocarbons-Technology: Saudi Aramco Yanbu Refinery. https://www.hydrocarbons-technology.com/projects/aramco-yanbu/

[349] IEA Bioenergy: Advanced Biofuels- Potential for Cost reduction (2020). https://www.ieabioenergy.com/wp-content/uploads/2020/02/T41_CostReductionBiofuels-11_02_19-final.pdf

[350] European Commission, Joint Research Center. What is limiting the deployment of cellulosic ethanol. https://www.mdpi.com/2076-3417/9/21/4523

[351] European Commission Final Report-Building up the future (2017). https://ec.europa.eu/transparency/regexpert/index.cfm?do=groupDetail.groupDetailDoc&id=33288&no=1

[352] Biofuels watch: Dead end Road- The false promises of cellulosic biofuels. http://www.biofuelwatch.org.uk/wp-content/uploads/Cellulosic-biofuels-report-low-resolution.pdf

[353] IEA: Advanced Biofuels- What holds them back (2019). https://www.irena.org/-/media/Files/IRENA/Agency/Publication/2019/Nov/IRENA_Advanced-biofuels_2019.pdf

[354] Ethanol Producers Magazine: Bloomberg Survey- Cellulosic ethanol will be cost competitive by 2016. http://ethanolproducer.com/articles/9658/survey-cellulosic-ethanol-will-be-competitive-by-2016

[355] Congressional Research Services: The Renewable Fuel Standard- Cellulosic Biofuels (2015). https://www.lankford.senate.gov/imo/media/doc/The%20Renewable%20Fuel%20Standard%20Cellulosic%20Biofuels.pdf

[356] Congressional Research Service: The Renewable Fuel Standard- An Overview (2020 update): https://fas.org/sgp/crs/misc/R43325.pdf

[357] U.S. EIA: EPA finalizes Renewable Fuel Standards for 2019, reflecting cellulosic biofuels shortfalls. https://www.eia.gov/todayinenergy/detail.php?id=37712

[358] Biofuels watch: Dead end Road- The false promises of cellulosic biofuels. http://www.biofuelwatch.org.uk/wp-content/uploads/Cellulosic-biofuels-report-low-resolution.pdf

[359] European Commission Final Report-Building up the future (2017). https://ec.europa.eu/transparency/regexpert/index.cfm?do=groupDetail.groupDetailDoc&id=33288&no=1

[360] U.S. EPA: Lifecycle Greenhouse Gas Results. https://www.epa.gov/fuels-registration-reporting-and-compliance-help/lifecycle-greenhouse-gas-results ; Note: average emissions data for cellulosic fuels corn stover and switchgrass is provided.

[361] IPCC (2019): Special report on climate change and land. https://www.ipcc.ch/srccl/chapter/summary-for-policymakers/

[362] BP statistical review of world energy 2019. https://www.bp.com/content/dam/bp/business-sites/en/global/corporate/pdfs/energy-economics/statistical-review/bp-stats-review-2019-full-report.pdf

[363] Our World in Data: Energy. https://ourworldindata.org/energy

[364] European Biomass Industry Association. Challenges related to biomass. https://www.eubia.org/cms/wiki-biomass/biomass-resources/challenges-related-to-biomass/

[365] IPCC report: Renewable energy sources and Climate change mitigation. https://www.ipcc.ch/site/assets/uploads/2018/03/SRREN_Full_Report-1.pdf

[366] IPCC (2019): Special report on climate change and land. https://www.ipcc.ch/srccl/chapter/summary-for-policymakers/

[367] European Academies Science Advisory Council: Multi-sustainability and functionality in the European Union's forests (2017). https://easac.eu/fileadmin/PDF_s/reports_statements/Forests/EASAC_Forests_web_complete.pdf

[368] Public transporation.org. http://www.publictransportation.org/about/

[369] Note: Vehicle miles = 2 (round trip) * 15 (distance) *4 (number of vehicles) = 120 miles; CO_2 released = (120 * 400)/1000 = 48 Kg

[370] Note: Vehicle miles = 2* 15 *1 = 30 miles; CO_2 released = (30 * 400)/1000 = 12 Kg. This calculation assumes that the total distance traveled between (to and from) work and home for car-pooling is exactly 30 miles each day. In reality, there will be some additional small amount of CO_2 released due to the fact that car-pooling will require some additional miles travelled (i.e. will require few additional miles for picking up and dropping passengers at desired locations). This information is not added purposefully herein because it will complicate the calculations without adding any additional value (i.e. will not change the basic conclusion).

[371] Note: Vehicle miles = 2* 15 *4 = 120 miles; CO_2 released = (120 * 226)/1000 = 27 Kg

[372] U.S. Department of Transportation. Public transportation's role in responding to climate change (2010). https://www.transit.dot.gov/sites/fta.dot.gov/files/docs/PublicTransportationsRoleInRespondingToClimateChange2010.pdf

[373] Note: This is a low-end estimate based on the 2010 U.S. Department of Transportation study. Please see Appendix for more information.

[374] Note: Public concern is expected about shared transportation due to an outbreak such as COVID-19. However, these short-term disruptions can be practically handled if and when they so arise. For example, by expanding use of tele-communication and by using private vehicles if travel is essential during such times and so on, during the affected time period. The proposals related to expanded shared transportation does not entirely eliminate ownership of private vehicles, but it does decrease the need for multiple vehicles per household.

[375] IPCC Report: Carbon dioxide capture and storage (2005). https://www.ipcc.ch/site/assets/uploads/2018/03/srccs_wholereport-1.pdf

[376] U.S. National oceanic and atmospheric administration, Earth System Research Laboratories: Trends in atmospheric CO_2. https://www.esrl.noaa.gov/gmd/ccgg/trends/

[377] IPCC Report: Carbon dioxide capture and storage (2005). https://www.ipcc.ch/site/assets/uploads/2018/03/srccs_wholereport-1.pdf

[378] Note: Please see section 3.1.11

[379] U.S. Department of Energy. Carbon capture opportunities for natural gas power systems. https://www.energy.gov/sites/prod/files/2017/01/f34/Carbon%20Capture%20Opportunities%20for%20Natural%20Gas%20Fired%20Power%20Systems_0.pdf

[380] Report for U.S.DOE by RAND corporation: Understanding cost growth and performance shortfalls in pioneer process plants. https://www.rand.org/pubs/reports/R2569.html

[381] Biofuels watch: Dead end Road- The false promises of cellulosic biofuels. http://www.biofuelwatch.org.uk/wp-content/uploads/Cellulosic-biofuels-report-low-resolution.pdf

[382] U.S. EIA: EPA finalizes Renewable Fuel Standards for 2019, reflecting cellulosic biofuels shortfalls. https://www.eia.gov/todayinenergy/detail.php?id=37712

[383] IPCC Report: Carbon dioxide capture and storage (2005). https://www.ipcc.ch/site/assets/uploads/2018/03/srccs_wholereport-1.pdf

[384] IPCC Special Report: Global warming of 1.5º C. https://www.ipcc.ch/sr15/chapter/chapter-4/

[385] U.S. Energy.gov offices: Fuel Cells https://www.energy.gov/eere/fuelcells/fuel-cells

[386] USDRIVE: Fuel Cells technical team roadmap (Nov. 2017). https://www.energy.gov/sites/prod/files/2017/11/f46/FCTT_Roadmap_Nov_2017_FINAL.pdf

[387] IEA: The future of hydrogen. https://www.iea.org/reports/the-future-of-hydrogen

[388] U.S. EIA: Cost and performance characteristics of new generating technologies (2020). https://www.eia.gov/outlooks/aeo/assumptions/pdf/table_8.2.pdf

Note the very high total overnight cost of fuel cells relative to other technologies.

[389] Energy.Gov Site: What is geothermal energy. Please see section 2.4: Technical & non-technical barriers to geothermal development.
https://www.energy.gov/sites/prod/files/2019/05/f63/2-GeoVision-Chap2.pdf

[390] http://www.renewables-info.com/interesting_energy_articles/why_dont_we_use_more_geothermal_energy.html https://www.energysage.com/about-clean-energy/geothermal/pros-cons-geothermal-energy/

[391] U.S. EIA: Cost and performance characteristics of new generating technologies (2020).
https://www.eia.gov/outlooks/aeo/assumptions/pdf/table_8.2.pdf

[392] National Renewable Energy Laboratory (2018): U.S. Solar photovoltaic system cost benchmark Q1 2018.
https://www.nrel.gov/docs/fy19osti/72399.pdf

[393] Note: Only the solar-distribution technology capital cost information was not directly available from the U.S. EIA 2020 report. The missing capital cost information for solar-distributed was obtained by multiplying the solar-utility capital cost value from the 2020 U.S. EIA report with the capital cost ratio of solar-distributed to solar-utility from the NREL (2018) report. Solar-distributed capital cost was estimated by averaging the capital costs for residential and commercial solar energy applications.

[394] Note: Capacity factor is a ratio of the actual output to the capacity output of the plant over a period of time. Please see Section 3.1 for more information. The ratio is important as it provides information about the utilization of a plant that is realistically possible.

[395] U.S. EIA: Levelized cost and levelized avoided cost of new generation resources (2020).
https://www.eia.gov/outlooks/aeo/pdf/electricity_generation.pdf

[396] U.S. EIA: Levelized cost and levelized avoided cost of new generation resources (2019).
https://www.eia.gov/outlooks/archive/aeo19/pdf/electricity_generation.pdf

[397] NREL. Annual Technology baseline Concentrated Solar (2018 NREL estimate used for capacity factor of CSP; 2018 NREL

capacity factor value is much higher than average 2019 value from EIA; NREL value instead of EIA was used herein to give benefit of doubt advantage to solar/storage). https://atb.nrel.gov/electricity/2018/index.html?t=sc

[398] Note: The comment in the 2020 U.S. EIA report on levelized cost estimation related to their assumption of capacity factors is provided for reference purpose: *"EIA evaluated LCOE and LACE for each technology based on assumed capacity factors, which generally correspond to the high end of their likely utilization range. This convention is consistent with the use of LCOE to evaluate competing technologies in baseload operation such as coal and nuclear plants"*

[399] U.S. EIA: Levelized cost and levelized avoided cost of new generation resources (2020). https://www.eia.gov/outlooks/aeo/pdf/electricity_generation.pdf

[400] U.S. EIA: Levelized cost and levelized avoided cost of new generation resources (2019). https://www.eia.gov/outlooks/archive/aeo19/pdf/electricity_generation.pdf

[401] National Energy technology Laboratory: Cost and performance baseline for fossil energy plants (2015). https://www.netl.doe.gov/projects/files/CostandPerformanceBaselineforFossilEnergyPlantsVolume1aBitCoalPCandNaturalGastoElectRev3_070615.pdf

[402] National Renewable Energy Laboratory (2018): U.S. Solar photovoltaic system cost benchmark Q1 2018. https://www.nrel.gov/docs/fy19osti/72399.pdf

[403] Note: Concentrated solar (CSP) is used as a **representative** for solar with storage **from this point onwards**. CSP costs are presented only for 8 hours storage in the EIA report. However, these costs should be reasonable for prioritization between technologies (considering the Tiered analysis approach discussed in Chapter 5).

[404] Note: For majority of the technologies, the LCOE data is directly from the U.S. EIA 2020 report (references are provided in the text corresponding to the Figure). The 2019 U.S. EIA, NETL (2015), and NREL (2018) reports were used to fill the missing data using a straight-forward ratios methodology. For e.g. the missing information for solar-distributed in terms of 2019

$/MWh was obtained by multiplying the solar-utility LCOE value from the 2020 U.S. EIA report with the LCOE ratio of solar-distributed (residential & commercial) to solar-utility from the NREL (2018) report. Due to some difference in LCOE assumptions in the different studies, this is not perfect; however, it is appropriate for comparing technologies for establishing Tiers (as discussed in Chapter 5).

[405] IEA: Global Energy and CO_2 status report 2019. https://www.iea.org/reports/global-energy-co2-status-report-2019/emissions

[406] IEA: Tracking the decoupling of electricity demand and associated CO_2 emissions. https://www.iea.org/commentaries/tracking-the-decoupling-of-electricity-demand-and-associated-co2-emissions

[407] U.S. National Energy technology Laboratory: Life cycle greenhouse gas emissions. Natural gas and power production. https://www.eia.gov/conference/2015/pdf/presentations/skone.pdf

[408] Annex III: Technology specific cost and performance parameters. Climate Change 2014: Mitigation of Climate Change. Contribution of Working Group III to the Fifth Assessment Report of the Intergovernmental Panel on Climate Change. https://www.ipcc.ch/site/assets/uploads/2018/02/ipcc_wg3_ar5_annex-iii.pdf#page=7

[409] Note: The cost analysis in this book is in **excellent agreement** with a recent related MIT study. MIT Energy Initiative, Insights into Future Mobility (2019): http://energy.mit.edu/wp-content/uploads/2019/11/Insights-into-Future-Mobility.pdf

[410] Note: The initial investment cost per avoided CO_2 ton per year for the proposed technology solution was estimated using data from Figure 18,19 & 21. The total cost per avoided ton of CO_2 was estimated using data from Figures 20 & Figure 21. For more information, please see Appendix.

[411] Note: Concentrated solar (CSP) is used as a **representative** for solar with storage **from this point onwards**. CSP costs are presented only for 8 hours storage in the EIA report. However, these costs should be reasonable for prioritization between

[412] technologies (considering the Tiered analysis approach discussed in Chapter 5).

[412] Note: Data from Figures 22 & 23 used for the initial investment cost per avoided CO_2 ton per year for hybrid and battery electric vehicles. The total cost per avoided ton of CO_2 was estimated using data from Tables 11 & 14 & Figure 23. For more information, please see Appendix.

[413] Note: Data from sections 3.2.3 & 4.2.1. For more information, please see Appendix.

[414] Note: The relative cost ratio between conventional light duty vehicles, hybrid and battery electric vehicles for the same trim is expected to be similar in different countries based on published retail prices.

[415] Note: The estimations were based on Transport Van and Transit Bus options, with both using conventional fuel (at 70% vehicle occupancy). For more information, please see Appendix.

[416] Note: The favorability ratings are based on relative favorability between the different technology solutions. The reference technology (which is to be replaced) serves as an important calibration point. The rating is directly based on the data provided in the previous chapter.

[417] U.S. EIA: How much of the U.S. CO_2 emissions are associated with electricity generation (2019). https://www.eia.gov/tools/faqs/faq.php?id=77&t=11

[418] U.S. EIA: What is U.S. electricity generation by energy source (2019). https://www.eia.gov/tools/faqs/faq.php?id=427&t=3

[419] U.S. EIA: Annual energy outlook 2020. https://www.eia.gov/outlooks/aeo/data/browser/#/?id=2-AEO2020&cases=ref2020&sourcekey=0

[420] Note: Solar with storage favorability ratings are also directly applicable to wind-onshore with storage due to similarities in the different characteristics.

[421] U.S. Bureau of Transportation statistics: https://www.bts.gov/content/number-us-aircraft-vehicles-vessels-and-other-conveyances

[422] U.S. EIA: Fast facts on transportation greenhouse gas emissions. https://www.epa.gov/greenvehicles/fast-facts-transportation-greenhouse-gas-emissions

[423] Tesla website: Model 3 retail price for trims with different driving ranges- Higher driving range equals higher retail price. https://www.tesla.com/model3/design#battery

[424] Note: For the analysis undertaken in this study, the driving range for battery electric vehicles has been purposefully been allowed to be *only* ~200 miles; i.e. the retail price has been used for the lower driving range trim/model for battery electric vehicles. For example, Tesla Model 3 with a driving range of ~220 miles priced at ~$35,000 is used in this study for comparing with a Toyota Camry with a driving range of 493 miles. This obviously results in an unfair comparison, considering that the conventional and hybrid light duty vehicles have an average driving range of over 400 miles. But as discussed in the text, benefit of doubt has been given to battery electric vehicle technology by including large potential advances that could occur in the near term that could allow electric cars to deliver 400 miles of driving range at the current lower priced models/trim.

[425] Note: In other words, it has **already** been assumed that technology advances in battery technology in the very near future will allow for a price reduction from $47,000 to $35,000. Price obtained from https://www.tesla.com/model3/design#battery (accessed Aug. 27, 2020).

[426] Note: Currently for the same trim, the retail price of a battery electric car is about 60% higher than conventional car. For an aggressive reduction, the price difference needs to reduce to less than 20%. As an example- In case of Tesla Model 3, an aggressive cost reduction corresponds to vehicle with a retail price of ~$28,000 for a driving range of 400 miles. Note the current retail price of Tesla Model 3 with 325 miles driving range is $47000. https://www.tesla.com/model3/design#battery (accessed Aug. 27, 2020).

[427] Note: Essentially, the top tier low-carbon technologies for the next phase (after 10 years) can again be determined by using the approach outlined in this book. For example, it is possible that a technology solution that is currently Tier 3 may become a top tier technology due to major technology breakthroughs in the next 10 years.

[428] Note: Unlike the high CO_2 reduction costs for battery electric light duty vehicles for private use, the costs are expected to be moderate for battery electric vans and buses levels (i.e. for high occupancy shared transportation applications).

[429] IEA Technology Report. Transforming industry through CCUS (2019). https://www.iea.org/reports/transforming-industry-through-ccus

[430] IEA: Tracking the decoupling of electricity demand and associated CO_2 emissions. https://www.iea.org/commentaries/tracking-the-decoupling-of-electricity-demand-and-associated-co2-emissions

[431] IEA: Global Energy and CO_2 status report 2019. https://www.iea.org/reports/global-energy-co2-status-report-2019/emissions

[432] Our World in Data. Natural gas prices. https://ourworldindata.org/grapher/natural-gas-prices

[433] IEA (2020): World Energy model. https://www.iea.org/reports/world-energy-model/techno-economic-inputs

[434] IRENA (2019): Renewable generation costs in 2018. International Renewable Energy Agency. https://www.irena.org/-/media/Files/IRENA/Agency/Publication/2019/May/IRENA_Renewable-Power-Generations-Costs-in-2018.pdf

[435] Fraunhofer Institute for solar energy systems. Levelized cost of electricity renewable energy technologies study (2013). https://www.ise.fraunhofer.de/content/dam/ise/en/documents/publications/studies/Fraunhofer-ISE_LCOE_Renewable_Energy_technologies.pdf

[436] The Energy & Resources Institute (2019): Exploring electricity supply mix scenarios to 2030. https://www.teriin.org/sites/default/files/2019-02/Exploring%20Electricity%20Supply-Mix%20Scenarios%20to%202030.pdf

[437] U.S. EIA: International Energy Outlook 2019. https://www.eia.gov/outlooks/aeo/data/browser/#/?id=15-IEO2019&region=4-0&cases=Reference&f=A

[438] IEA Technology Report. Transforming industry through CCUS (2019). https://www.iea.org/reports/transforming-industry-through-ccus

[439] U.S. EIA: International Energy Outlook 2016. https://www.eia.gov/outlooks/ieo/pdf/transportation.pdf
[440] International organization of motor vehicle manufacturers. Vehicles in use. http://www.oica.net/category/vehicles-in-use/
[441] IEA: Transport. https://www.iea.org/topics/transport
[442] Global gasoline price. https://www.globalpetrolprices.com/gasoline_prices/
[443] Global electricity price. https://www.globalpetrolprices.com/electricity_prices/
[444] U.S. EIA: Coal and the environment. https://www.eia.gov/energyexplained/coal/coal-and-the-environment.php
[445] U.S. EIA: Natural gas and the environment. https://www.eia.gov/energyexplained/natural-gas/natural-gas-and-the-environment.php
[446] IPCC report: Renewable energy sources and Climate change mitigation. https://www.ipcc.ch/site/assets/uploads/2018/03/SRREN_Full_Report-1.pdf
[447] U.S. EIA: Nuclear power and the environment. https://www.eia.gov/energyexplained/nuclear/nuclear-power-and-the-environment.php
[448] U.S. EIA: Solar energy and the environment. https://www.eia.gov/energyexplained/solar/solar-energy-and-the-environment.php
[449] U.S. EIA: Wind energy and the environment. https://www.eia.gov/energyexplained/wind/wind-energy-and-the-environment.php
[450] U.S. Congressional Research Service (2020 Report): Electric vehicles: A primer on technology and selected policy issues. https://fas.org/sgp/crs/misc/R46231.pdf
[451] U.S. DOE: Alternative fuels data center. Emissions from hybrid and plug-in electric vehicles. https://afdc.energy.gov/vehicles/electric_emissions.html
[452] U.S. EPA: Economics of biofuels. https://www.epa.gov/environmental-economics/economics-biofuels#impacts

[453] Note: This can be easily seen from the cost comparison data provided for the different technology solutions and the corresponding rating in terms of Tiers.

[454] IPCC, 2014: *Climate Change 2014: Synthesis Report. Contribution of Working Groups I, II and III to the Fifth Assessment Report of the Intergovernmental Panel on Climate Change.* https://www.ipcc.ch/site/assets/uploads/2018/02/SYR_AR5_FINAL_full.pdf

[455] U.S. Congressional Budget office. The budget and economic outlook: 2020 to 2030. https://www.cbo.gov/publication/56020

[456] World Bank Poverty database (2015 data). http://iresearch.worldbank.org/PovcalNet/povDuplicateWB.aspx Total global population living under 5.5$/day: ~3.4 billion in 2015

[457] Note: By the end of the year 1950, the global cumulative CO_2 emissions from fossil fuel combustion had exceeded 200 billion tons. Remarkably, these extremely large levels were so low from a *threshold* perspective at that time, that even after the speculation that CO_2 could cause warming, *the related impact was grossly misunderstood until 1950*. This is clear from the fact that the two key researchers, Arrhenius in ~1900 and Callendar in 1930s/1940s, who had speculated that CO_2 release from human activity would cause warming, believed that this effect could actually be *beneficial for mankind*.

[458] Note: In the later part of the twentieth century, concerns were raised about global warming and potential issues, but no significant (*call to action*) alarm was raised by the global scientific community. The global consensus grew strong enough to raise a significant alarm only in the beginning of the twenty first century after 1000 billion tons of CO_2 had been released (i.e. after an extraordinarily large implementation of fossil-fueled technologies). This can be considered as the true threshold level for the comprehensive agreement about the severity of the CO_2 problem.

[459] IEA Technology Report. Transforming industry through CCUS (2019). https://www.iea.org/reports/transforming-industry-through-ccus

460 IEA Technology Report. Transforming industry through CCUS (2019). https://www.iea.org/reports/transforming-industry-through-ccus

461 IEA: Global Energy and CO_2 status report 2019. https://www.iea.org/reports/global-energy-co2-status-report-2019/emissions

462 U.S. EIA: International Energy Outlook 2016. https://www.eia.gov/outlooks/ieo/pdf/transportation.pdf

463 International organization of motor vehicle manufacturers. Vehicles in use. http://www.oica.net/category/vehicles-in-use/

464 IEA: Transport. https://www.iea.org/topics/transport

465 U.S. EIA: International Energy Outlook 2016. https://www.eia.gov/outlooks/ieo/pdf/transportation.pdf

466 World Economic Forum. Speed of energy transition. http://www3.weforum.org/docs/WEF_the_speed_of_the_energy_transition.pdf

467 Note: Governments should primarily rely on a systematic prioritization analysis for supporting only the most efficient technologies via policy decisions.

468 Note: Early adopters are important for transitioning to new technologies. This provides data for evaluating the true (at scale) potential of the technologies. Also, there is no significant downside considering that the cost is borne by entities that can afford it. In other words, even if the technology does not have potential, there is no significant loss for the society.

469 Note: For example- a) Since, CO_2 accounts for only about 75% of the global greenhouse gas emissions, solutions will also be required for reducing the other greenhouse gases as well. b) Social education of the global population is critical for ensuring controlled population growth and behavior changes to minimize food, material and energy waste. c) Forests, which play a critical role in the CO_2 cycle, are being destroyed; related solutions will also be important.

470 Note: Since, greenhouse gases are long-lived (up to several hundred years), they stay for sufficient time in the atmosphere to get well mixed. As a result, their concentration in the atmosphere is roughly the same anywhere in the world and is independent of the location of the source.

[471] Netherlands Environmental Assessment Energy report "Trends in global CO₂ and total greenhouse gas emissions; 2018 report", December 2018, *PBL report 3125.*
https://www.pbl.nl/en/publications/trends-in-global-co2-and-total-greenhouse-gas-emissions-2018-report

[472] Note: This considers the inherent constraints such as available resources for a given country.

[473] Note: Drastic, rapid reduction will not allow the use of systematic prioritization and will thus result in a significant use of highly inefficient Tier 3 & 4 solutions.

[474] Note: Budget deficits are ballooning even in advanced economies such as the United States, and further significant increase can cause tremendous economic pain to future generations.

[475] Note: Over the past several decades there has been a large move of the manufacturing industry from advanced economies to China. This is sub-optimal from the viewpoint of greenhouse gas emissions considering the relatively much higher emissions from the much larger coal use for electricity generation in China.

[476] Note: This is based on the well-established fact that a net efficiency advantage is required for net job creation.

[477] Note: This follows from the fact that on a percentage basis, U.S. and EU combined produce only about 22% of the global greenhouse gas emissions currently.

[478] Note: Unlike for EU and U.S., the population is expected to grow significantly for the rest of the world over the next decades. Moreover, the energy consumption (and thereby emissions) is also expected to grow much more rapidly for the rest of the world considering that a large fraction of its population will move from poverty/lower middle class to the middle class (i.e. there will be a large increase in standard of living).

[479] Note: Any benefit from the 20% lower CO_2 emissions will be felt by all countries around the globe; i.e. while the costs are local, benefits are mostly global.

[480] European Commission. Adaption to Climate change.
https://ec.europa.eu/clima/policies/adaptation_en

Made in the USA
Middletown, DE
05 April 2021